D1612538

The
Cosgrave
legacy

The
Cosgrave
legacy

by

Stephen Collins

BLACKWATER PRESS

Editor

Deirdre Bowden

ISBN

0 86121658 X

© 1996 Stephen Collins

Produced in Ireland by
Blackwater Press
c/o Folens Publishers
8 Broomhill Business Park
Tallaght
Dublin 24

*A catalogue record for this publication is available
from the British Library.*
Collins, Stephen. The Cosgrave Legacy.

While considerable effort has been made to locate all holders of copyright material used in this text, we have been unable to contact some of these. Should they wish to contact Blackwater Press, we will be glad to come to some arrangement.

Printed in Ireland at the press of the Publisher.

CONTENTS

ACKNOWLEDGEMENTS

I would like to thank all the people who generously gave up their time to talk to me during the preparation of this book and provided me with their reminiscences of the Cosgrave years. I would particularly thank Peter Barry, John Bruton, Liam Burke, Richard Burke, Conor Cruise O'Brien, Barry Desmond, James Dooge, Brendan Halligan, Paddy Harte, Muiris Mac Conghail, Maurice Manning, Michael Mills, Ted Nealon, Richie Ryan and Dick Walsh for talking to me about the period.

A special word of thanks is due to Ursula Halligan who made her unpublished thesis 'The Cosgrave Coalition 1973–77' available to me. Her interviews with Liam Cosgrave were an important source and her thesis illuminated many aspects of his career. My thanks also to my cousin, Charles Lysaght, who supplied me with the unpublished memoirs of his aunt, the late Moira Lysaght. Barry Desmond trawled through his files and came up with a lot of useful material covering Liam Cosgrave's period in politics.

I would also like to thank the staff of the National Library, the Oireachtas Library and the National Archive for their usual help and courtesy during my research. *The Irish Times* and the *Irish Independent* libraries kindly made their picture files available to me.

Desmond Fisher read a draft of the book and made very valuable suggestions as to how it could be improved while Maurice Manning gave me access to his work in progress on the life of James Dillon, read the final version of the book and made some vital corrections. Any errors or omissions that remain are entirely my own responsibility.

A special word of thanks to my wife Jean for her helpful advice throughout and to my children Eoin, Niamh and Catherine for their patience.

I would also like to thank Deirdre Bowden of Blackwater Press for her care and attention to detail while doing a very efficient editing job and John O'Connor for commissioning the book in the first place.

The book does not contain footnotes but the sources are generally cited in the text, except for the occasional unattributable quote.

Stephen Collins, November 1996

In memory of my grandfather William Farrell.

PROLOGUE

AT THE top of the blue-carpeted stairs leading to the Dáil chamber in Leinster House there is a long landing connecting the more modern part of the building to the nineteenth century town house of the Dukes of Leinster. Along both sides of this landing hang portraits of former leaders of the State, facing each other across the wide stairway.

The first painting on the left is a portrait of William Thomas Cosgrave, president of the Executive Council from 1922 to 1932. On the other side of the landing, directly facing W.T., is a picture of his son, Liam Cosgrave, Taoiseach from 1973 to 1977. Father and son face each other across the heads of the Dáil deputies trooping in and out of the chamber; few ever give either picture a passing glance.

The portrait of W.T. is that of a serene white-haired man with a twinkle in his eye who looks content with his life and work. He is dressed in the formal attire of his day with the high wing collar he favoured, but he looks remarkably relaxed and wears a benign smile. By contrast the painting of the son conveys a stiffer personality. He is dressed in a sombre grey suit and no smile breaks through his flinty demeanour.

The two men were very close throughout their lives and Liam Cosgrave has said that he cannot recall any subject on which they disagreed. One close political associate of Liam summed up his fundamental approach to politics in the light of his attachment to his father. 'At times of crisis de Valera used to look into his own heart to see what the Irish people felt. I think that in a pinch Liam Cosgrave always asked himself what his father would have done.'

As far as the son is concerned W.T.'s towering achievement was his role in creating the institutions of this State. Liam showed on one notable occasion that he was prepared to sacrifice his own career and vote with a Fianna Fáil Government when he felt that the party which he led was misguidedly putting the State in danger.

The lives of W.T. and Liam Cosgrave encapsulate the political history of Ireland in the twentieth century. Between the two of them they participated in every major political event that shaped the Ireland we know today. W.T. attended the founding of Sinn Féin in 1905 and he subsequently carved out a reputation for himself as a reforming politician on Dublin Corporation. He fought in 1916 and was one of the first Sinn Féin MPs elected to the House of Commons as the tide of history swept the Irish Parliamentary Party to oblivion in the aftermath of the Rising.

A Minister in the first Dáil and a vital supporter of Michael Collins and Arthur Griffith during the Treaty debates, the unassuming W.T. was landed with the task of leading the fledgling State through a bitter Civil War and its first decade of freedom when his two heroes died within ten days of each other in August, 1922. Despite the fact that his Government was full of men of enormous talent it was Cosgrave who was selected in 1922 to lead the country through its darkest hour. More than any other political leader he is entitled to take credit for establishing the basic democratic norms which have characterised a free Ireland.

On W.T. Cosgrave's death in November, 1965, John Healy in his *Irish Times* Backbencher column was uncharacteristically emotional: 'So long as there is a blue uniform on O'Connell Bridge; so long as the green of a soldier's uniform is; so long as legal men argue and so long as men and women armed with the right and the might of the ballot box sit in Dáil Éireann, so long will William T. Cosgrave be remembered.'

As Liam Cosgrave grew to manhood his father's political influence was in decline and his great achievements were belittled and then forgotten. W.T. retired from active politics in the 1940s, unable to counter the political dominance of Eamon de Valera and Fianna Fáil, the very people he had defeated in the Civil War. Liam took up the torch, getting elected to the Dáil at the exceptionally young age of 23. He rose rapidly in the ranks of Fine Gael and was a Minister before the age of 30.

Elected leader of his party at the age of 45 he had to endure a long time in the political wilderness and barely survived the repeated attempts of his internal enemies to remove him from the leadership. He hung on tenaciously and was rewarded by taking over as Taoiseach in 1973 and following his father's footsteps to the top of the political ladder.

Like his father before him Liam presided over a Government of all the talents. That such an ordinary-seeming individual should lead a Government containing so many intelligent and dynamic politicians was often a cause of wonder. Like his father he too had to deal with an armed threat to the State during his term of office and his attitude to it was unyielding.

It is a remarkable record that father and son, with such similar temperaments and personalities, should both have been rulers of this State. Neither of them gained anything material from politics but they both did the State some service. While in power they were both very much taken for granted and even undervalued by their own supporters but they share another characteristic: As time passes both their records appear much more impressive than their contemporaries ever gave them credit for. With hindsight, modesty may be given its due, while the fatal attraction of the loose-lipped demagogue begins to pall.

1

THE REBEL

WILLIAM Thomas Cosgrave born in Dublin in 1880, was the eldest son of Thomas Cosgrave, a publican and grocer, of 174 James' Street, and his wife, Brigid Nixon. Cosgrave senior was involved in politics as a member of the Board of Poor Law Guardians, the forerunners of the local authorities. The Cosgrave's were originally from Co. Wexford and, according to family tradition, one of them was executed in the 1798 Rebellion. They moved to Castledermot, Co. Kildare, during the nineteenth century and that is where the Dublin branch of the family originated.

W.T. Cosgrave grew up in a reasonably comfortable middle class environment in the last few decades of the nineteenth century. W.T. was one of three children; he had one brother Philip and a sister May. His father died when he was just nine years old and his mother married again. Her second husband, Tom Burke, who came originally from Seskin in Co. Tipperary started work at 174 James' Street as the pub manager before marrying Mrs Cosgrave. There were two children by the second marriage, Frank (known as Goban) and Joan. The business was modestly successful and the Cosgrave-Burke's were part of the growing Catholic middle class in Dublin.

W.T. was educated like many boys of his background by the Christian Brothers at Francis Street, near his home. As a boy he served Mass in the local Catholic church, beginning an interest in religion which was to last all his life. After primary school he transferred to the O'Brien Institute on the north side of the city which was also run by the Christian Brothers. He left school at 16 and went to work. His lack of higher education was something he felt as a drawback in later life but at the time he was happy to begin working in the family business.

A family friend, Moira Lysaght, whose family were in the same business, years later recalled her impressions of 174 James' Street as a child. She remembered it as a much smaller business-cum-family house than her own. 'It faced the main entrance of the South Dublin Union and having entered the hall door to the left of the shop, on the first landing with its red-shaded light I can clearly seen in memory's eye the regal figure of Mrs Burke, with her halo of snow-white hair.'

Miss Lysaght recalled more than half a century later how in the early years of the century her family often went walking in the Phoenix Park where they were joined by Tom Burke while his stepson, W.T., rode in the park on horseback. 'As the latter galloped by on horseback, his golden hair flying in the breeze, Tom humorously commented "There goes John Gilpin."'

The Cosgrave children all possessed the same refined handsome appearance, white and golden hair, and quick, rich-speaking voices, according to contemporaries. W.T. and his brother Phil worked in the pub and shop as assistants to their stepfather, Tom. He was a pleasant, bombastic country man who in appearance resembled King George V. He usually dressed well in grey and black striped trousers, conventional black coat and bowler hat. He was a very different man from his step children whom he irritated constantly with his bantering remarks.

One evening in the Cosgrave-Burke home around the turn of the century was remembered by Miss Lysaght at the time of W.T. Cosgrave's death in 1965:

> 'We were seated with our backs to the wall at the far side of the dining room table and facing the fireplace before which stood the resplendent figure of Willie with his golden hair and equally golden moustache. [After the Rebellion his head and face were shaved.] In deep, studied tones he held us spellbound, recounting a ghost story about "the headless coach" which words and rolling delivery still ring in my ears. In the background the step father, Tom, impatient at the length of the recital, kept on muttering – "Will the bloody fellow ever shut up?"'

The atmosphere on social occasions among these relatively prosperous Dublin publicans and grocers at the beginning of the twentieth century, with games of charades or forfeits for the children and dancing of 'the lancers' and 'the quadrilles' by the adults, is reminiscent of the life-style captured by James Joyce in his short story *The Dead*. Reflecting that comfortable life-style W.T. kept a horse from the time he was a young adult. He told his son years later that he once rode to the Meath hunt with 400 followers. Politics, though, would soon intrude on the Cosgrave-Burke's comfortable life, as it also does in *The Dead*.

Not simply content to lead the life of a Dublin publican W.T. from an early age inherited his father's interest in politics but he found the Irish Parliamentary Party, which represented the broad sweep of constitutional Nationalist opinion, too tame. He attended the first annual convention of Sinn Féin in the round room of the Rotunda in December 1905. Joining the new party was a bold step for a young man like Cosgrave most of whose contemporaries were content to support the Irish Party or even back the publicans' organised interest on Dublin Corporation.

Sinn Féin emerged out of a loose grouping called the National Council which was established in 1903 to protest at the visit to Dublin of King Edward VII. The movement got the backing of the Corporation, which refused to present an address to the King. Some of the councillors then formed a group committed to a more Nationalist programme and also pledged to do something about the appalling social conditions in Dublin at the time. At the inaugural meeting of Sinn Féin organised by Arthur Griffith, the moving spirit behind the movement, these councillors were joined by people like Patrick Pearse, Oliver St John Gogarty and Cosgrave in launching the new party. As this stage Cosgrave was a mere foot soldier and was not called on to speak, unlike his larger-than-life friend, Gogarty, who addressed the gathering with an oratorical flourish. The best line of the day, however, was delivered by a priest, Fr Harpur from Wexford, who came up with the phrase 'Curse your concessions England — We want our country.'

W.T. became actively involved in the Dublin party organisation which made a determined attempt to win a number of seats in the Corporation elections of January 1906. The party, which was still known as the National Council, did well in the capital, winning six seats on the Corporation. It was led by Alderman Tom Kelly, who was committed to reforming the corrupt dealings of the Corporation. In Ushers Quay ward, where Cosgrave lived, the party was narrowly defeated by a sitting councillor who represented the publicans' interest. W.T. then founded a branch of Sinn Féin in his own area and became the driving force in the local organisation.

At this stage Sinn Féin was still very much a minority Nationalist party and Irish politics was dominated by John Redmond and the

Parliamentary Party. When one sitting MP, Charles Dolan, decided to join the new movement he resigned his seat in Leitrim and fought the by-election as a Sinn Féin candidate. Dolan was well beaten by Redmond's candidate winning 1,157 votes as against 3,103 for the party's man.

It was not an encouraging start and Sinn Féin stayed out of the two national elections of 1910 prompting John Redmond to say that he would 'crush Sinn Féin in the palm of his hand.' In local Dublin politics Sinn Féin fared a bit better and in 1909 W.T. Cosgrave was the candidate for Ushers Quay. He signed a party pledge committing himself to a range of policies including the non-recognition of the British parliament, protection for Irish industry, re-afforestation, the setting up of an Irish consular service, educational reform and the establishment of an independent civil court system. W.T. was elected to the Corporation along with six of his colleagues and they formed an important grouping on the city council.

A little over a decade later an *Irish Times* reporter wrote:

'In those days Sinn Féin was an unpopular creed so for the time being Mr Cosgrave turned his attention to municipal reform and became a member of Dublin Corporation. Here he joined the little party led by Alderman Tom Kelly which set out to abolish jobbery and corruption in the public life of the city. He quickly mastered the intricacies of public finances, becoming chairman of the Finance Committee and gaining a huge respect for the skill and thoroughness in which he presented annual estimates.'

He made housing issues a priority in a city whose tenements were notorious at the time. One tangible memorial to Cosgrave's influence on the City Council was a decision he initiated to build Corporation housing estates in the city. One of these developments was the estate now known as Ceannt's Fort in his home area. W.T. later told Ernest Blythe that in his actions on the Corporation he was 'a little bit of a leftist.'

Although he can hardly have anticipated it at the time, his role on Dublin Corporation gave W.T. a very good training for life as a political leader in independent Ireland. It also helped to save his life after the 1916 Rising when his reputation as a reforming politician played a part in having his death sentence commuted.

Side by side with his activity in local Dublin politics Cosgrave continued his involvement with the Irish-Ireland side of Sinn Féin. The Sinn Féin newspaper records his attendance at the weekly meetings of the Craobh Eamonn Mhic Gearailt branch of Sinn Féin which were held in the family premises at James' Street. Griffith was a frequent guest speaker at branch meetings while Cosgrave himself regularly spoke at them. Even at this stage he didn't waste words and in a style which was to become characteristic of him he preferred to make short, pointed and witty contributions rather than engage in the long-winded oratorical type of speech so common at the time.

Sinn Féin was still very much a fringe party when the two general elections of 1910 gave John Redmond and his Parliamentary Party the balance of power in the House of Commons. They used that position to extract the third Home Rule Bill from Asquith's Liberal government. Ireland was plunged into crisis as Unionists, with the backing of the Conservative Party, went into open revolt and founded the Ulster Volunteer Force designed to frustrate the implementation of Home Rule. The UVF imported arms from Britain's enemy Germany and made ready to defy the democratic decision of the House of Commons. Constitutional politicians were gradually pushed aside as Nationalists responded by founding their own paramilitary force, the Irish Volunteers.

W.T. Cosgrave was now becoming a significant figure in Nationalist policies and when the Irish Volunteers were founded at the Rotunda in Dublin in November 1913, by Eoin MacNeill, he was among the dignitaries on the platform. As at the founding of Sinn Féin seven years earlier, Padraig Pearse was there too. Another to share the platform that day was Nationalist priest, Fr Eugene Sheehy, a great-uncle of Conor Cruise O'Brien.

Cosgrave's involvement with the Volunteers complemented his activity in Dublin politics. 'When the National Volunteer movement started he threw himself into it heart and soul. When the inevitable split came in 1914 he joined the Pearse group,' a journalist who covered city council meetings recalled. In the run-up to 1916 the Volunteers conducted regular drills and marches. W.T and his brother Phil were enthusiastic members of the organisation and they persuaded their step-brother, Goban, to join up as well. W.T., by now a respectable member of the Corporation, looked an incongruous figure as he marched out on manoeuvre in his Volunteers' uniform.

On Easter Sunday 1916, Miss Lysaght remembered being at a concert in the Fr Mathew Hall in Church Street at which Joan Burke, W.T.'s step-sister, sang *The West's Awake* and *The Minstrel Boy.* In the front was W.T. with other members of his family and at the interval Goban came in, walked rapidly up to W.T., spoke to him quietly and then left. Later the Lysaghts heard that he had been down the country as a dispatch rider bringing messages about the planned Rising.

Earlier that same Easter Sunday the Lysaghts on their usual Sunday morning walk in the Phoenix Park were warned by Tom Burke to 'be careful tomorrow and don't go out.' This indicates that the Cosgrave-Burke family were all too keenly aware of what was about to happen. W.T.'s defence at his court martial after the Rising, when he was sentenced to death, was that he had no idea what was going to develop when he marched out on Easter Monday but Miss Lysaght's recollections give a different picture.

W.T. was a member of the 4th Dublin Battalion of the Irish volunteers with the rank of Lieutenant. On Easter Monday morning Cosgrave joined the rest of the battalion at 11 a.m. in Emerald Square close to Guinness Brewery. Of a nominal battalion strength of 700 only 120 men turned out. 'Today you are going into action. An Irish Republic has been declared and we are marching on the South Dublin Union,' their commanding officer Comdt. Eamonn Ceannt told his men. The South Dublin Union, now St James' Hospital, sprawled over 52 acres with its own streets, alleyways, residences, wards, and even churches as well as wide open fields, all surrounded by a high wall and with a population of 3,282 people on that Easter Monday morning. The objective of taking the Union was to prevent British troops coming to the relief of Dublin Castle.

Max Caulfield interviewed W.T. in the early 1960s for his definitive account of the Rising published before the fiftieth anniversary. According to this account the battalion moved off from Emerald Square at 11.35 a.m. with Ceannt leading a party of ten cyclists to the Union. Cosgrave guided the main party, under the command of Cathal Brugha, as he knew the area intimately and they moved through side streets and back alleys in order to avoid being challenged.

Ceannt made his way through the back entrance at midday with his cyclists and marched through the Union to the main gate where Brugha and Cosgrave had taken control without a fight. Ceannt spread his men thinly across the vast area to the consternation of Cosgrave.

'Look, isn't this hopeless. Surely we can't hope to hold the whole Union, we haven't got the men,' Cosgrave remarked to Brugha.

'What do you suggest then?' responded Brugha sarcastically.

Cosgrave pointed to the night nurses' home, a solid three-story stone building on the west side of the main courtyard built at right angles to James' Street.

'It's the strongest building in the Union and its in the right position. From the back we could control MacCaffrey's, Mount Brown, Brookfield Road and even the Rialto Gate,' responded Cosgrave.

'Get the men in at once. Ceannt will want to make that headquarters,' said an impressed Brugha.

Around noon 100 British soldiers of the 3rd Royal Irish, bayonets at the ready, marched up the road towards the Union. They had been ordered to relieve Dublin Castle. Confused fighting broke out at the entrance to the Union with casualties on both sides. The British then took up positions on the roof of the Royal Hospital and sent an attacking party around to the Rialto Gate. They opened up on the defenders around 1 p.m. After ferocious fighting at the Gate, in which the officers commanding the attacking party — Capt. Warmington and Lieut. Ramsay — were killed, the attackers eventually overwhelmed the defences and the volunteers surrendered. At 2.30 p.m. 50 soldiers dashed through the entrance from the canal and fought their way across open ground to Hospitals 2 and 3.

'By mid afternoon both sides had suffered heavy losses. Ceannt had come off worst for most of his outposts had been driven in. Yet he had done all that could be expected of him. The Royal Irish Regiment were still held up,' says Caulfield.

One of the casualties that first day of the Rising was W.T.'s step-brother, Goban, who had loyally followed in his footsteps into the 4th Battalion. He was firing from a window in the Union when he was hit by a bullet through the neck. W.T., who was nearby, rushed to the aid of his step-brother but he died instantly. The death of Goban had a profound effect on W.T. and he blamed himself then and in later years for involving his sibling in the fighting.

On that first night of the Rising the Volunteers in the South Dublin Union said the Rosary before trying to catch some sleep. Lieut. Cosgrave dozed off but was wakened by a sentry who whispered:

'They are out there digging a trench,' pointing towards MacCaffrey's Estate. Cosgrave went over to the window.

'Where?' he asked.

'There just in front. Don't you see it.'

He looked again and sure enough there did seem to be a trench there. Revolver in hand he stole quietly from the Nurses' Home and crept over the grass. Then he realised that the 'trench' was a tarmacadamed path.

'It's only an ould path,' he reassured the sentry when he returned to the Nurses' Home.

'What about the noise then, I heard them digging. Listen.' Cosgrave listened and thought he could hear someone digging. He set off to investigate again and finally discovered the cause of the noise — a loose window blind flapping in the breeze.

On Tuesday morning Ceannt's men improvised a flag, painting an emerald harp on a yellow window blind and nailing it to a long pole. This was raised from an upper window of the Nurses' Home as the garrison stood to attention and sang *A Nation Once Again.* The military reacted by opening up with furious fire from the roof of the Royal Hospital. None of the rebels was hit, the flag was undamaged but a woman sitting in her home on James' Street reading a book and a holidaymaker from Belfast walking along the South Circular Road were both shot dead.

On Thursday there was a big battle for the Nurses' Home which by this stage was garrisoned by just 27 men. A major attack began at 3 p.m. with each side having an exaggerated idea of the other's strength. The British forced their way into the lobby and Ceannt thinking the game was up decided to retreat.

Cosgrave told Caulfield that a definite order to retreat was given.

'It was given to me by Capt. Douglas ffrench Mullen and I understood that it was a definite order from Vice Comdt. Brugha who was upstairs and in a position to see where the British were.'

The rebels were in retreat when a bomb was tossed over a barricade which was holding up the British. The bomb wounded Brugha who managed to drag himself to the bottom of the stairs and turn back to hold off the attackers single handedly with his 'Peter the Painter' revolver. Meanwhile the rest of the rebels had retreated to a dormitory where Cosgrave was arguing with Ceannt that the British had not in fact broken through and that they should return to continue the fight. Ceannt was not convinced and the rebels dejectedly waited for the end. Then they heard a lone voice singing *God Save Ireland* in short snatches. It was Brugha who in between singing opened fire at the barricade. It roused his comrades who sheepishly returned to man the barricade with him. The military never broke through. So Thursday night passed away with the city blazing away on the eastern skyline.

On Friday the GPO garrison surrendered. The South Dublin Union still held out and MacDonagh, after his surrender, asked to be driven there, where he had a discussion with Ceannt and they both surrendered at the same time. Cosgrave walked out with his head bowed down, grieving for his step-brother, Goban, and not knowing what fate awaited him.

W.E. Wylie, the lawyer appointed by the State to act as prosecuting counsel at the court martial of the rebels, recorded his surprise at finding Cosgrave as one of the prisoners on trial for his life. He had never met him before but had heard of him as a member of Dublin Corporation and as a man who was always ready to help the poor of the city.

'I got a shock when I saw him standing there in the green uniform of the Irish Volunteers, with a sergeant's stripes on his arm. I opened the conversation by asking him if he had any idea of the position he was in and he said he had not and asked if it was serious. I told him that the last three men who were tried had all been condemned to death and would be shot in the morning, and that shook him up a bit.

'I asked him if he had any defence and he said that he had never heard of the rebellion until he was in the middle of it. He assured me, and I believed him, that when he marched out on Easter Monday morning he thought he was merely going out on a route march, that he was suddenly told to take men into a hut in the South Dublin Union and hold it and before he knew what happened he was in the middle of a battle. The Royal Irish from Richmond Barracks had rushed the hut and captured him with the others.

'I told him he would have an opportunity of making a full statement and he then asked me if he could call evidence of character. I said certainly and that I would adjourn the case to the next day and have his witnesses present. If I remember correctly he asked for Mr James Gallagher, Lord Mayor, Surgeon MacArdle and Mr Lorcan Sherlock. I told the police sergeant to have them at court at 9 a.m. next morning and they duly arrived.'

After the evidence had been heard Wylie told the court that the accused wanted to make a statement and call evidence.

'I turned and asked Cosgrave to say whatever he wished.

'"I would rather you did it for me," he said. And so I launched out into a speech for the defence and then examined the three witnesses as regards Cosgrave's character.

'It seems a rather strange procedure when written down but none of us thought it in the least peculiar. I have always believed that in prosecutions it is the prosecutor's duty to present the case as fairly as he can and I stuck firmly to that rule. There should be no such thing as "winning" a prosecution. Let the jury understand that they are the guardians of the peace and the upholders of the law of the land and give the prisoner a perfectly fair run.'

As the case closed General Blackadder, president of the court martial, called Wylie back and asked: 'Is that a decent man and was he in your opinion rushed into this?'

'Yes, sir,' replied Wylie.

'Thank you,' said the general. 'We will recommend a reprieve.' Cosgrave was sentenced to death but reprieved. Along with his brother, Philip, he was sent to Dartmoor prison, where conditions were very poor before being sent on to Lewis Prison, in Wales where most of the rebels were held. Although public opinion in Dublin was initially against the Rising the executions changed the atmosphere and there were soon calls for the release of prisoners. In January 1917, Dublin City Council passed a motion calling specifically for Cosgrave's release. 'Mr Cosgrave was chairman of the Finance Committee and had won the respect of every man who had met him. Would anyone seriously suggest for a moment that Willie Cosgrave was a criminal?' read the motion.

2

MINISTER FOR LOCAL GOVERNMENT

W.T. COSGRAVE was released from prison in January 1917 and returned home to a very different Ireland from the one he had left less than a year before. The men of 1916 were now regarded as heroes rather than villains by a substantial segment of the population and a broad Nationalist front was taking shape under the banner of Sinn Féin.

By the time Cosgrave came out of jail Sinn Féin and a range of radical Nationalist groups had decided to test the mood of the electorate by encouraging Count Plunkett to run in the Roscommon North by-election on 3 February against the Parliamentary Party. Plunkett, the father of executed 1916 leader, Joseph Mary Plunkett, won the election, giving Sinn Féin its first seat in the House of Commons. Such was the confused political situation that it was only after his election victory that Plunkett was reluctantly persuaded to adhere to Griffith's policy of abstention from Westminster.

At another by-election in May in Longford South, Rising veteran, Joe McGuiness narrowly defeated the Party and in July, Eamon de Valera was elected for Clare East, following the death of Major Willie Redmond, MP, on the Western front. Cosgrave was then asked by Sinn Féin to stand as its candidate at a by-election in Kilkenny city in August 1917. W.T. was the first official Sinn Féin candidate put into the field. The other three victorious candidates were not Sinn Féin members but 'advanced' Nationalists of one kind or another who found the Sinn Féin label handy in the confused political situation of 1917.

Cosgrave had the help of legendary political organiser, Dan McCarthy, for his by-election campaign. McCarthy had run the failed Sinn Féin campaign in Leitrim in 1908 but had shown his prowess in the three by-elections of 1917, particularly in East Clare. Cosgrave had the support of the *Kilkenny Journal* which declared that 'the issue before the voters of Kilkenny is whether Kilkenny stands for Ireland a nation or for Ireland as a West British province.' The newspaper editorial rejected the suggestion that Sinn Féin stood for 'red ruin and revolution' saying the party represented nothing of the kind.

In a hard fought but not noticeably bitter campaign Cosgrave made a number of characteristically short speeches. 'We have come asking you to put your mark for the right of the Irish people to a new Ireland and an Ireland no longer under the domination of a foreign government.' Other prominent figures like Eamon de Valera and Eoin MacNeill campaigned for Cosgrave, making much longer speeches in his favour than the candidate himself.

In the event Cosgrave won the contest by 772 votes to 392. When the result was announced in the council chamber his defeated Nationalist Party opponent John Magennis expressed all the pent up frustration of the average Redmondite, describing the result as 'a victory for intolerance, low, mean, lying and scurrilous abuse, terrorism and intimidation of the grossest type.' W.T. didn't respond to the criticism but said the campaign had been 'an exercise of national self-restraint typical of the Irish race.'

After his victory Cosgrave went out onto the balcony of the courthouse where he was joined by de Valera. 'A scene of wild enthusiasm was witnessed,' when the two men appeared, according to the *Kilkenny Journal*.

The authorities became seriously alarmed at the fourth Sinn Féin victory in a row and the result was followed by nationwide raids and arrests under the Defence of the Realm Act. Among the prisoners were Thomas Ashe, Austin Stack and Fionan Lynch. They went on hunger strike in Mountjoy and, after force-feeding, Ashe died in the Mater Hospital on 5 September. His death added considerably to the anti-British mood in the country; Ashe's body lay in state for three days in the Pro Cathedral and 30,000 people followed the coffin to Glasnevin.

The huge funeral was a potential flash-point for a confrontation with the military because the Volunteers were determined to mount a guard of honour for the coffin. Cosgrave helped to defuse the problem by going to see the Dublin city treasurer, a man called Eyre, whom he knew well through his Corporation activities. Eyre in turn went to see the commander of the British troops in Dublin, Sir Bryan

Mahon, and he agreed to confine his soldiers to barracks during the funeral. A few years later Cosgrave appointed Sir Bryan as a senator in the Irish Free State.

The political allegiance of the Irish people was now slipping inexorably away from the old Parliamentary Party. In its place the Volunteers, the IRB and Sinn Féin merged together into a broad Nationalist front under the Sinn Féin banner. From the beginning there were differences between the Sinn Féin group of which Cosgrave was a prominent member, committed to Griffith's policy, and the revolutionaries of the IRB who had masterminded the rebellion of 1916. The Volunteers were somewhere in the middle with members like Cosgrave drawn from Sinn Féin and others like Collins from the IRB.

With the label Sinn Féin being applied to all the separatist factions de Valera decided to contest the presidency of the party against Arthur Griffith in October 1917. Griffith stepped down rather than push the issue to a vote and de Valera was elected. For the next four years it appeared that non-violent Sinn Féin and the militant armed Republicans were at one but tensions always lingered beneath the surface and a clash between the two was inevitable at some stage.

When a general election was called in 1918 Sinn Féin swept the boards. The party won 73 seats as against 6 for the Parliamentary Party and 26 for the Unionists. In terms of seats the result was an overwhelming victory for Sinn Féin but there was not total unanimity among the electorate. With Sinn Féin being unopposed in a number of constituencies, due in some cases to intimidation, nearly one third of the electorate did not get a chance to vote and of the votes cast Sinn Féin won just 47%. In Kilkenny Cosgrave, like many of his colleagues around the country, was elected unopposed. By the time of the election he was back in jail, having been arrested along with 71 other Sinn Féin leaders, including de Valera, as a result of the 'German plot' of April 1918. The alleged plot between the Sinn Féin leadership and the Germans for another Rising was widely regarded in Ireland as a concoction by the authorities and the jailing of the Sinn Féin leadership was a huge boost to the party's electoral campaign.

Fulfilling their pledge to abstain from Westminster the Sinn Féin MPs met in the Mansion House in Dublin on 21 January 1919, and constituted the First Dáil. In the absence of many leading Sinn Féin personalities, including Cosgrave and de Valera, who were still in Lincoln Jail, Cathal Brugha was elected temporary president of the

Dáil. He selected four Ministers, Eoin MacNeill for Finance, Michael Collins at Home Affairs, Count Plunkett, Foreign Affairs and Dick Mulcahy for Defence.

On the same day as the first Dáil met another incident took place which was also to have a vital bearing on the future of Ireland. At Soloheadbeg in Co. Tipperary a group of Volunteers led by Dan Breen ambushed and killed two policemen, opening a guerrilla war against the forces of the Crown. The Soloheadbeg ambush shocked opinion across the Unionist–Nationalist divide and the killings were denounced from the pulpit of the local parish. Arthur Griffith made no public comment but according to a close associate, Desmond Ryan, he frowned on the killings. There was something symbolic in the fact that on the same day as the Dáil first met the Volunteers, soon to become known as the IRA, committed a brutal act of violence. The seeds of a later struggle for the soul of Ireland, between the ballot box and the bullet were sown on that fateful day, 21 January 1919.

De Valera escaped from Lincoln jail on 3 February and the Dáil met for the second time on 1 April. Brugha resigned his temporary position and de Valera was elected president of the Dáil. On 2 April he announced his cabinet: Griffith, Home Affairs; Brugha, Defence; Plunkett, Foreign Affairs; Countess Markievicz, Labour; MacNeill, Industry; Collins, Finance; and Cosgrave, who had been released from prison by that stage was appointed to head the Department of Local Government. W.T. was now one of the leaders of the independence movement.

His experience as a member of Dublin Corporation and in Sinn Féin local administration made him admirably suited to the post. Ernest Blythe, who first got to know Cosgrave in 1919, explained years later why W.T. became such a popular figure as Minister for Local Government.

> 'It was not long till I discovered that he was an enemy of all pomposity, which wakened in him a spirit of mischievous humour, and that he was an expert at puncturing it with a whimsical comment or a seemingly innocent query. He has often been described as a modest man and rightly so. He never showed the slightest ambition to be at the head of affairs or to claim, much less monopolise, the limelight.'

Throughout his period of office he was almost constantly on the run and had to work underground. Cosgrave's office, which was generally located in the back rooms of private houses, was moved constantly between Clare Street, Parnell Square and Exchequer

Street. Members of his family were arrested and jailed on several occasions and his office was raided continually. He evaded arrest by assuming a number of disguises and by keeping on the move. Moira Lysaght remembered seeing him on Merchants' Quay one day with his hair dyed black and she recalled hearing that a Miss Drago regularly coloured his hair to protect the disguise.

As well as becoming a Minister of the Dáil in 1919 Cosgrave took another eventful step. He married Louisa, daughter of his colleague on Dublin Corporation, Alderman Flanagan of Portmahon House in Rialto, the next parish to St James'. Flanagan was a leading member of the old Parliamentary Party in Dublin and was a wealthy property owner. The Flanagans were well known for other reasons. Louisa had three brothers all of whom were well-known characters in Dublin but the best known of them was the Bird Flanagan.

Oliver St John Gogarty, who was no shrinking violet himself, found the Flanagans a bit too eccentric for his taste.

> 'Any mention of the Bird Flanagan makes me uneasy. He is one of three brothers who would be better had they remained in Turgenev. Characters such as these are to be found both in the Russian author and in Dublin's fair city. Who is the Bird? Well let me try to tell you. He went to a fancy dress ball in Earlsfort Terrace skating rink dressed as the Holy Ghost and supported by two holy women. In the middle of the floor he laid an egg the size of a football. The management interposed; he and his supporters went out clucking. But the name the Bird stuck to him since the incident of the egg.'

Ulick O'Connor believes that the Bird was in fact the victim of a rival practical jester who carried out the ice rink performance but one way or another the name stuck.

The exploits of the Bird became part of Dublin folklore. On one occasion he rode his horse into the lobby of the Gresham Hotel where he requested a drink for his horse. That incident is still commemorated in the name of the Bird Flanagan bar in the hotel. W.T., whose sense of humour was very dry by comparison, had married into a family who were legends in their own lifetime but the Flanagans were well off. After his marriage to Louisa, W.T. purchased Beechpark in Templeogue where he was to live for the rest of his life. The couple had two sons, Liam and Michael. Liam, the eldest, was born on 13 April 1920, at a time when W.T. was a wanted man with a price on his head.

Cosgrave was typical enough of the Sinn Féin leadership who were generally middle class and mainly Dublin based but he was a little older than most of his colleagues and through his activity on the Corporation he had far more practical political experience than any of them. W.T., as Minister for Local Government, helped to develop support for Sinn Féin on other local councils and many of them were persuaded to shift allegiance from the British administration in Dublin Castle to the Dáil, even though Sinn Féin remained a minority on most councils.

Some of Cosgrave's early schemes were to investigate the possibility of organising a municipal milk service and the purchase of the Freeman's Journal. His department advised local government bodies to apply for all possible British grants while they still could, particularly when it came to funds for public housing.

Local elections in urban areas, held under proportional election, which was introduced by the British to minimise Sinn Féin strength, were set for 15 January 1920, and the result reflected a high degree of diversity among the urban electorate. Sinn Féin did well but it was not the overwhelming victory of the general election. Of the 1,186 seats Sinn Féin won 560, Labour 394 and the Unionists 355. The Home Rulers clung on to 238 seats and Independents of all kinds 269. The figures for the percentage share of the vote are even more illuminating. Out of the 322,244 votes cast Sinn Féin won 27.1%, closely followed by the Unionists with 26.7%, Labour took 18%, the Home Rulers 15% and Independents 14%. It was an indication that in urban areas, at least, the electorate was by no means committed to an Irish Republic as the only desirable outcome of the independence struggle.

The county council elections which followed in June of 1920 delivered a much more emphatic result for Sinn Féin with the party winning majorities in 29 of the 33 councils. Many seats were uncontested and the party was unchallenged in rural areas. The council elections provided an antidote to the somewhat disappointing urban results.

In the meantime the Volunteers, now called the Irish Republican Army, stepped up their campaign of guerilla war and the country was gradually engulfed in a wave of violence as the British responded with the counter-terror of the Black and Tans and the Auxiliaries. As the authorities began to round up Sinn Féin leaders Cosgrave was arrested again in March 1920. He was released from prison at the end of April but was hospitalised in mid May and did not resume his duties until July.

With many councils repudiating British authority grants were cut off. A circular sent by Cosgrave in September 1920, declared:

'The stoppage of grants in aid of local taxation by the enemy government is a last despairing attempt to bribe the people of Ireland back into slavery.'

At this stage Cosgrave had his headquarters in the General Council of County Councils office in Parnell Square. Under constant threat of discovery by the authorities he received messengers who delivered letters and minutes from the various county councils and met council members who were brought to his offices blindfold.

W.T. had been provided with an assistant Minister, the brilliant and mercurial, Kevin O'Higgins. W.T. needed back-up for not only was he not in the best of health at this time but he was by now a well known figure in Dublin and the police were in a position to shadow him everywhere he went to frustrate his activities. With the appointment of O'Higgins the Department of Local Government now consisted of the Minister, the Assistant Minister, a clerk, a typist and an office boy. Cosgrave and the abrasive O'Higgins had a strained relationship. As Terence de Vere White pointed out the two men were 'diametrically opposed to one and another in temperament, intellect and outlook.' At times they did complement each other. Whenever an abusive letter needed to be written Cosgrave would say 'Here, Higgins, you're a cross-grained divil, you had better deal with this fellow — and for God's sake work off some of your spleen on him, instead of on me.'

The political activity of the Dáil took place against the background of escalating violence. 'Bloody Sunday' on 21 November with the killing of 14 alleged British intelligence officers on the orders of Collins marked an escalation of the campaign of violence. That same afternoon the Auxies retaliated by going to Croke Park and shooting dead 12 of the spectators gathered for a football match between Tipperary and Dublin. Griffith was appalled by the violence initiated by the Collins hit squad. 'We cannot defend this,' he told Sinn Féin colleagues.

In the aftermath of 'Bloody Sunday' Collins warned Cosgrave that he had heard from his top spy in the Castle, David Neligan, that the Minister for Local Government was to be arrested. W.T. decided that in the circumstances it was futile for him to continue with the work of his department and he disappeared for almost two months. One day O'Higgins came into the office to find a note from his chief directing him to stop the work for the time being as Cosgrave had left Dublin. O'Higgins refused to act on his chief's instructions and continued to work on in the department, provoking a row with his Minister when he returned to his duties.

Cosgrave's disappearance became an issue of controversy in the political battles of later years. Long after the event Robert Barton said of W.T. that he was 'so elusive that he could hardly ever be found by his colleagues'. Quoting a number of stories from the time Arthur Mitchell in his book *Revolutionary Government in Ireland* says:

> 'According to one account Cosgrave had ceased going to his office to avoid arrest. Upon receiving complaints Collins sent a message to Cosgrave to open the offices. Cosgrave told the messenger "Tell Collins that I am not going to be shot for him".'

Tim Pat Coogan puts down W.T.'s reclusive period as a reaction to the horrors of Bloody Sunday. The evidence suggests that he disappeared on the advice of Collins rather than on his own initiative. Soon after de Valera returned to Ireland he got Cosgrave to resume his position. Richard Mulcahy claimed O'Higgins had a low opinion of his chief's capacity for leadership at this time. As an indication that Cosgrave was right to be concerned about his personal safety a reward of £3,500 for information leading to his capture was announced by the British in March. An even bigger reward of £10,000 was offered for Collins, Mulcahy and Brugha.

De Valera returned from a long 18-month absence in the United States in December 1920 to find the political and military situation transformed. Cosgrave returned to his desk at the end of January 1921, and quickly established a rapport with de Valera in the cabinet. Coogan quotes de Valera as telling Frank Gallagher that at this period Cosgrave became 'nearer to me in a personal sense than anybody in the cabinet,' and he put Cosgrave's attachment to him on a par with that of Frank Aiken. 'Cosgrave was the one who called at de Valera's office to take him to lunch and performed other small, necessary services such as ensuring that he got his hair cut,' says Coogan.

An important political initiative was taken by the British through the Government of Ireland Act, 1920. The Act finally delivered on the promise of Home Rule but in the shape of two parliaments, one for the 26 counties of the South and the other for the North. A bridge between the two parliaments was proposed in a Council of Ireland which would draw elected politicians from both. The Act got a cold response from Sinn Féin because it came nowhere near the party's demand for independence. The powers given to the two parliaments were limited, with control of finance and foreign affairs retained at

Westminster. However, the Sinn Féin leadership didn't grasp the long-term significance of partition which was institutionalised in the Act. Elections in May 1921, saw all 124 Sinn Féin candidates elected unopposed in the South. W.T.'s brother, Philip joined him in the Second Dáil. In the North the election was a different story. All constituencies were keenly contested and the Unionists won a clear majority in the 52-seat assembly. At the opening of the Northern parliament at Stormont in June King George V undertook a political initiative in calling for reconciliation which led to a breakthrough in the search for a solution.

British prime minister, Lloyd George, abandoning his policy of trying to 'catch murder by the throat' followed up on the King's initiative and his proposal for a truce was accepted by Sinn Féin on 11 July. There followed a lot of delicate manoeuvering by Lloyd George and de Valera who met four times in Downing Street during July. The wily Lloyd George described negotiation with de Valera as akin to 'picking up mercury with a fork' but the president of the Dáil eventually accepted an invitation for a conference in London to settle the Anglo-Irish issue once and for all.

However, when it came to the composition of the Irish negotiating team de Valera dropped a bombshell — he announced to his startled cabinet colleagues that he would not be travelling. In a decision which was to have an incalculable effect on the history of Ireland in the twentieth century he claimed it was better that he should hold himself in reserve as a symbol of the Republic. Griffith, Collins and Cosgrave voiced their opposition to de Valera's decision at cabinet, providing a hint of the terrible divisions to come. Whatever the closeness or otherwise of Cosgrave's relations with de Valera during the spring and summer of 1921 they were strained by this development.

Cosgrave didn't just oppose de Valera at cabinet, he came out in the open in the Dáil on 14 September and objected to the decision. He was immediately rebuked by a strong de Valera supporter, Dr Pat McCartan, who accused him of being out of order in opposing a cabinet motion in the Dáil. Cosgrave, however, stood his ground. He told the Dáil that 'this was a team they were sending over and they were leaving their ablest player in reserve. Now it was not usual to leave the ablest players in reserve. The reserve would have to be used some time or other and it struck him now was the time they were required.'

Surprisingly Kevin O'Higgins immediately got to his feet to oppose his senior colleague and support de Valera. He told the Dáil he was fully convinced that the President should not go to London in order to safeguard the Republic and preserve its symbolic head. Demonstrating, not for the first time, his political naïvety O'Higgins sided with the more doctrinaire Republicans like Countess Markievicz and Mary MacSwiney against Cosgrave. Michael Collins briefly put on the record his belief that de Valera should have been part of the delegation and said he did not want to go himself. By this stage objections were too late and de Valera had no difficulty getting his way with the Dáil.

Cosgrave's reservations stemmed from the fact that he was aware de Valera was already working on the formula of external association to get over the problem of the Republic. Back in June de Valera had asked Griffith to get him out of the strait-jacket of the Republic. Now in September he told Griffith 'there may have to be scapegoats'. De Valera later said that he was using Griffith as bait for Lloyd George to entice him towards the Irish position. Cosgrave, much more wily than Griffith, clearly had an inkling of de Valera's strategy from the start and did his best to head him off. Despite their difference of opinion de Valera still believed Cosgrave was an ally he could count on in all circumstances.

The Dáil delegation led by Griffith and Collins spent two months in intensive negotiations with the British and finally agreed to the terms of a treaty which essentially conferred dominion status, akin to that of Canada, on the 26 counties. The Treaty was agreed on the night of 5 December without reference back to de Valera or the cabinet in Dublin. In the early hours of the morning, after the Treaty was signed, Collins, gripped by a sense of foreboding wrote:

'When you have sweated, toiled, had mad dreams, hopeless nightmares, you find yourself in London's streets, cold and dank in the night air. Think — what I have got for Ireland. Something which she has wanted these past 700 years. Will anyone be satisfied at the bargain? Will anyone? I tell you this — early this morning I signed my death warrant. I thought at the time how odd, how ridiculous — a bullet may just as well have done the job five years ago.'

As Collins was pacing the streets of London first word of the signing reached Dublin. Journalist and historian Desmond Ryan, who participated in the 1916 Rising, the War of Independence and the Civil War describes the scene in a Dublin newspaper office as the news of the Treaty came in.

'It was late and the remaining subs had already put on their hats and coats. Half their number had gone home. All the evening rumour had chased rumour but now the Chief was wrestling to fit in the unexpected news at the stone below, scanning the reversed type, killing the least important stories and listening with knit brow and eyes aglow to the yeas and nays of the printing room foreman. The formes were locked and the presses started to the taps of hammers on the leaden semi-cylinders from the foundry, false starts and then a hum. Wearily, less wearily the machines sang: peace, Peace, PEACE! A white cataract swirled from the presses to the waiting vans. Peace! The posters shrieked on the building's front. One word, five deep black letters. PEACE!'

The popular mood may have been for peace but the signing of the Treaty came as a shock to de Valera, as much because the signatories had not consulted him before signing, as anything else. He decided immediately to reject the agreement in the belief that he could carry the cabinet with him. Cosgrave suddenly found himself in a pivotal role as the nation held its breath and waited for the three cabinet members, Collins, Griffith and Barton, who had signed the Treaty, to return home. Three others — de Valera, Stack and Brugha — were strongly opposed to it; Cosgrave was the man in the middle. De Valera decided on a pre-emptive strike before the signatories even came home and he called a meeting of the four cabinet Ministers who were in Ireland. When the cabinet met on 7 December de Valera announced that he was going to sack the three Ministers who had signed the Treaty.

Stack and Brugha had no hesitation in supporting de Valera but Cosgrave, who carefully avoided expressing any view one way or another on the merits of the Treaty, surprised his three colleagues by maintaining that it would be wrong to condemn the delegates without a hearing. De Valera was taken aback by Cosgrave's opposition to his proposed sacking but he conceded that the three deserved a hearing and agreed to postpone a decision until they had returned. He took this cautious approach in an attempt to keep Cosgrave on his side so that he could out-vote the three plenipotentiaries when they returned. It was one of the few times in his political life when de Valera was outsmarted, because Cosgrave clearly anticipated his game. It was a decisive moment in Irish history and many years later Cosgrave told his son Liam that it was one of the most significant cabinet meetings he had ever attended.

If de Valera had pressed ahead and sacked the three negotiators the Treaty might have been strangled at birth and Irish history would have been very different. As it was Cosgrave bought the signatories time and he kept the political options open long enough to out-manoeuvre the militants. By giving the Treaty a breathing space of another 24-hours he also allowed time for a groundswell of popular opinion, fuelled by the press, to continue developing in its favour.

The critical cabinet meeting took place the following day in the Mansion House and it lasted for more than five hours. As well as the seven cabinet Ministers Duggan, Duffy, Childers and Kevin O'Higgins attended the meeting. Griffith and Collins were unambiguously behind the Treaty while the other signatory, Barton, although doubtful, felt obliged to vote in favour as he had signed it. With de Valera, Stack and Brugha implacably opposed Cosgrave's was the crucial vote. He had no hesitation in backing the Treaty, much to de Valera's annoyance.

As the cabinet meeting was going on in the Mansion House Frank Gallagher was briefing journalists in an adjoining room. They were oblivious to the furious row among Ireland's leaders about the fate of the country going on within earshot. 'Just as the room filled with enquiring journalists came angry voices. To every question from the pressmen I had a voluble answer. They did not perceive the raised voices, which in my ears were again and again an orchestration to what I was saying.'

The cabinet decided by a majority of four to three to recommend the Treaty to Dáil Éireann and the Irish people. De Valera, however, made it clear that he would be opposing the Treaty and he told his colleagues he would be issuing a statement to the press.

In the emotional debate on the Treaty which lasted from 14 December 1921 until 10 January 1922, W.T. Cosgrave was his usual practical, level-headed self. Before the debate began he gave his private assessment of what the row was all about. 'Everybody wants to lap up the milk but nobody wants to recognise the cow,' he told Michael Hayes. In the debate itself he poked fun at de Valera, who was bitterly disappointed that Cosgrave had turned the balance of power against him in the cabinet. Attacked for not wanting to rid Ireland of all British influence he rejoined:

'The best colleagues play foreign games. The President can bear me out in that [applause]'

a reference to Dev's passion for the British game of rugby rather than gaelic football and hurling. Cosgrave continued with a dig at Stack and Brugha.

'At the race meetings one sees the Union Jack. I believe the Minister for Home Affairs [Stack] can bear me out in that [applause]. I don't know what the Minister for Defence [Brugha] does in his idle moments. I cannot get him to bear me out in anything.'

Despite their growing differences Cosgrave still respected de Valera and Stack but his attitude to Brugha was very different.

'I believe, sir, the loss of the President to the Free State, should this instrument be approved, would be a terrible loss. I believe the loss of the Minister for Home Affairs and the Minister for Finance would be equally irreparable, I know the Minister for Defence. My own conviction is that except for war he is not worth a damn for anything else.'

W.T.'s attitude to his former colleague from the South Dublin Union in 1916 gave a hint of the Civil War bitterness to come. However, in this, his first major contribution to the debate on 21 December he was happy that his sense of humour had lightened up the proceedings.

'Whether I have made a case for signing the Treaty or not, I think Dáil Éireann is in better humour now than when I started and I now formally approve, recommend and support the Treaty,' he concluded.

Recalling the Treaty debate a few months later an *Irish Times* journalist referred to Cosgrave's capacity to lighten the gloomy atmosphere.

'One day the whole Assembly was bored to mental paralysis. Member after member had droned out his contribution to the musty discussion on constitutional quibbles which nobody understood and in which none but the man who was speaking took the slightest interest. Tempers were jagged, nerves were on edge; as time progressed bitter taunts began to be hurled across the room. Then Mr Cosgrave got up and in a moment the whole atmosphere was changed. A ripple of half suppressed mirth greeted his opening sallies and in a twinkling his apparent flippancy had the whole Dáil laughing without restraint. Even Mr de Valera could not resist the well pointed witticism of the jocular gentleman from Kilkenny, as Mr Cosgrave was nicknamed half an hour later by Mr Cathal Brugha, and when his speech was finished not only had several new supporters been gained for the Treaty but the danger signals had disappeared and everyone was in good humour again.'

While his speech had more humour than most he did make some very serious points. Not only did he refer to the North, which most TDs ignored completely, he showed a rare grasp of the essential contradiction in militant Irish Nationalism between the drive for sovereignty on the one hand and the desire for unity on the other.

> 'One question that has not been put at all is this: If you could have a choice for a Republic with twenty six counties, would you have it or a Dominion for the whole of Ireland. If such a choice were put up my money would be on the Dominion, not *per se* on the Dominion, but because it would effect that unification that ought to be effected in Ireland.'

His assessment about the prospects of Unionists accepting a Dominion may have been optimistic but Cosgrave at least recognised a problem which didn't rate in the contributions of most other deputies. Sean McEntee was the only anti-Treaty deputy to deal in any detail with the North but Cosgrave was the only one who identified the nub of the problem for Irish Nationalists. When the vote was taken on 6 January 1922, the Treaty was approved by 64 votes to 57 and de Valera resigned the Presidency. De Valera spoke of the four glorious years and national discipline and then overcome with emotion he sat down, buried his face in his arms and wept. His action released the pent-up emotions of his fellow deputies and almost every one of them was soon sobbing openly.

When the Dáil resumed on 9 January de Valera offered his government's resignation and rejected Collins' offer of cooperation. To try and preserve the unity of the Dáil a formula was devised for parallel government structures. On 10 January Griffith was proposed and elected as president of the Dáil and promised to function as president of the Republic. He named his cabinet from pro-Treaty deputies with Collins remaining as Minister for Finance and Cosgrave, Minister for Local Government.

Two days later Griffith, acting in his capacity as chairman of the Treaty delegation, summoned members of the House of Commons of Southern Ireland to a meeting on 14 January and in less than an hour the 60 pro-Treaty deputies present elected a Provisional Government which had Collins as chairman and Cosgrave in his Ministry of Local Government. Neither Griffith nor Mulcahy were members of the Provisional Government but they worked closely with it. It was thus with two structures of government, a divided Dáil and a split IRA that the country lurched towards Civil War.

3

MORAL DESOLATION

THE Provisional Government set up headquarters at Dublin's City Hall, because of its easy access to Dublin Castle, the seat of the British administration. Kevin O'Higgins graphically summed up the mood in those early months of 1922 describing himself and his Government colleagues as 'simply eight young men in the City Hall standing amidst the ruins of one administration, with the foundations of another not yet laid, with wild men screaming through the keyhole.'

There was some escape from the anxiety as W.T. Cosgrave told Ulick O'Connor years later for his biography of Oliver St John Gogarty.

> 'On most afternoons of the week Gogarty and Collins would drive out for tea to Beechpark, the house of Vice-President Cosgrave which was situated at the foot of the Dublin hills in Templeogue. Here, for an hour or so, they could forget the atmosphere of doom that was gradually gathering about public life in the county during those fateful months. Collins would roar with laughter at Gogarty's sallies, particularly when Gogarty said something more than usually irreverent that caused a shadow to flit across the face of the Vice-President, who had a Dublin man's sense of humour but was inclined rather to piety.'

Remembering those days the elderly W.T. told O'Connor 'I often thought that pair of rascals took more delight in shocking me than in talking serious business when they came out to tea.'

In the six months after the Treaty as the Government struggled with the drawing up of a new Constitution the country drifted towards civil war. Rory O'Connor, the leader of the anti-Treaty military wing, repudiated the authority of the Dáil on 28 March and he received the reluctant support of de Valera. Shortly after midnight on 13 April

O'Connor and the Irregulars, as the armed Republicans were now called, seized the Four Courts in Dublin.

The Catholic hierarchy issued a joint statement two weeks later condemning the rise of intimidation, sabotage and murder adding:

'Like the great bulk of the nation we think that the best and wisest course for Ireland is to accept the Treaty and make the most of the freedom it undoubtedly brings ... the cause of all our present scandals and turmoil is the unconstitutional policy of certain leaders who think themselves entitled to force their views upon the nation, not by reason but by firearms.'

With an election arranged for the end of June, Collins and de Valera signed a pact that would allow thepro and anti-Treaty factions to return to the Dáil in their existing strength. Neither man appears to have understood the workings of proportional representation because such a pact was simply not feasible in multi-seat constituencies with other parties and Independents also entitled to enter the fray.

The British were seriously worried by the pact and asked for a formal meeting with the Irish side. Griffith who had been opposed to the pact in the first place was not anxious to go to London to defend it. He was eventually persuaded to go but he asked that Collins, Cosgrave, O'Higgins and Duggan should go with him to confront the British delegation of Lloyd George, Churchill, Birkenhead, Austen Chamberlin and Hamar Greenwood. Collins was also anxious that W.T. should travel suggesting that 'Cosgrave and his oil can' would come in handy at the conference. The meeting was tense to begin with and the temperature rose when Churchill demanded to know if the Irish side intended to stick by the Treaty.

An angry Griffith jumped to his feet and told the British that he had no intention of dishonouring his word and would stand by the Treaty. 'Griffith spoke to them like a virgin who had been affronted by a rude remark,' Cosgrave told his friends when he returned to Dublin. At the meeting Cosgrave intervened to cool things down; he explained to the British that political realities dictated the necessity of the pact. As a normal election was impossible it was the only way they had of testing public opinion for the Treaty. As conversation then became general Cosgrave suddenly asked Churchill, who had been taking a very severe line, how he was feeling after a recent fall from a pony during a polo match.

'Instantly Winston Churchill's manner changed; here was somebody who had more than an official interest in him, a kindly solicitude for him personally. From that moment his manner changed; he became sympathetic,' according to Padraig Colum in his biography of Griffith.

When it came on 25 June 1922, the election proved a decisive decision by the electorate in favour of the Treaty. Despite widespread intimidation by the Irregulars the pro-Treaty panel of candidates polled nearly twice as many votes as the anti-Treaty panel. If the votes of Labour, the Farmers' Party and Independent candidates are added into the pro-Treaty total the result was even more decisive with less than 22% of the electorate voting against the Treaty.

After the election result the Provisional Government issued an ultimatum to the Irregulars to leave the Four Courts and release a hostage they were holding there. The Republicans refused and the Civil War began with an attack on the Four Courts by the Free State Army. The garrison surrendered after three days but in the course of the fighting the Public Record Office, and much of its invaluable collection of historical documents, was destroyed. Street fighting took place in Dublin and O'Connell Street was again left in ruins, only six years after 1916. In a major military offensive the Free State forces drove the Irregulars out of all the major towns by the end of August, with sea borne landings in Cork and Tralee being part of the operation. After that the Irregulars took to guerrilla warfare and terrorism.

Collins took temporary leave from his position as chairman of the Provisional Government to concentrate on winning the war and Cosgrave was elected by his colleagues as cabinet chairman in his place while Griffith continued on as president of Dáil Éireann. The first meeting of the third Dáil was postponed on a number of occasions, pending the stabilisation of the military situation.

Following the outbreak of hostilities at the end of June President Griffith and the members of the Provisional Government, whose lives were now in constant danger, were compelled to live together under military guard in the newly acquired Government Buildings, formerly the Department of Agriculture in Upper Merrion Street. As the war intensified some Ministers were also forced to live in Government Buildings with their families for protection.

'O'Higgins told Churchill how, when he went on the roof at night to get air and lit a match, a sniper's bullet shot the cigarette out of his hands,' Terence de Vere White wrote in his biography of O'Higgins:

'On their return from their honeymoon Kevin O'Higgins and his bride had set up house in Terenure in the Dublin suburbs, which he called Dunamace after the rock near his boyhood home. It proved to be no fortress and when rumours of an attack on it reached the Government, Mrs O'Higgins had to leave at a moment's notice and take refuge with a neighbour. Shots were fired into the house and, the following morning, it was closed up and the young wife moved into the safety of Government Buildings.'

This strange existence of cabinet Ministers and their families, cooped up behind armed guards in the imposing Government Buildings on Merrion Square, heightened the sense of siege. Gogarty, a lifelong friend of Griffith and Cosgrave describes going there in early August 1922 after he had heard worrying reports about Griffith's health. 'Arthur Griffith lay on a small mattress in a room off the Ministry of Justice high up in the Government Buildings, as the place intended for a College of Science in the days of the British Administration was now called,' wrote Gogarty remembering the scene in *As I was Going Down Sackville Street.*

He recalled his sadness that Griffith had to be guarded by Scots soldiers recruited into the Free State Army because Irishmen could not be trusted.

'If you wished to see him as a medical attendant you had to put your face into a large leather box-like grille and hold it against the revolver of the sentry on duty before the door was opened. When you were admitted into the Hall you found yourself in a small chamber, walled by bullet-proof sheets of steel. Search and interrogation preceded your admittance. The lift was not working, neither were the charwomen. Through dirty marble halls and up dirty staircases of a building never designed for dwellings, at last you reached the fourth storey. A long corridor led to the Ministry. Past both, you reached the small closet where Arthur Griffith lay. At a glance you recognised a man who was very ill. He had a solicitor administering to him. The hour was nine o'clock of a morning. My mind was made up at once. Out of this he must be taken.'

Gogarty had Griffith brought to 96 Lower Leeson Street, a nursing home run by the Sisters of Mercy, but it was too late. The first leader of an independent Ireland died of a stroke the following morning.

Cosgrave was shattered when he heard of Griffith's death, particularly as it came so soon after threats had been made by the Irregulars to shoot Government Ministers. On the day of his leader's death W.T. sat down in his office and wrote a memo, left in the files of his department, which was clearly designed to be published if he was murdered by Republicans. The full text is worth quoting because it sums up Cosgrave's deep religious faith and his absolute commitment to democracy.

'Now under the shadow of the great national calamity, the death of President Arthur Griffith, comes the news that members of the Government are on the list to be shot. This is misguided patriotism on the part of those who have been unequal to the shock of war. The people who so act are irresponsible and must not be allowed to cow or awe the people of Ireland. Even if the members of the Government are shot and die others will be found to take their places. None of us could be indispensible. The country has not yet discovered the true worth of our successes. The people must discover them. I believe Genl. Collins is one of the greatest men Ireland has produced. A statesman and a soldier — and there are others also in the Government and in the Army. My place will be easily filled. I am sorry for my people, my wife, my children, my mother and family. They all suffered during the late war and did not grumble — others suffered too and did not grumble. They did not suffer in vain. Hard times are coming but they — the people of Ireland — will endure, but they must prevail against any minority seeking to order their will or their life, save under the laws which the people's representatives pass. I willingly forgive those who think I should be shot and those who take part in such shooting and I ask forgiveness of all those I have offended. I thank all who helped me and without whose help any work in which I was engaged would have been valueless. I thank all who prayed for me and helped me whom in life it was not possible to even thank. I thank the Archbishop and all his priests and all my colleagues and friends and acquaintances and if it can do any good I ask those who are in arms against the Government to consider if it be not possible to come to agreement with the nation. No member of the Government wishes to continue any war on any section. I ask for obedience to the parliament of the Irish nation and may God in His infinite mercy forgive me my sins and pardon my shortcomings. 12.8.22. Liam T. Mac Cosgair.'

Cosgrave gave the oration at his Griffith's graveside three days later. Uncharacteristically bitter W.T. took a sideswipe at de Valera when describing Griffith's sterling qualities.

'He abhorred those magicians of political metaphysics who say one thing and mean another. At no time during his life, during the period that anyone here knew this man, did he ever say yes when he meant no or say no when he meant yes and when he signed the Treaty with the enemy, whom he had encountered and fought during the last 30 years, he meant to keep it. His signature was his bond for the honour of the nation on whose behalf he had pledged his word.'

Cosgrave then went on emotionally:

'He died a sorrowful man, and if it were not for the greatness of his heart and the magnificence of his mind he would have died a broken-hearted man, for within the last few months of his life he looked out upon the moral desolation which, for the time being darkened his country and stained its name both at home and abroad — a moral desolation not merely in the ordinary acceptance of the term in which people think of dishonesty and disregard of individual rights, of reckless murder and general insincerity, but also the moral desolation in a blindly dishonest outlook and attitude towards the national position and the effect on the nation's Treaty of Peace.'

Ten days later on 22 August came the dreadful news of Collins' death at Beal na Bláth. The cabinet met that night in Cosgrave's office and an immediate concern was to ensure that there would be no military reprisals. Collins' body was brought back from Cork to Dublin by boat and lay in state in City Hall. He was buried in Glasnevin alongside Griffith, Parnell and O'Connell. Cosgrave again had the painful duty of delivering the oration at the graveside of a dead Irish leader for the second time in less than two weeks. He was now the obvious successor to Griffith and Collins but W.T. was not the only name considered by the leaders of the pro-Treaty party. Richard Mulcahy and Eoin MacNeill were asked by supporters to put their names forward. Kevin O'Higgins, who never had an easy relationship with Cosgrave, pressed Mulcahy.

'O'Higgins' idea was that I should be the head of the Government,' wrote Mulcahy, 'but there was no move to discuss that and as far as I was concerned the position with regard to the Army was that I didn't believe that the Army could be handled by anyone except myself after Collins' death. Therefore, the question of my taking over the Government would be an utter impossibility at that time.'

Terence de Vere White says that while O'Higgins favoured Mulcahy the support for Cosgrave was so strong that he withdrew his opposition. O'Higgins, though, is reputed to have sneered that 'a Dublin corporator would make Ireland a nation once again.' On the Republican side there was a misguided view that Cosgrave and his colleagues would not be able for the task facing them. 'Collins' loss is one which they cannot fill. The enemy's position from the point of view of military and political leadership is very bad — we are at present in a much better position,' wrote Liam Lynch at the end of August.

On 9 September the Third Dáil met for the first time and Cosgrave was proposed and elected as President of the Executive Council. He spelled out his credo clearly and succinctly:

'It is my intention to implement the Treaty as sanctioned by the vote of the Dáil and the electorate, insofar as it was free to express an opinion, to enact a constitution, to assert the authority and supremacy of parliament, to support and assist the national Army in asserting the people's rights, to ask parliament, if necessary, for such powers as are deemed essential for the purpose of restoring order to suppress all crimes, to expedite as far as lies in the power of the Government the return of normal conditions throughout the country.'

Cosgrave maintained an outward reluctance to accept the leadership and at his first meeting with Northern Ireland prime minister, James Craig, he protested: 'You know, I've been pushed into this. I'm not a leader of men.' This self-effacing judgement should not be taken too seriously. Winston Churchill, who knew something about the qualities needed in a leader of men said:

'The void left by the deaths of Griffith and Collins was not unfilled. A quiet potent figure stood in the background sharing, like Griffith, the dangers of the rebel leaders without taking part in all that they had done. In Cosgrave the Irish people found a chief of higher quality than any who had yet appeared. To the courage of Collins he added the matter-of-fact fidelity of Griffith and a knowledge of practical administration and state policy all his own.'

Cosgrave typically laughed off Churchill's assessment and told friends with a twinkle in his eye that the only reason he had been described as 'a chief of higher quality' than any of the others was because he had taken the trouble to ask after Churchill's health after a fall from a pony during the tense negotiations of May 1922.

One of the finest historians of the period, Irish-American, Joseph Curran got it about right:

'Cosgrave's self-assessment was too modest, for in his quite commonsensical way he made an effective leader. He delegated authority wisely, handled Ministerial disputes even-handedly and was, on the whole, an ideal chairman. His colleagues valued his advice and steadiness and long before he left office his competence and wit had made him personally very popular with voters.'

On the day he was elected President of the Executive Council by Dáil Éireann in succession to Michael Collins on 9 September 1922, *The Irish Times* published a perceptive profile:

'Mr W.T. Cosgrave is a man who has succeeded very well in keeping out of the limelight of publicity. That perhaps is his best title to fame but he has other qualities in addition to his modesty and is regarded by those who know him as one of the soundest men in Ireland today. It would be hard to imagine anybody who is less true to what we used to consider the Sinn Féin type than Mr Cosgrave. It is not only that he does not dress in the regulation way — trench coat, leggins and slouch hat and the rest of it; but he has a thoroughly Conservative face. He is neither a wild-eyed revolutionary nor a lank-haired poet. He dresses generally in sombre hues, wears a bowler hat and looks rather like the general manager of a railway company. His hair is his most striking feature. It is very fair, turning now to grey and he wears it straight up on his head à la Pompadour.

'His manner is most unassuming. Unlike so many of the new school of Irish politicians he does not believe in talking and has an excellent capacity for work. During the tiresome debates on the Treaty which occupied Dáil Éireann for so many bleak winter days at the tail end of last year, Mr Cosgrave was one of the very few who managed to keep his sense of proportion intact. Others raved and ranted. His was always the soft answer that, we are told, turneth away wrath, but the Premier-elect has a knack of spicing his remarks with a dry and somewhat pawky humour which incensed some of his opponents hugely. A few of his speeches were delightful.

'But behind all Mr Cosgrave's kindly levity there is a rock of common sense. He is undoubtedly the most capable man in the new Irish Parliament and that may be said without the slightest contradiction of any of his colleagues. As Premier of the Free State he has a formidable task before him but in one way he is almost the ideal choice because he has no violently extremist past to live down and with him the problem of saving face does not arise.'

Padraig Colum, a long-time friend and political ally provides the following pen-picture of W.T. as he took over the leading role in the Dáil in the autumn of 1922:

'With his faintly coloured hair and moustache — his hair standing up in a sort of crest — his pale face and prominent eyes, he does not look a forceful man. His head tilted to one side gives the sense of something drooping in his physique. A painter or sculptor looking at him would note how finely and delicately his chin and mouth are modelled. He speaks leaning forward, his hands on the barrier before him; his delivery becomes like a series of pistol shots, each word shot out, each word reaching its mark. He is sociable as becomes a Dublin man and abundantly witty. His wit is a Dublin wit. It is founded on a very exact estimate of character. He can reveal character in a mordant phrase. Before his humour, before the phrase that springs up in his speech pretentiousness of all kinds falls away.'

Ernest Blythe, who served him in government for a decade, recalled how Cosgrave put his warm personal qualities and quirky sense of humour to great political advantage. With a cabinet of strong individuals Cosgrave was able to defuse tense situations and find a compromise where none seemed possible.

'One of the most difficult feats of persuasion which he carried out became necessary when a small group of pro-Treaty deputies declared on the enactment of the Free State constitution that they would not take the oath and would thereby exclude themselves from the Dáil. With the Civil War still in progress and at a critical stage such an action could have had a very serous consequences indeed. There seemed to be no way of persuading the recalcitrant when Mr Cosgrave, without disclosing his intention to anyone put his own plan into operation. He announced that though having no personal objection to the oath he had decided not to take it and to leave the Dáil with the others as he considered that he had done his bit and someone else should carry on. His cabinet colleagues were aghast at his attitude and Kevin O'Higgins condemned it angrily and bitterly. Mr Cosgrave, however, refused to relent and allowed himself to be well and truly lumped with the others. Finally after a heated debate the non-juring group of whom Mr Cosgrave was now the obvious leader retired to another room to consider the arguments which had been put forward by the majority. After half a hour they returned and announced that out of consideration for their colleagues they would take the oath and remain in the Dáil. By this little excursion into dramatics Mr Cosgrave averted a minor political crisis which might have had major consequences. But Kevin O'Higgins, who had been completely taken in, was not mollified for several days.'

During September 1922 the Civil War intensified and Mulcahy proposed that the Army be given the power to try and punish a wide range of offences. After long discussion at cabinet the details of an Emergency Powers Bill were agreed. This provided for the setting up of military tribunals which would try cases involving a range of offences against people and property. The tribunals were empowered to impose the death penalty for serious offences, including the possession of weapons.

When the Bill was introduced in the Dáil Cosgrave told deputies that 'those who persist in those murderous attacks must learn that they have got to pay the penalty for them.' In response to suggestions from the Labour leader, Tom Johnson, Cosgrave announced an amnesty on 3 October to give Republicans a chance to surrender before the new provisions came into effect. Few availed of the option and the special powers came into effect on 15 October, the day after the amnesty expired.

The first executions took place a month later when four young men found guilty of carrying unauthorised arms in Dublin were shot by a firing squad. A week later an execution took place which elevated the Civil War into a new phase. Erskine Childers was captured at his cousin's home in Wicklow in possession of a handgun, given to him by Michael Collins. He was tried and convicted by a military court and executed the following morning.

Cosgrave vigorously defended the execution of Childers in the Dáil on 28 November and he outlined the basis of his Government's policy:

'What do we want? We want simply order restored to this country. We want all arms under the control of the people who elected us and who can throw us out tomorrow if they so desire. We want that the people of this country only shall have the right to say who are to be armed and who are not; and we are going to get the arms if we have to search every house in the country.'

Maintaining that the same law had to apply to the 'intellectual' Childers as applied to the four 'poor men's sons' who had been executed a week earlier Cosgrave went on ...

'People who rob with arms are going to be brought before military courts and found guilty. Persons robbing at the point of the gun will be executed without discrimination. This is going to be a fair law, fairly administered and administered in the best interests of the country for the preservation of the fabric of society ... We are going to see that the rule of democracy will be maintained no matter what the cost and no matter who the intellectuals that may fall by reason of the assertion of that right.'

The response of the Irregulars to the emergency powers came on 30 November when the IRA chief of staff, Liam Lynch, sent instructions to all Battalion OCs for operations against the enemy. No less than 14 categories of people were directed to be 'shot at sight', including all members of the Provisional Dáil who had voted in favour of the Emergency Powers Act. Republicans were also ordered to kill members of the Senate, High Court judges, journalists and proprietors of hostile newspapers and even 'aggressive Free State supporters'. The homes and offices of all these people were also to be destroyed as were the homes of 'imperialist deputy lieutenant of the county types', who mostly were Protestants. There followed a series of outrages by Republicans against politicians, journalists and ordinary citizens.

As the Civil War escalated Cosgrave had to face other problems. A constitution had to be drafted and enacted to put the operations of the Government and the Dáil on a legal basis. A police force was hurriedly established and in a courageous and imaginative move the new Civic Guard was established as an unarmed force in contrast to its predecessor the RIC. This was one of the most important moves Cosgrave made in legitimising the institutions of the new state. On 6 December, the first anniversary of the Treaty, the new constitution was enacted by the Dáil. The Irish Free State formally came into being and the provisional Government ceased to exist. Cosgrave was formally re-elected by the Dáil to the position of president.

The Republican response to the new constitution was swift. The day after it was enacted two Dáil deputies were gunned down on their way from their Dublin hotel to Leinster House. Sean Hales was killed and Padraic Ó Máille, the Leas Ceann Comhairle, was wounded in an outrage which shocked the nation. Cosgrave and Mulcahy were both visibly shaken and angry when they heard the news, according to newspapers. The murders threatened to undermine Irish democracy because some Dáil deputies fled Dublin for their lives after the shooting. Cosgrave knew that if the Dáil itself wilted in the face of terror then democracy could not survive. He ordered the secret service to go after the fleeing deputies and bring them back to Dublin. He then met each of the worried TDs individually and appealed to them not to be deterred from their patriotic duty.

By this stage Cosgrave had already stamped his authority on the Dáil and was known by his own supporters as 'The Boss.' Sean MacEoin, who initially feared W.T. was not strong enough to conduct the war after Collins' death, conceded years later that after a couple of months the military was convinced that 'Cosgrave had the punch that was needed.' On the night of 7 December all his authority was required to calm his panicking deputies. A story was told of one TD from Cork who resisted threats of execution by the secret service if he left Dublin and only agreed to stay because he feared Cosgrave's wrath.

Having met his wobbling TDs Cosgrave then chaired a critical cabinet meeting to consider the Government's next move. Mulcahy, who was Army Chief of Staff and Minister for Defence, submitted a proposal from the Army Council for the immediate execution of four imprisoned IRA leaders, Rory O'Connor, Liam Mellows, Richard Barrett and Joe McKelvey. After a discussion Cosgrave went around the cabinet table to ask each Minister individually if he approved of the executions. Of the Minister's present Blythe, MacNeill and FitzGerald backed Mulcahy, McGrath questioned the policy but only O'Higgins initially baulked. Rory O'Connor had been best man at his wedding only a year before and he felt terrible anguish at having to agree to the executions but agree he finally did. He was swayed by the argument that if the cabinet did not act ruthlessly there would be more assassinations and TDs would start to resign, turning the Executive Council into a dictatorship.

The next morning the four IRA leaders, one from each province, were taken out and executed at Mountjoy Jail. There was outrage among Opposition TDs who accused the cabinet of personal vindictiveness when the decision was announced to the Dáil later that day. 'Personal spite, great heavens, vindictiveness, one of these men was a friend of mine,' said O'Higgins before he broke down in tears, unable to continue.

Cosgrave was calmer telling deputies that it had been impossible for the cabinet to consult the Dáil before acting but he defended the action.

> 'There is an elementary law in this case. The people who have challenged the very existence of society have put themselves outside the Constitution and only at the last moment, not thinking there was such infamy in this country, we safeguarded this Dáil and the Government and the people of Ireland from being at the mercy of these people ... There is only one way to meet it and that is to crush it and show them that terror will be struck into them.'

The Government's decision was supported by 39 votes to 14.

Donal O'Sullivan, the clerk of the Senate later wrote:

> 'However this action of the Executive may be regarded from the ethical standpoint it proved to be an effective deterrent, for no other member of the legislature was assassinated during the progress of the Irregular campaign.'

However, a host of outrages followed rapidly. On 10 December the house of Deputy McGarry in Dublin was burned down and his young son, aged 7, died from burns. An inquest jury later returned a verdict of 'wilful murder'. On 28 December a landmine destroyed the music warehouse of Deputy McCullough blowing the whole front of the house into the street.

On the night of 13 January Cosgrave's own home at Beechpark was burned to the ground by Republicans. Young Liam Cosgrave was just three at the time but his earliest childhood memory is of that night and the bitter, acrid smell of burning timber. Liam went to live with his relatives in James' Street while Louisa and young Michael went to stay at her father's house. W.T. mostly lived in Government Buildings but also spent some time at the Curragh camp where he was safe from attack. A few weeks later Dr T.F. O'Higgins, father of Kevin O'Higgins, was murdered at his home in Stradbally, Queens County (Laois). His body was riddled with bullets in the presence of his wife and 17-year-old daughter. Cosgrave's uncle, Patrick, was murdered by Republicans at the family home in James' Street.

There was also an orgy of burning and destruction of some of the country's finest houses which sent some truly patriotic Irish people into exile in despair. Examples of this campaign were the destruction of Kilteragh House, owned by Horace Plunkett, the burning of the historic Moore Hall in Mayo, the destruction of one of the finest libraries in the country at the ancestral home of Senator John Bagwell in Clonmel, the burning of Desart Court in Co. Kilkenny. The homes of all these people were attacked because of their connections with the Senate.

The Catholic Church came out unequivocally on a number of occasions during the Civil War. In October 1922, Cardinal Logue issued another joint pastoral denouncing the Republican campaign in very trenchant terms:

'A section of the community, refusing to acknowledge the Government set up by the nation, have chosen to attack their own country as if she were a foreign power ... They have wrecked Ireland from end to end. All those who in contravention of this teaching participate in such crimes are guilty of grievous sins and may not be absolved on Confession nor admitted to Holy Communion if they persist in such evil courses.'

In the early months of 1923 the Government continued its executions policy to deal with Republican outrages. A refinement of the policy which brought a lot of success was to sentence Republicans to death but to suspend the sentence as long as there were no further outrages in the area concerned. This policy helped to speed up the end of the Civil War. By April there were 13,000 Republican prisoners in jails and camps throughout the country.

With the Irregulars on the defensive an attempt was made by de Valera to negotiate an end to the Civil War. At the end of April, following the death of Liam Lynch and the capture of Austin Stack, he asked two Independent senators to mediate with the Government and arrange a peace conference, asking Cosgrave to accept six principles which would underpin the talks.

Cosgrave refused to accept the six points or accede to the request for a conference but gave the two senators a document to put to de Valera. This document outlined the Irish Government's peace terms based on the following principles:

'(a) That all political issues whether now existing or in the future arising shall be decided by the majority vote of the elected representatives of the people.

'(b) As a corollary to (a) that the people are entitled to have all lethal weapons within the country in the effective custody or control of the Executive Government responsible to the people through their representatives.

'The acceptance of these principles and practical compliance with (b) by the surrender of arms to be the preliminary condition for the release of prisoners who shall be required to subscribe to (a) and (b).'

De Valera refused to accept the terms and Cosgrave defended them to the Dáil:

'We have said from the very beginning that we are prepared to wipe the slate clean but we are not prepared to take any risk with regard to the possession of arms by people who do not realise their responsibilities as citizens.'

By this stage the Irregulars were in no position to bargain and on 24 May Aiken ordered the IRA to stop fighting and dump arms. De Valera issued a stirring message to the IRA hailing them as the 'Legion of the Rearguard' who had saved the nation's honour. The Civil War was over.

4

BUILDING THE STATE

WITH the Civil War finally over Cosgrave faced the cold reality of trying to build a state from the rubble of dreams shattered by fratricide and destruction. The sheer physical damage to the infrastructure of the country was immense and it took enormous sacrifices and a huge effort of national will to rebuild the fabric of the state. In the absence of Republicans, who refused to recognise the legitimacy of the Dáil, Cosgrave had a strong majority in parliament. While no formal party structure existed among his supporters a whip was appointed to coordinate their voting strength and they acted to all intents and purposes like a political party. In January 1923, a convention of pro-Treaty deputies took place in Dublin to discuss the formation of a party and in April 1923, Cumann na nGaedheal was launched at a meeting in the Mansion House in Dublin. Cosgrave delivered an opening address outlining the party's policy which included the playing down of differences, denominational, social and class, as the basis on which the Free State might develop.

When the Civil War formally ended in May Cosgrave decided to call a general election. It was held in September, and Cumann na nGaedheal emerged as the largest party with 63 seats out of 153. It was not an overall majority but as Republicans, who won 45 seats, decided to continue their boycott of the Dáil it gave Cosgrave a comfortable working majority. However, the total vote for parties who accepted the Treaty, at less than 70%, showed a significant slippage since the pact election of a little more than a year earlier.

In the Dáil Cosgrave was an effective speaker, as he had demonstrated during the Treaty debates, but he was not an orator and

had little time for wordy speeches. His cabinet colleague Ernest Blythe
recalled his style:

> 'Mr Cosgrave was a ready and effective speaker in the Dáil or on a
> public platform but he was not much inclined to prepare elaborate
> formal addresses. When such was necessary he resorted to team work
> and showed himself in advance of other politicians here by having
> orations prepared by ghost writers who, however, were given his
> detailed personal instructions.

> 'On one occasion when he had delivered a stirring address at the
> cenotaph on Leinster Lawn, the Most Rev. Dr Fogarty, Bishop of
> Killaloe, who had come to Dublin for the ceremony said to him as
> they walked away:

> '"I congratulate you, Mr President, on your speech; it was very fine
> indeed."

> '"Actually," replied Mr Cosgrave, "I think it was splendid" adding as he
> enjoyed the bishop's look of astonishment, "I didn't write a word of
> it."'

Another cabinet colleague, Eoin MacNeill, who was one of
Cosgrave's speech writers, recalled in a memoir how he drafted
Cosgrave's address to the League of Nations in 1923. 'I had the
gratification of seeing it printed afterwards in an American book as an
example of Mr Cosgrave's oratory,' wrote MacNeill. Cosgrave
generally behaved in cabinet as first among equals rather than as a
charismatic leader. Brian Farrell in his perceptive *Chairman or Chief*
puts W.T. into the chairman category. In a cabinet of intellectuals like
O'Higgins, Paddy Hogan and Eoin MacNeill, Cosgrave did not give
the impression of a forceful leader of men. Yet it would be a serious
mistake to take his own self-effacing assessment of his role too
seriously. During the Civil War and throughout the 1920s it was
Cosgrave, rather than any of his more brilliant Ministers, who kept the
Government going as a cohesive unit and he was not known by his
colleagues as 'The Boss' for nothing.

Blythe believed W.T.'s ability to find a compromise was his greatest
strength.

> 'Though he came into national politics by shouldering a rifle in 1916
> and graduated by sharing responsibility for guerilla warfare against
> the British forces and by heading our Irish Government during the
> Civil War, he was essentially a man of peace, preferring stratagem to
> violence and persuasion to a showdown. When as happened from
> time to time his cabinet was sharply divided on an issue of importance

Mr Cosgrave was adept at finding compromise acceptable to both sides.'

The major problem faced by Cosgrave and his colleagues was the damage to the country's infrastructure wrought by the Civil War. In its determination to prove that Ireland was capable of self-government the Cosgrave government ran a tight fiscal policy as it re-built the country. Ernest Blythe, as Minister for Finance, went into Irish folklore for his decision to cut a shilling off the old-age pension in 1924 and to cut the salaries of teachers and other public servants by 10%. The nature of the cuts became a millstone around the Government's neck and, ironically, the very people whose Civil War activities made the austere measures necessary were the ultimate political beneficiaries.

The Government had many positive things to its credit. The decision to build the electricity-generating plant at Ardnacrusha and the establishment of the Local Appointments Commission to remove patronage from state appointments helped lay the new state on a firm foundation. Socially progressive legislation such as the control of rents and mortgages and the division of tens of thousands of acres of land under Patrick Hogan's Land Act of 1923 helped to improve the lot of ordinary people but did not have any lasting political impact and the Government was increasingly regarded as out of touch with the concerns of ordinary people as the 1920s wore on.

Even the style of dress adopted by Ministers served to alienate them from the voters. The wearing of formal morning suits, wing collars and top hats was the normal dress code for people of their position at the time but it gave the Government a distant air. W.T. was often portrayed by Republican propaganda as a West Brit which was ironic given his strong Nationalist sentiments but his dress code served to reinforce the image.

W.T.'s religious conviction was the bedrock of his life. He attended Mass and Communion every day and, like a great many people in Ireland at the time, said the Rosary every night. It is said that during the 1920s when younger members of the Free State Government visited Beechpark in the evening they were expected to join in the nightly recitation of the five decades of the Rosary. During the War of Independence Cosgrave had proposed to de Valera that a theological commission should be established to vet the decisions of the Dáil. After independence he considered handing over the site of the General Post Office in Dublin for the building of a Catholic Cathedral as there was no Catholic cathedral on any main street in Dublin due to the penal laws.

Cosgrave travelled to Rome on a number of occasions as President of the Executive Council and it was a habit he was to continue in and out of government. His loyalty to the Papacy went hand in hand with his piety and he was accorded a number of papal honours and allowed to establish an oratory in his house where Mass could be said each morning.

His close friend, the far from pious Oliver St John Gogarty, wrote facetiously that W.T.'s 'piety greatly embarrassed His Holiness, the Pope.' Gogarty travelled with the President in 1924 on one of his visits to Rome, as part of a group led by Bishop Fogarty of Killaloe, another good friend of Cosgrave's. At an audience with the Pope the leading members of the group received medals from His Holiness but through an error Gogarty was presented with the medal intended for the President. The writer refused to part with it asking Cosgrave with mock seriousness.

'Do you question the Pope's infallibility?'

On a more serious note, Cosgrave moved to ban divorce in the Irish Free State when the Attorney General, Hugh Kennedy, sought clarification as to whether it would continue to be allowed on the British model. W.T. consulted Dr Byrne the Archbishop of Dublin, and asked him to get the views of the hierarchy on the matter. Not surprisingly the hierarchy expressed its opposition to divorce and Cosgrave had no hesitation in introducing a bill in the Dáil banning divorce. He told the Dáil:

'I consider that the whole fabric of our social organisation is based upon the sanctity of the marriage bond and that anything that tends to weaken the binding efficacy of that bond to that extent strikes at the root of our social life.'

Many modern commentators have, with the benefit of hindsight, tended to mock Cosgrave for his piety but in the context of the newly-independent Ireland it was not that surprising. Historian, Ronan Fanning, puts Cosgrave's adoption of elements of Catholic social teaching as the civil law in context:

'In the light of successive centuries of British repression of, and discrimination against, Irish Catholics (particularly in regard to property and position) together with the ingrained anti-Catholicism of nineteenth century Britain, it is hardly surprising that a certain Catholic triumphalism became a hallmark of the Irish Free State.

Those who too readily deride that triumphalism, moreover, should recall that just such anti-Catholic prejudice and discrimination, in a particularly virulent form, remained a distinguishing feature of that part of Ireland still within the United Kingdom.'

Critics of Cosgrave's piety also ignore his personal lack of sectarian impulses. He faithfully stood by the agreement of 1922 to appoint representatives of Southern Unionism to the Senate despite severe criticism from Fianna Fáil throughout the 1920s who claimed he was involved in a Masonic plot with Protestant members of the Seanad. W.T also offered to appoint the last leader of the Nationalist Party, John Dillon to the Senate but the offer was spurned. 'I will not serve with people who have blood on their hands,' Dillon is said to have replied.

The infamous Dunbar-Harrison case provides an interesting example of the pressures Cosgrave was under. In 1930 the Local Appointments Commission appointed a Protestant, Letitia Dunbar-Harrison, to the vacant position of Mayo County Library. The County Council refused to ratify the appointment on the alleged grounds that Miss Dunbar-Harrison did not speak Irish, but nobody was in any doubt that the reason was that she was a Protestant. The Government responded by dissolving the County Council and appointing a Commissioner in its place who duly appointed Miss Dunbar-Harrison to the post. The political reaction from Fianna Fáil was one of outrage at the appointment. De Valera maintained that if the functions of the appointee were merely those of an attendant handing out books then religious affiliation would not matter. 'On the other hand, if the whole idea behind the scheme was that the librarian should go into the homes of people, and into the schools, and push the scheme, if instead of her duties being passive they were active, the position was an entirely different one.'

With his political opponents playing a discreet sectarian tune Cosgrave also came under pressure from Archbishop Gilmartin of Tuam but he wrote to the prelate as follows:

'As I explained to Your Grace at our interview, to discriminate against any citizen — or exercise a preference for a citizen — on account of religious belief would be to conflict with some of the fundamental principles on which this State is founded.'

With pressure mounting on all sides, though, Cosgrave eventually opted for a political fudge and in December 1931, Miss Dunbar-Harrison was transferred from Castlebar to the Department of

Defence library in Dublin. This incident shows some weakness on Cosgrave's part but not sectarianism. Critics of his piety would also do well to note that Fianna Fáil in the late 1920s hounded him for allowing 'immoral publications' to circulate in Ireland and demanded even more rigorous censorship than that in operation.

His religious piety did not prevent Cosgrave from remaining a close friend of the irreverent and bohemian Oliver St John Gogarty all his life. Gogarty, who was appointed to the Senate by Cosgrave, had a narrow escape from death in 1923 when he was taken by Republican gunmen to a house in Chapelizod to be murdered. Gogarty escaped by jumping into the freezing Liffey and he promised an offering of swans to the river in return. This promise he fulfilled at the Trinity boat club a year later.

On 24 March 1924, after a champagne lunch in the Shelbourne Hotel, Gogarty, members of his family and friends including Cosgrave, W.B. Yeats and Lennox Robinson went to the Zoo, where the swans were lodged pending their release on the river. 'It was typical that Mr Cosgrave should have honoured the occasion by his presence. A Dubliner, like Gogarty, he shared his delight in gesture, and was not above taking part in a little myth-making,' wrote Ulick O'Connor in his biography of Gogarty.

In October 1923, Cosgrave suffered a great personal loss when his brother, Philip, died at the age of 38. The two had always been close and Philip had followed W.T. into the Volunteers, was condemned to death in 1916 and elected to the Dáil in 1921. He was governor of Mountjoy as well as a TD for his home area of Dublin when he died unexpectedly. He attended a political meeting in College Green, at which W.T. was the main speaker, caught a chill and died two day later. It was a body blow to W.T. who had now lost his brother and step-brother within the space of a few years.

Despite the end of the Civil War intermittent violence from Republicans occurred throughout the 1920s but it was not the only problem which faced Cosgrave. Towards the end of 1923 and early in 1924 he had to deal with mounting discontent in the Army and battles for supremacy among his own cabinet Ministers, particularly O'Higgins and Mulcahy whose differences crystallised around the Army issue.

The immediate cause of the problem was that the Army which had grown to a 57,000 men during the Civil War was being reduced in size. The issue came to a head at the end of February 1924 when the cabinet decided to demobilise or demote senior officers. This provoked a mutiny by some senior officers.

In the midst of the crisis Cosgrave became ill and was absent from critical cabinet meetings. It has never been explained how ill Cosgrave was and whether it was real, merely diplomatic or a serious mental crisis. His political enemies suggested that W.T. was not able to handle the strain and simply opted out but, given what he had been through in the Civil War, that is not very probable. One way or another, O'Higgins, as vice-president of the Executive Council, took control and chaired seven cabinet meetings between 18 and 22 March. Decisions were taken not only to seek the resignations of senior Army officers, including the chief of staff, but to sack Mulcahy as well. The Minister for Defence decided to try and sort out the mess by resigning himself, thus averting a major crisis for the Government.

Going on cabinet papers it would appear that the decision on the sackings was taken without consultation with Cosgrave and that he first learned of it in the newspapers. He did intervene with his colleagues after the sackings to suggest an extension of the time limit on the surrender of stolen material by the original mutineers and this was ultimately agreed. By the end of the episode two Ministers, Mulcahy and McGrath, had departed the Government and McGrath and another eight TDs actually left Cumann na nGaedheal. What Cosgrave was doing during the crisis is difficult to establish but he appears to have been in political difficulty and unable to restrain O'Higgins from taking a dominant role, whether through illness or weakness it is difficult to say.

He may have been operating another variation of the manoeuvre described by Blythe during the row over the Free State constitution in an attempt to keep both sides together or he may simply have been unable by reason of illness to intervene. Ronan Fanning concludes:

'While due allowance must be made ... for Cosgrave's conception of his role as conciliatory chairman it is indisputable that O'Higgins forced through a more uncompromisingly constitutionalist line in Cosgrave's absence, than had been followed in his presence.'

Professor Joe Lee has a different interpretation, seeing the whole episode as a power-play by O'Higgins:

'Cosgrave salvaged what he could by frustrating, from his hospital bed, the ambition of O'Higgins to become acting Minister for Defence, by assuming the office himself. Cosgrave held Defence for eight months before appointing the relatively safe Patrick Hughes as his successor. He managed within a year to dismiss O'Duffy, who seemed to be more intent on exacting loyalty to himself than to the Government, and confined him solely to his former police responsibilities. Finally, Cosgrave recovered sufficient ground to bring Mulcahy back into the cabinet as Minister for Local Government, following the general election of June 1927, and thus provide himself with some balance once more against O'Higgins.'

In October 1924, McGrath and eight other disillusioned back-benchers resigned from the Dáil in protest at the affair. Cosgrave refused to be panicked and called all nine by-elections for 13 March 1925. Cumann na nGaedheal won seven of the by-elections and that was the last of the Army crisis.

In the early 1920s the Cosgrave Government had a number of achievements to its credit. Despite W.T.'s initial scepticism about the need to develop a pampered diplomatic service, Ireland joined the League of Nations and Cosgrave led the Government delegation to Geneva in September 1923.

There were also notable economic achievements during the 1920s. The Shannon hydro-electric scheme was built at Ardnacrusha, in defiance of economic orthodoxy. The sugar beet industry was developed with factories at Carlow and Thurles. Paddy Hogan as a dynamic Minister for Agriculture began improvement in livestock breeding and expanded trade, and the country saw the first increase in population since the famine. Hogan also introduced the Land Act of 1923 which marked the final transfer of the land of Ireland from the landlords to the tenant farmers.

The Government, though, was dogged by crises in security and Anglo-Irish relations. One embarrassing, if inevitable, setback was the report of the Boundary Commission provided for in Article 12 of the Treaty. The expectation of the Treaty signatories had been that the Boundary Commission would hand large portions of the North where there were Catholic majorities over to the Free State. However, following the blood letting of the Civil War there was no public mood in the Free State for confrontation with the North. Cosgrave appointed one of his senior Ministers, Eoin MacNeill, to the Boundary Commission which was chaired by an English-born South African, Mr Justice Feetham, and the editor of the *Northern Whig*, J.R. Fisher. MacNeill found himself in a minority position but mysteriously failed to keep Cosgrave informed of what was happening. In November 1925 the *Morning Post* newspaper revealed that the commission was about to recommend the transfer of Catholic South Armagh to the Free State and Protestant East Donegal to the North. Cosgrave rushed to London where he quickly did a deal with British prime minister Stanley Baldwin and James Craig to suppress the report. The *status quo* on the border was retained with the South preferring to keep East Donegal rather than gain South Armagh. As part of the deal the liability of the Free State for the British national debt was cancelled but Cosgrave agreed to continue the payment of the land annuities.

The Boundary Commission débâcle was a setback for Cosgrave and his Government and it was followed in May 1926, by a political challenge at home. Eamon de Valera broke away from Sinn Féin and established Fianna Fáil in anticipation of a general election the following year. That election came in June 1927, and it represented a stern rebuff for Cosgrave. Cumann na nGaedheal lost 16 seats and ended up with 47 TDs. Fianna Fáil performed very impressively winning 44 but as the party was still committed to an abstentionist policy Cosgrave was still able to hold on to the reins of government.

The murder of Kevin O'Higgins on his way to Mass in Booterstown on 10 July changed the political scene fundamentally. The day O'Higgins was murdered is a childhood memory the seven-year-old Liam Cosgrave never forgot. He vividly remembered years later how his mother was convinced that W.T. too had been killed because he was delayed so late that night conferring with government colleagues. W.T.'s anxiety when he did come home made a profound impression on the young Liam.

Cosgrave responded by the introduction of a harsh Public Safety Bill and, more significantly, the Electoral Amendment Bill in the wake of the murder. The Electoral Bill required that in future all Dáil candidates would have to take the oath of allegiance to the Crown, otherwise they would be ineligible to become candidates. This confronted de Valera with a critical dilemma. Either Fianna Fáil now agreed to take the oath or they would not be in a position to contest the next election. De Valera responded by leading his party into the Dáil in August and taking the oath as an 'empty political formula.' Accepted wisdom has it that Cosgrave's intention was to force Fianna Fáil into democratic politics through the Electoral Bill but Bertie Smylie, later a famous editor of *The Irish Times*, recalled years later that Cosgrave reacted with shock when he told him 'Dev is going in'.

Fianna Fáil's entry to the Dáil now left Cosgrave in a minority and de Valera did a deal with the Labour Party and the National League whereby he agreed to support a Labour minority government led by

Tom Johnson once Cosgrave was defeated in a vote of confidence. Fianna Fáil and Labour were so confident of forcing Cosgrave out of office in August 1926, that they didn't even muster their full quota of TDs on the day of the confidence motion. A Labour TD, T.J. O'Connell was at a teachers' conference in Canada and didn't bother to come home with the newspapers speculating that Cosgrave would lose by 73 votes to 69.

On the day of the debate the figures began to change as some Redmondite and Independent TDs began to have second thoughts about backing an unholy alliance of Fianna Fáil and Labour. The key to the vote turned out to be Alderman John Jinks, TD for Sligo, who has gone into folklore because of what happened. Jinks, a member of the National League Party led by Willie Redmond, was known to be unhappy at his leader's decision to bring down Cosgrave. Major Bryan Cooper, a former Unionist who now supported W.T., brought Jinks to a nearby hotel and plied the Sligo-man with drink. Jinks then disappeared from the precincts of Leinster House and mysteriously ended up on the Sligo train when the division was called in the Dáil. The vote was tied at 71–71 and the Ceann Comhairle gave his casting vote in favour of the Government. Cosgrave had survived by the skin of his teeth thanks to the disappearance of Jinks.

Cosgrave won two by-elections at the end of August and with Fianna Fáil and Labour still licking their wounds from the failed attempt to oust him, he dissolved the Dáil and called a general election for September. The result saw Cumann na nGaedheal increase its strength from 47 to 62 seats but Fianna Fáil also increased from 44 to 57. Labour and the other smaller parties took a hammering and the two big parties were left to confront each other in the Dáil.

Cosgrave was now under increasing pressure both inside and outside the Dáil but he didn't lose his nerve. The Government worked away doggedly at home and with great success in international affairs, particularly at the Imperial Conference of 1931 where McGilligan broadened the scope of Irish independence and proved that the Treaty could indeed be used as a stepping stone to complete freedom.

Meanwhile Fianna Fáil began to build its support base after entering the Dáil. Its economic programme was based on the principle of protectionism and the party focused its attacks on Agriculture Minister, Paddy Hogan, for his reforms aimed at making Irish agriculture competitive in a free trade environment. One of the issues Fianna Fáil focused on in particular was land annuities, the payments made to the British Exchequer by Irish farmers, in return for the loans to buy out their land under the various Land Acts. The issue represented a combination of Nationalist rhetoric and economic self-interest as far as farmers were concerned.

A sardonic *London Times* reporter noted at the end of 1927 how Fianna Fáil was ruthlessly going after the farmers' vote:

'A protected paradise is not the wildest or most dangerous of Fianna Fáil's promises to an electorate which is a curious mixture of shrewdness and credulity. When Mr Hogan, unfolding his admirable programme of benefits for farmers, says *"O fortuantos nimum sua si bona norint"*[1], Mr de Valera and his friends send back from a hundred platforms the sinister echo *"No rint"*. They tell the people that Fianna Fáil's accession to power will mean the end of land purchase annuities and already the effect of this reckless promise on a community of struggling small farmers has been very mischievous.'

With Fianna Fáil concentrating on economic issues the Government appeared obsessed with security concerns as the IRA continued to engage in sporadic outrage and murder. The Public Safety Acts of 1927 and 1931 and the Jurors' Protection Act gave the Government drastic powers and allowed military tribunals to try terrorist offences. Cosgrave and his Ministers vigorously defended the need for such measures but the electorate grew increasingly weary of the security emphasis.

Fianna Fáil cleverly expanded its Republican appeal by adding to its policy practical promises based on voter self-interest. For farmers it was the abolition of the land annuities and for the urban working class it was the promise of jobs through a protectionist policy. Cosgrave called a general election for February 1932 and went to the country promising stability and continuity.

With Fianna Fáil and the IRA hand in glove during the election campaign Cosgrave's tactics became essentially negative. 'The Shadow of a Gunman — Keep it from your door,' read one Cumann na nGaedheal poster. Another had a red flag superimposed on a tricolour with the message 'We want no reds, keep their colour off your flag'. A newspaper ad read 'The gunmen are voting Fianna Fáil, the Communists are voting Fianna Fáil'. The most famous poster of all read 'Devvy's Circus, absolutely the greatest road show in Ireland today — Señor de Valera, world famous illusionist, oath swallower and escapologist. See his renowned act: Escaping from the strait-jacket of

1. "O fortunate are those who know how well off they are."

the republic. Frank F. Aiken, fearsome fire eater. Shaunty O'Kelly, the man in dress clothes. Monsieur Lemass, famous tight rope performer, see him cross from the Treaty to the Republic every night. Performing frogs, champion croakers, marvelous trained sheep.'

On platforms around the country Cumann na nGaedheal speakers had difficulty getting a hearing as the campaign got increasingly disruptive and the IRA put its muscle behind the Fianna Fáil campaign. Government speakers were shouted down with opponents demanding 'Who started the Civil War?' and 'Who ordered the execution of Rory O'Connor?' A standard Cumann na nGaedheal reply to such hecklers was 'And how many banks did you rob?'

While both Fianna Fáil and Cumann na nGaedheal were staunchly Catholic the hierarchy and the parish priests tended to support the Government with many curates backing de Valera. On his tour of the country W.T lunched with the Bishop of Kerry on 1 February, he visited the Catholic and Church of Ireland Bishops of Limerick the following day, the next day he had tea with his old friend Bishop Fogarty of Killaloe and then went to meet Bishop Harty of Cashel. Michael O hAodha recalled how as a child he heard Bishop Fogarty preaching at Mass in Ennis during the 1932 campaign when Cosgrave was a member of the congregation.

'So we can only pray that all the saints in heaven, the cherubim, seraphim and choirs, shall join with Saint Flannan to plead before the golden throne that God may look down on all the Dalcassians gathered here in this ancient see of Killaloe to ask before God's altar for divine protection and guidance for our great President, W.T. Cosgrave, to whom we extend a *céad míle fáilte* to Ennis.'

At Cosgrave's final election rally at College Green in Dublin on 14 February passions boiled over as rival supporters fought each other on the streets and the Gardaí had difficulty in quelling the riot. 'There were cheers and counter cheers, scuffles took place among the crowds, free fights developed and batons were drawn,' reported the *Irish Independent.*

When the election took place on 16 February the voters opted for change rather than a continuation of the old regime. Fianna Fáil increased its share of the vote from 35% to over 45% while Cumann na nGaedheal slumped from 39% to 35%. In terms of seats de Valera had 72 while Cosgrave won 57. It was a shattering blow to Cosgrave and Cumann na nGaedheal to lose an election to the forces they had defeated in the Civil War ten years earlier but a younger electorate was looking to the future, not the past.

The Dáil assembled at 2.30 p.m. on Tuesday 9 March 1932. De Valera entered Leinster House accompanied by his son, Vivion, who had a revolver in his pocket. A number of other senior Fianna Fáil TDs were armed as they entered the Dáil chamber. Frank Aiken had earlier handed out revolvers to some of his colleagues and rumour has it that even heavier weapons were on hand in case of an Army coup. James Dillon always claimed in later years that he saw a senior Fianna Fáil politician assembling a machine gun in a telephone booth at the back of the chamber.

The belief in Fianna Fáil that a coup was possible demonstrated how severely they still misjudged Cosgrave. True enough some wild men on the Government side had talked about a coup, particularly the Garda Commissioner, Eoin O'Duffy. Ernest Blythe was also rumoured to be in favour of a coup but there was no widespread sympathy for such a move in Cumann na nGaedheal and Cosgrave was not prepared to countenance it. He asked colleagues where the rumours were coming from and was told about O'Duffy whom he had never liked or trusted in the first place.

Tim Pat Coogan recalls that Cosgrave was always very wary of O'Duffy:

'In fact, Cosgrave had only persuaded my father [Eamonn Coogan] to act as deputy commissioner in the first instance because he convinced him that a counter balance was needed to someone whom he regarded as a wild man.'

Cosgrave himself took the opening of the sixth Dáil calmly. Maurice Manning describes the opening in his forthcoming biography of James Dillon, quoting Dillon as saying: 'Before the vote, far from being engaged in any frantic plotting, Cosgrave was upstairs playing pontoon with the former Education Minister, John Marcus O'Sullivan.'

In an assessment of Cosgrave's achievement Professor Joe Lee criticised him for political ineptitude by shifting to the right in the mid-1920s rather than coming to an accommodation with Labour. He added:

'Cosgrave had responsibility thrust upon him in frightening circumstances, which would reinforce his natural caution. His vision was limited, his instincts conservative. He had neither a capacious intellect nor a commanding personality. What he did have was a basic

W.T. Cosgrave addresses an election meeting in 1918.

W.T. (centre) arriving at University College Dublin on January 6 1922, for the vote on ratification of the Treaty.

Members of the Second Dáil outside the Mansion House in August, 1921. W.T. in front row (fourth from right) with Arthur Griffith and Michael Collins on his left and Kevin O'Higgins on his right.

At the funeral of Michael Collins in August 1922. W.T. walks between Eoin MacNeill and J.J. Walsh.

During the Civil War with 'The Blacksmith of Ballinalee' General Sean MacEoin and Surgeon McArdle.

*With Mr Justice W.E. Wylie, the man who prosecuted him after the 1916
Rising. At the Horse Show in 1923.*

After the Civil War a happy family picture. With wife Louisa and children. Liam (with the pony) and Michael.

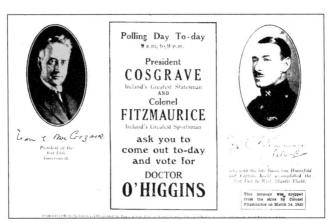

By-election leaflet for T.F. O'Higgins in Dublin North in 1929. W.T. and trans-Atlantic flight hero, Col. James FitzMaurice, endorse the candidate.

W.T. as leader of the Opposition addressing an Army recruitment meeting in 1939.

Portrait of W.T. in retirement.

With wife Louisa in the 1950s.

Father and son. At the Phoenix Park races in 1959.

decency, a sense of public service, and sound judgement on matters of state. He was essentially a moderate, who had to learn and did learn, however reluctantly, the fundamental lesson on which the survival of civilised public life depends, that moderates must be prepared, in the last resort, to kill in defence of moderation. It was due in large measure to him that things did not fall apart, that the centre did hold, that not so many but so few of the rough beasts slouching through the Ireland of the twenties would reach their blood-soaked Bethlehems. And Cosgrave would do the ship of State one final service, by the manner in which he quietly left the bridge and handed over the wheel to the rival captain. Bitter though it was in party terms — indeed precisely because it was so bitter in party terms — it was his finest hour.'

While Professor Lee's assessment is basically generous it is also quite contradictory. Cosgrave is faulted for his innate conservatism and his lack of a commanding personality but is praised for his decency, judgement, moderation and his willingness in the last analysis to kill to protect the values he believed in. Yet is clear that his strengths derived from the attributes Prof. Lee describes as his faults. It is precisely because he was practical and self-effacing, did not have any desire to be a demagogue or engage in intellectual gymnastics that Cosgrave was so successful in laying the foundations of the Irish State and fighting off the blood-thirsty beasts who sought to devour her at birth. Ireland was the only newly independent country in Europe after the First World War which remained a democracy throughout the twentieth century and for that Cosgrave must take a lot of the credit. Not only did he, and his colleagues in Cumann na nGaedheal, ensure that democracy survived the threat of Republicans in the Civil War but the manner in which he handed over power to his arch enemy, de Valera, after the people had spoken in 1932, was, as Lee acknowledges, his ultimate achievement.

An unlikely but telling tribute to W.T.'s contribution to Irish democracy came from de Valera. Tim Pat Coogan retails a conversation between de Valera and his son Vivion after Fianna Fáil had been in power for a few years. Vivion was complaining about Free Staters in conventional Fianna Fáil style when his father stopped him. 'Yes, yes, we said all that, I know. I know. But when we got in and saw the files ... they did a magnificent job, Viv. They did a magnificent job.'

5

HARD TIMES

W.T. COSGRAVE was 51 and his son Liam 12 when Cumann na nGaedheal lost office in 1932. W.T. would never again serve in government and all his great political achievements were behind him, although of course he could not have known that at the time. The political atmosphere became increasingly sour and intimidating during 1932. De Valera's decision to throw open the jails and release all the IRA prisoners appeared to confirm Cumann na nGaedheal suspicions that Fianna Fáil and the IRA were virtually the same.

Immediately he left office Cosgrave and his supporters found it difficult to exercise their basic political rights. In May 1932, W.T. was shouted down at a rally in his Cork constituency. Violence was encouraged by the *Irish Press* which had been established by de Valera to back the Fianna Fáil case in 1931. 'Free speech was governed by certain conditions, one of which was that no party advocating foreign domination was entitled in any country to misguide the people,' thundered the newspaper, justifying the breaking up of Cumann na nGaedheal meetings.

IRA leader, Frank Ryan, summed up the Republican attitude towards political opponents even more trenchantly than the *Irish Press*:

> 'No matter what anyone says to the contrary, while we have fists, and boots to use, and guns if necessary, we will not allow free speech to traitors.'

It was against this background that the Army Comrades Association was founded early in 1932 to protect Cumann na nGaedheal supporters from IRA harassment. T.F. O'Higgins, a brother of the late Kevin O'Higgins, assumed leadership of the movement in August 1932. In January 1933, with Anglo-Irish relations deteriorating rapidly and violence on the streets increasing, de Valera called a snap election and this time he won an overall majority. At a time of Anglo-Irish confrontation Cosgrave and Cumann na nGaedheal were portrayed as the 'anti-national' party, while Fianna Fáil grabbed the public imagination as the patriotic party.

Now secure in power de Valera dismissed O'Duffy as Garda Commissioner. O'Duffy in turn took over the leadership of the ACA which had adopted the blue shirt as its uniform and rechristened itself as the National Guard. A plan by O'Duffy to lead a great parade to Dublin in August was met head on by de Valera. He reintroduced Cosgrave's anti-terrorist measures which Fianna Fáil had spent so much time denouncing and he banned not only the march but the National Guard. O'Duffy backed away from confrontation and cancelled the march.

In September 1933, a demoralised Cumann na nGaedheal agreed to merge with the Blueshirts and the Centre Party to form a new political entity known as Fine Gael. O'Duffy, who was not even a TD, was elected leader of the new party with W.T. its leader in the Dáil. The excitable and unstable O'Duffy adopted the trappings of European fascism but he was an incompetent leader who quickly alienated even his strongest supporters. Why Cosgrave agreed to his leadership is puzzling. He clearly had no faith in O'Duffy's abilities but given the demoralisation among his own supporters and the insistence of the Centre Party on a new leader he felt he had no choice but to give way.

'It is clear that Cosgrave was not especially enthusiastic about the whole idea and it seems that his reservations were shared by some of his frontbench colleagues, most of all by Patrick Hogan,' wrote Maurice Manning in his definitive study of the Blueshirts. Cosgrave's decision to work for a merger was influenced by his belief that Opposition unity was essential at all costs. He was convinced that Fianna Fáil was out to smash all opposition and unless the various groups came together they might all perish. Neither the Centre Party nor the National Guard was anxious to have him as their leader so to bring about Opposition unity he decided to forego the leadership. There was also a group within Cumann na nGaedheal which was anxious to replace Cosgrave as leader. The feeling among the disgruntled element was that under his leadership the party had lost two elections within a year and seemed to be making little progress. It

was felt that a more vigorous and extrovert type of leadership, such as
O'Duffy's, was necessary to counter de Valera.

An insight into the feelings of an ordinary Cumann na nGaedheal
supporter at the drift of Irish politics at the time is given by Terence de
Vere White in his memoir *A Fretful Midge*.

> 'In the early years of the Irish Free State Mr William T. Cosgrave had
> the thankless task of keeping law and order in a country which
> dislikes law but likes litigation and chafes at all orders except Holy
> Orders. Mr Cosgrave's Government executed many of those who took
> up arms against it. The young and brave murdered, looted and
> burned — but these events only offended those who suffered
> personally. The country, as a whole, forgot and forgave them. Mr
> Cosgrave was never forgiven for his executions. The quality which
> finally destroyed him was modesty. Soon after Mr de Valera took office
> his opponents gathered together under the leadership of one whom
> most of them did not know, a certain General O'Duffy. With a
> humility as praiseworthy as it was misguided, the experienced
> Cosgrave stood down for this futile person who had won local
> celebrity as chief of police.'

O'Duffy was a disaster as party leader and he gave the opponents of
Fine Gael plenty of ammunition to portray the new party as a fascist
organisation. Street violence between the Blueshirts and the IRA was
now a feature of political life. O'Duffy's colleagues found him
impossible to work with and eventually he resigned as leader of Fine
Gael in 1934. Cosgrave was then elected in his place facing the thankless
task of attempting to rid Fine Gael of its image as a crypto-fascist
organisation while trying to oppose an increasingly rampant Fianna Fáil
in the Dáil. It was galling for Cosgrave to watch de Valera taking on the
mantle of the defender of law and order and democracy against the
threat posed by the Blueshirts but the sure political footwork of Fianna
Fáil left him with no answer.

> 'Many Blueshirts, perhaps most, saw themselves as essentially
> moderate, founded to defend constitutional freedoms against the IRA
> threat, though the toughs amongst them happily contemplated a
> dictatorship. They were not pervasively anti-democratic in principle but
> they allowed themselves to be manoeuvred into a position where Fianna
> Fáil were able to pose as hereditary democrats and denounce the
> Blueshirts as potential dictators. They were less adept than Fianna Fáil
> in exploiting the fascistic rhetoric of Nationalism,' considered Joe Lee.

Another political battle faced by Cosgrave was his opposition to the
new constitution produced by de Valera. The Fine Gael leader wrongly

regarded it as a document designed to give de Valera the powers of a dictator. Dev decided to kill two birds with the one stone and he called a general election for the same day as a referendum on his Bunracht na hÉireann.

There was a significant slippage in the Fianna Fáil vote from almost 50% to 45% and the party lost eight seats. Fine Gael gained 5% to 35% but did not win a single extra seat, thanks in large measure to a radical revision of the constituencies designed to protect the Fianna Fáil position. The referendum too was passed but with a small enough majority, 56%, backing it.

Fianna Fáil was back as a minority government again and had to rely on Labour to govern. This delicate position allowed Cosgrave a decisive input into the choice of the nation's first president. Douglas Hyde was first suggested by Cosgrave after Fianna Fáil and Fine Gael each vetoed lists put up by the other. Hyde proved acceptable and he was elevated to Áras an Uachtaráin without an election being necessary.

The following year de Valera successfully negotiated the end of the economic war and the transfer of the Treaty ports to Irish jurisdiction. He again went for a snap election to capitalise on the achievement and the move paid off handsomely. Fianna Fáil won 51.9% of the vote, its best ever performance, before or since, and the party had 77 TDs in the 138 member Dáil — a comfortable majority. Fine Gael slipped back to 33% and lost three seats in the process. The party had now clearly lost its majority status and was condemned to play second fiddle to Fianna Fáil.

It was in this atmosphere of disillusion, bitterness and violent street politics that W.T.'s eldest son, Liam, grew up. Like his father before him he attended the Christian Brothers in Synge Street. However, when he was old enough for secondary school he moved on to Castlenock College, a boarding school which was decidedly more middle-class in atmosphere and which attracted the sons of large farmers from around the country. In later life Cosgrave has expressed more affection for Synge Street than Castlenock but he fitted in well at his school and became a prefect in his final year.

Cosgrave's relationship with his father was very close all through his life. Even as a teenager he talked politics incessantly with W.T., often staying up late into the night discussing the issues of the day. He joined Fine Gael at the age of 17 and spoke at his first public meeting in the same year, 1937, during the general election campaign. The election coincided with the return of the Blueshirts from Spain but Cosgrave declared years later 'I was never a Blueshirt; and neither was my father'.

Religion was the mainstay of W.T.'s life and it gave him great comfort during his years in the political wilderness. He and Louisa travelled to Rome regularly and in 1934 they brought Liam to the city for the first time. All three had an audience with the Pope and it made a huge impression on the 14-year-old future Taoiseach. Like his father he remained a devout Catholic all his life and visited Rome regularly as an adult.

After his Leaving Certificate Liam decided to study law and enrolled at the Kings Inns. He attended some courses in UCD as part of his studies and still recalls the brilliance of Paddy McGilligan's lectures on Constitutional law. He did well, but not brilliantly, at the Kings Inns and was called to the bar in 1943. Friends from that era remember that the Cosgrave home was a very open one with friends of Liam welcome to call at any time. Tennis evenings were held during the summer with W.T. often taking a active part.

Liam surprised his family by joining the Army in 1940 in response to the Government's appeal for volunteers following the outbreak of the Second World War. He regarded it as his duty to join up even though his father is said to have had reservations about it. In typical Cosgrave fashion he modestly joined up as a private soldier but was promoted to Lieutenant after a few months. From his time as a soldier he developed a strong loyalty to the Army which was to be a feature of his political outlook. In September 1996, he marched proudly in uniform alongside his old comrades in a parade to commemorate the 50th anniversary of the ending of the Emergency. He continued his studies at Kings Inns while he was in the Army.

Despite his close relationship with his father Liam again surprised W.T. in 1943 by deciding to seek a Fine Gael nomination for the Dáil. He was elected at the very young age of 23 and for a short period he was a member of the House alongside his father, who was still leader of Fine Gael. Liam's decision to enter politics in County Dublin caused consternation in the household of Desmond FitzGerald (father of Garret) because it led to the end of Desmond's political career. The disappointment and resentment in the FitzGerald family was so intense that some people in Fine Gael have traced the poor relationship between Cosgrave and Garret FitzGerald which almost led to a split in Fine Gael in the late 1960s, to this incident.

A confused version of this event is to be found in Garret FitzGerald's autobiography *All in a Life* which despite a number of factual errors indicates the level of hurt felt by the FitzGeralds. After stating that Desmond FitzGerald stood for the Dáil in 1944 along with H. P. Dockrell, Garret continues:

'A third candidate was 24-year old Liam Cosgrave, son of W.T. Cosgrave, who had retired from the party leadership the previous year. Liam Cosgrave's nomination came as a surprise and was received with enthusiasm neither by H.P. Dockrell or my father. My father was not given to showing resentment, however, and accepted the situation gracefully enough. My mother was less patient. Her comments were distinctly acid, especially when Fine Gael won only one seat in Co. Dublin and the single TD elected for the party was Liam Cosgrave.'

FitzGerald's recollection is faulty on a number of counts. As Liam Cosgrave was first elected in 1943 he was a sitting TD when Desmond FitzGerald was nominated to contest Dublin County for Fine Gael in 1944. In 1943 Cosgrave secured the nomination for Dublin County and joined Henry Morgan Dockrell, Patrick Joseph Roe and Mary Ennis on the Fine Gael ticket. Cosgrave polled very well winning 11,099 votes on his first outing. Dockrell and himself took two Fine Gael seats, Fianna Fáil won two with Sean Brady and Patrick Fogarty while James Tunney (father of James chairman of the Fianna Fáil parliamentary party in the 1980s) won a seat for Labour.

It was the following year in 1944 when a second general election was called within the space of 12 months that Desmond FitzGerald, who lost his Seanad seat in 1943, secured a Fine Gael nomination to run with Liam Cosgrave. At this stage Cosgrave and Dockrell were the sitting TDs and contrary to what Garret says both were re-elected in 1944.

Cosgrave walked away with the Fine Gael vote, polling a whopping 12,322 first preferences. Dockrell won a respectable 6,488 first preferences but FitzGerald was humiliated, winning just 1,978 votes. This electoral setback clearly impacted on the FitzGerald family. Despite Desmond FitzGerald's important role in the founding of the State his political career was over at the early age of 56 and his financial circumstances were difficult for some time. He died in March 1947.

The Fine Gael vote was down considerably in 1943 but so was the Fianna Fáil vote. De Valera came back in a minority government and waited his opportunity to pounce again. The mood of those elections is captured by Terence de Vere White, a party supporter at the time.

'Ireland, judging by Wicklow was neutral to the core and had no qualms of conscience about it. It was also apparent in 1944 that the former Unionists who had rowed in behind Mr Cosgrave were beginning to change their allegiance. In Greystones in which Protestantism, golf and bridge absorb the waking hours of the residents, I had confidently expected to capture all the votes for the commonwealth candidate. I did nothing of the kind. A local clergyman was reported to have advised his flock to vote for Mr de Valera, as he was less bigoted than Mr Cosgrave. Mr de Valera is indeed above reproach in matters of religious tolerance but Mr Cosgrave had been at pains to put in the Senate the parson's co-religionists and Mr de Valera's friends had been equally zealous to burn down their houses. The parson's intervention was a sad example of how soon eaten bread is forgotten.'

W.T. Cosgrave, disappointed and disillusioned by politics, decided to step down as party leader before the 1944 General Election. W.T. and Liam were in the Dáil together for less than 12 months and following the departure of his father from politics the Cosgrave mantle fell on the young TD who was appointed to the party's front bench.

The 1944 election result was a bitter disappointment to Fine Gael. The party had polled reasonably well under W.T. Cosgrave the previous year but the decision of de Valera to call a snap election less than a year later on the pretext of a Dáil defeat caught the Opposition parties on the wrong foot and Fianna Fáil romped home to a comfortable majority. Fine Gael were in total disarray in the 1944 campaign with the new party leader Richard Mulcahy not even a member of the Dáil when Cosgrave stood down. Mulcahy did make it back to the Dáil in 1944 but his party fared disastrously winning just 20% of the vote.

De Valera returned as Taoiseach with a comfortable Dáil majority and his reputation as the shrewdest politician in the country enhanced by his decision to go for a snap election in less than a year in office. It was the third time he had won an overall majority by this formula of holding two elections in less than 12 months, the earlier ones being in 1933 and 1938.

After the 1944 election Mulcahy appointed young Liam Cosgrave to the front bench at the age of 24. Cosgrave in typical fashion later played down this rapid promotion saying that it had happened 'at a time when front-bench talent was thin on the ground.' Two years later he was chairman of the Dáil Committee on Public Accounts, a position normally reserved for the Opposition. All in all it was a very rapid rise up the political ladder.

Like any young man of his age Liam Cosgrave liked to relax. Horse racing was a favourite pastime and he travelled to race meetings around the country with friends from the political and legal worlds. He also did the round of parties among people of his own social group in Dublin and he was not averse to having an occasional drink in a pub.

Vincent Browne tells a story about Liam's participation in a paper chase in south County Dublin during the mid-1940s. A group including Liam repaired to a public house, stayed for longer than they had intended and became a bit boisterous. Somebody found a goose in a nearby field; the bird was captured and brought into the pub and offered a drink. There was general hilarity when the goose took with relish to drinking stout and in the uproar some damage was done to the furniture in the pub.

> 'The young TD became very agitated about the disreputable behaviour and insisted on the ejection of the goose and the departure from the premises. He was heard to remark to a dissenting friend: "It's all right for you but it's my bloody constituency." "TD incites goose to wreck pub," quipped another companion.'

Liam clearly did not want to be tarred with the same brush as his uncle the Bird Flanagan.

Despite his senior position on the Fine Gael front bench young Cosgrave got embroiled in a controversy with Mulcahy who was in favour of Ireland continuing to remain in the Commonwealth. This was a popular view in Fine Gael, particularly with the Parliamentary Party element but also with Cumann na Gaelers like Mulcahy and Eamonn Coogan. Liam Cosgrave, though, never forgot his father's Sinn Féin origins and was always very suspicious of the British. In 1946 he told the Dáil:

> 'So far as this country is concerned the one major problem is partition. So long as partition continues, harmonious and cordial and friendly relations between this country and Great Britain can never be established on the basis on which they might rest if partition ceased to exist.'

Because of differences on this issue and an instinctive lack of sympathy between the two men, relations between Mulcahy and young Cosgrave were never close. There may well have been resentment on

Mulcahy's part that the son of his former leader had so quickly forced his way into such a senior position at such a young age.

After the Emergency, as the Second World War was so quaintly named in Ireland, disillusionment with Fianna Fáil finally began to set in among the electorate. Fine Gael, however, was not the catalyst for political change. It was a new party, Clann na Poblachta, founded in 1946 by ex-IRA leader, Sean MacBride, which captured the mood for change. The party appealed to the more Republican section of the Fianna Fáil electorate, as well as to disgruntled teachers and, in October 1947, sensationally won two by-elections.

In an attempt to nip the Clann in the bud de Valera unexpectedly dissolved the Dáil in January 1948. Fine Gael tried to cash in on the mood for change and fought the campaign on the slogan 'Youth and Experience'. The party had plenty of experience but little youth so Liam Cosgrave looked forward with confidence to promotion if Fine Gael managed to get back into government after 16 years in the wilderness.

Dun Laoghaire was established as a constituency in 1948 and Cosgrave opted to run there rather than in Dublin County. He topped the poll in that election — a feat he was to repeat in every single election until he retired in 1981. He kept in very close touch with his constituents and attended virtually every Fine Gael branch meeting in his constituency throughout his political career. Cosgrave always remembered that his mandate as a politician came from the people of Dun Laoghaire and his attention to the minutiae of constituency business became legendary. His younger brother, Michael, who was a more outgoing personality, played a big role in most of his Dáil campaigns.

H.M. Dockrell lost his seat in 1948 but his son, Percy, ran in 1951 and was elected on Cosgrave's surplus. That pattern was repeated for nearly 30 years except on the occasions when the Cosgrave surplus was not large enough. A story told by a long-serving Fine Gael figure about the 1957 Election illustrates the relationship between Cosgrave and Dockrell:

'The count was in Rathmines town hall. Liam turned up early but went off somewhere for a while when he saw how the result was going. Then Percy Dockrell rolls in about 11.30 a.m. and asked me how it was going, because Percy wouldn't know what was happening. I told him it was going badly and he said "how badly". I said "Just about as badly as it can go" and Percy looked at me and said "You mean Liam doesn't have enough votes for me".'

6

FIRST MINISTRY

THE 16-YEAR political famine ended for Fine Gael in 1948 and provided Liam Cosgrave with the opportunity to get his first taste of Ministerial office. Initially, though, it was not clear that de Valera would be forced out of office. While the Fianna Fáil vote dropped to just under 42% the party had held on to power with the same share of the vote in 1943 and this time around they had actually one more TD than in that election with 67 Dáil seats out of 146.

Both Fine Gael and the new party, Clann na Poblachta, did very poorly in the 1948 election. Fine Gael slumped to its lowest share of the vote in the history of the state, before or since, at 19%, although it did manage to win one extra seat on transfers to give it a total of 31. The Clann which confidently expected to win over 20 seats actually won just 10 with 13% of the vote. With the two parties performing poorly, Labour split into two factions, another small party, Clann na Talmhan, holding seven seats and 12 Independents winning their way into the Dáil it seemed as if Fianna Fáil was the only party which could offer stable government.

The fragmented Opposition was united, however, by one theme. 'Put Them Out' had been a slogan during the campaign and after the election the various parties and factions came together to offer an alternative government to the Dáil. Fine Gael, Labour, National Labour, Clann an Poblachta and Clann na Talmhan together had 67 seats, exactly the same number as Fianna Fáil. A meeting of party leaders convened by Richard Mulcahy agreed on the formation of a government but there was one snag — Mulcahy was not acceptable as Taoiseach.

Mulcahy, as the commander of the Free State Army in the Civil War had responsibility for the executions policy which had led to the deaths of Sean MacBride's comrades in the IRA. MacBride felt he could not serve under Mulcahy but it was Bill Norton, the Labour leader, who raised the issue in the discussions, suggesting to Mulcahy that he should stand aside. The Fine Gael leader graciously put personal considerations aside, as he had done during the Army mutiny of 1924, and John A. Costello emerged from Fine Gael as an acceptable compromise for Taoiseach.

The fact that Costello and MacBride were senior colleagues in the Law Library helped to smooth the path. Then, as now, membership of that exclusive club frequently counted for far more among its members than mere party affiliation. With Costello as Taoiseach, MacBride, Minister for External Affairs and another eminent barrister, Paddy McGilligan, Minister for Finance, the lawyers were in all the top positions. The Dáil Independents had to be included in the deal and yet another barrister (non-practising), James Dillon, was a pivotal player in getting them on side. Expelled from Fine Gael because of his support for the Allies during the war, he was included in the cabinet as Minister for Agriculture representing the Independents. Fine Gael had six cabinet posts, including Taoiseach, Clann na Poblachta and Labour got two each, National Labour and Clann na Talmhan one each, with the other going to Dillon.

Even though he was only 28 Liam Cosgrave is said by some Fine Gael sources to have expected a cabinet position, but he says there is no substance in this claim. He was made a parliamentary secretary, as junior Ministers were then titled, but was a parliamentary secretary with a difference because not only was he Chief Whip he was also given the job of secretary to the Government. This came about because Sean MacBride had a deep distrust of civil servants in general and of the cabinet Secretary, Maurice Moynihan, in particular. Moynihan had been cabinet Secretary to de Valera since 1932 and was a very close confidant of the outgoing Taoiseach. In view of that Costello agreed to MacBride's request to exclude Moynihan from cabinet meetings and Cosgrave was given the task of acting as cabinet secretary.

Nearly 50 years later at the end of 1994 another Fine Gael Taoiseach, John Bruton, reinvented the position of secretary to the Government as a political appointment for Pat Rabbitte of Democratic Left. This time it had nothing to do with distrust of the cabinet Secretary, Frank Murray, who continued to attend cabinet meetings and carry out his normal functions, but all to do with political expediency. Democratic Left were given just one cabinet post for Proinsias De Rossa and the appointment of Rabbitte was designed to give them an unofficial 16th member of the cabinet.

The decision to make Liam Cosgrave secretary to the Government in 1948 placed a lot of responsibility on his shoulders, particularly since he was acting for a government with limited cabinet experience. Brian Farrell has written that the experiment was a mistake and that 'this departure from established procedure weakened both Taoiseach and cabinet and contributed to the breakdown of internal communications which was a feature of the last days of this government.' Given that the experiment was not repeated in 1954–57, during Costello's second government, it would appear that the Taoiseach agreed.

Cosgrave himself, does not accept Farrell's assertion that the absence of officials led to a breakdown in communication at cabinet. 'Mr Costello, the secretary to the Government and myself discussed and recorded all decisions taken at Government meetings,' he told Ursula Halligan in 1982, when she interviewed him for an MA thesis on his 1973–77 Government.

While Cosgrave may have been disappointed at not getting a full cabinet position his role as secretary to the Government gave him a powerful inside track. He was also appointed to the critical post of Chief Whip as well as parliamentary secretary to the Minister for Industry and Commerce, Dan Morrissey. As Morrissey had been ill during the election and was in and out of hospital during the first Inter-Party Government Cosgrave had to fulfill many of his functions for long periods.

Cosgrave was also made a member of the economic sub-committee of the cabinet which was established on MacBride's suggestion to 'undertake a complete survey of the whole economic position of the State and to make recommendations.' In contrast to the current situation where there are 15 cabinet Ministers and 17 junior Ministers the situation was that in 1948, despite the fact that there were so many parties in government, the cabinet was kept to 13 Ministers and there were only three junior Ministerial posts. Cosgrave's colleagues as parliamentary secretaries were Brendan Corish of Labour, who would nearly 30 years later be part of a government with him, and Mick Donnellan, of Clann an Talmhan.

As Chief Whip Cosgrave gained an invaluable insight into how a government of different parties can be made to work. 'It was a most interesting experience as it involved five parties and 12 Independents and as Government Whip there was no shortage either of work or experience in dealing with different people and situations,' he says.

This experience was to serve him in good stead when he became Taoiseach himself because he had a much greater appreciation than most other Taoisigh of the need to keep back-benchers on side. 'The Government majority in 1973 was only two, which was the lowest ever and involved close contact with every deputy supporting the Government,' he says.

Cosgrave enjoyed serving under Costello as Taoiseach and found him agreeable to work with. 'He was hard-working and considerate to those he had to deal with.' The controversial decision of the Taoiseach to declare Ireland a republic while on an official visit to Canada annoyed a lot of people in Fine Gael but Cosgrave was not one of them. 'In the Dáil debate on the Taoiseach's estimate in 1948 the late William Norton and James Dillon and myself all expressed support for the repeal of the External Relations Act.'

Because of his role at Industry and Commerce Cosgrave was kept doubly busy. That department had been built into an empire by Seán Lemass during the war and there was hardly an aspect of the nation's life that it did not touch. The Industrial Development Authority was established by Morrissey in 1949 but as he was ill Cosgrave had to pilot the legislation through the Dáil against very strong opposition from Fianna Fáil. Other major projects included the setting up of the Trade Board and the nationalisation of CIE, which also absorbed a lot of Dáil time.

Cosgrave got involved in a conflict with Norton over prices. On the advice of his officials he strongly resisted the Labour leader's attempt to establish a prices tribunal. His views were unpopular with the electorate and Norton won the day at cabinet. He had no problem accepting the majority decision but he never regretted his stance.

Cosgrave took part in negotiations with the British which led to the Anglo-Irish Trade Agreement of 1948 and during talks about coal the following year he met the future prime minister, Harold Wilson, who was then with the Board of Trade. He also had to deal with the North and took part in negotiations with Stormont Ministers about the Erne hydro-electric project and the Great Northern Railway. This involved the first direct talks with Northern Ministers since independence. Cosgrave visited Belfast to meet Northern Minister for Commerce, William McGreery, and Maynard Sinclair, Deputy Prime Minister and Minister for Finance, visited Dublin. 'These direct contacts were the first since the State was established and after the first Coalition left office Lemass and McGreery concluded the GNR agreement,' says Cosgrave.

The Foyle Fisheries Commission was another development at this time and it was one that became the model for the North–South bodies in the Framework Document of 1995. Cosgrave is proud of these little publicised achievements.

'These practical moves on cooperation were the first taken by an Irish Government and the Stormont Government. The Lemass–O'Neill talks much publicised, followed over a decade later. These talks were, of course, undertaken in the TV era and got widespread coverage whereas the earlier meetings received photographic and press coverage.'

Cosgrave, given his family tradition, had little time for the way Unionists ran Northern Ireland but neither did he approve of verbal Nationalism:

'I always held the view that the prime responsibility for conditions in the North of Ireland lay with the Unionist politicians who ignored and neglected for over 50 years the position of the Nationalist minority. Eventually the situation exploded in 1969. At the same time most of the talk from down here had no positive contribution to make and many were happy if verbal patriotism was accepted as the highest form of political martyrdom. I believed that practical measures to improve the situation like the Erne Scheme, etc., was the right way ahead. These, of course, should also have been accompanied by measures and policies in the North to provide a just and fair form of government from the minority. The ultimate objective being to unite Ireland.'

As Cosgrave and Morrissey carried out their talks with Northern Ministers on economic cooperation Sean MacBride launched an international blitz against partition which failed to achieve anything. The anti-partition campaign of the late 1940s and early 1950s only showed how insulated Ireland had been during the war from the realities of international politics and the campaign was an embarrassing failure. Cosgrave was impatient with MacBride. He publicly dismissed as 'nonsense' a statement by the Minister for External Affairs that conditions in Northern Ireland were as bad as in the communist countries in eastern Europe.

Cosgrave says that John A. Costello preferred his low key approach to the strident one of MacBride.

'Costello knew from views I expressed publicly and privately that I
regarded the line taken on partition between 1948–51 as counter
productive. Indeed, I gathered from him after the change of
government in 1951 that if we were returned to government he would
likely appoint me to External Affairs. He accepted that the views given
by me were realistic.'

As well as working extremely hard in two departments Cosgrave also
devoted himself to constituency work in his new constituency of Dun
Laoghaire. Jim Dooge, who served as Cathaoirlach of the Seanad in
the 1970s and was Minister for Foreign Affairs in Garret FitzGerald's
first government, as a young man served as Cosgrave's constituency
secretary from 1948 until 1954. He recalls:

'Liam was an amazing constituency man. He paid tremendous
attention to the constituency. In a sense we were building up a new
organisation in Dun Laoghaire–Rathdown. His attendance at his
branch meetings and his work for his constituents was absolutely
remarkable. Remember he had a desperate job as whip then. I think
that the Government had to get 10 out of 12 Independents to get a
majority. And Liam was chief whip so he had to be pretty efficient.
The Independents in the Dáil were a strange bunch.'

The Inter-Party Government of 1948–51 had a number of
achievements to its credit but it will go down in history as collapsing
because of a Church–State crisis, even though it actually collapsed for
other reasons. The real reason for the fall of the Government was the
decision of two Independents to withdraw their support from the
Government over the price of milk. It is arguable that hostility of the
farmers to James Dillon, rather than the hostility of the hierarchy to
Noel Browne brought an end to the first Inter-Party Government.
Nonetheless it was the débâcle of the Mother and Child Scheme
which fatally weakened a government already tottering because of
personality clashes at cabinet. The Mother and Child Scheme
achieved the status of a *cause célèbre*, mainly because Dr Browne
insisted on making a martyr of himself.

Browne became a cabinet Minister, at MacBride's insistence, on his
first day in the Dáil. The appointment caused astonishment not least
to the deputy leader of Clann na Poblachta, Noel Hartnett, whose own
claims were inexplicably overlooked. Browne, in a foretaste of his
entire political life, soon began to fight with his party leader and
relations between him and MacBride became impossible.

Briefly stated Browne's Mother and Child Scheme was designed to
provide free ante and post-natal care for mothers and free medical

care for children up to the age of 16, without a means test. The Catholic hierarchy opposed the complete absence of a means test in the scheme as marking an unacceptable level of state intervention in medicine.

In the autumn of 1950 Browne held a number of consultations with the bishops and believed for some reason that they would not oppose his scheme. His fatal move, though, was that in March 1951, he announced the scheme without cabinet approval. The bishops objected and Browne then agreed with his cabinet colleagues to abide by the hierarchy's judgement on whether the scheme was compatible with Catholic morality. The bishops said no, the cabinet agreed and Browne was ultimately asked to resign by Costello and MacBride.

While the controversy has come to be regarded as a clash between Church and State 'the decisive breach was between government colleagues rather than between government and the hierarchy,' according to Ronan Fanning who gives a detailed account of the incident in *Independent Ireland.*

Browne's own attempt to portray the affair as an effort by the Church and the medical profession to prevent poor women and children receiving free medical treatment is another distortion of the event that has gained common currency. It was rich women and children the church and the doctors wanted excluded from the scheme for whatever motive. 'There was a fundamental, long-term issue of principle also involved. If Browne's scheme succeeded, the strong likelihood was that private practice would gradually be superseded by a salaried state service. However hysterical and opportunistic the fears expressed in some medical circles, suspicion of the longer term potential autocracy of the State was by no means unwarranted,' according to Joe Lee.

Liam Cosgrave did not play a direct role in the crisis or make any public statement on the issue but he was present with important Ministers like Norton, Mulcahy, Dillon and Morrissey in the Taoiseach's office at the key moments. One story retailed by Vincent Browne is as follows:

> 'At one of the interminable meetings on the crisis a document written by Noel Browne on the alleged treachery of his party leader, Sean MacBride, was circulated for perusal. Cosgrave quietly left with the document under his arm and returned a short time afterwards. When asked later what he was doing out of the room he smiled wanly and replied that he had gone to have a copy made of the document in case it might come in useful at some future date.'

When the election came in June 1951 the first Inter-Party Government lost power but the fortunes of the different parties in government varied enormously. The Fine Gael vote rose significantly by 6% from its all-time low in 1948 and the party gained nine extra seats. It was back in business as the main alternative to Fianna Fáil who, while getting back into government as a minority, gained only one seat. The big loser was Clann na Poblachta which lost eight of its ten seats.

His term in office boosted Cosgrave's reputation significantly. 'It was in this position that certain qualities (which only those who know him suspected) came to light,' reported *The Leader.* 'He was unusual in that he gained the admiration of his departmental servants not for any subservience to the expert view but for his sympathetic but critical consideration of their advice. He was always willing and able to listen, to understand, reject and accept. He was, in fact, much better than they had expected from such a fledgling.'

In 1950 Liam Cosgrave, at the age of 30, married Vera Osborne, a member of a Kildare family well known in the horse racing world. Cosgrave's best man was Dick Finlay, whose brother Tom was later made president of the High Court by Cosgrave, having been appointed to the bench by Jack Lynch. The Cosgrave's had three children, Mary, Liam and Ciarain.

During the next three years in Opposition Cosgrave played an increasingly prominent role on the Fine Gael front bench. With most of his colleagues now getting on in years Cosgrave's experience, ability and enthusiasm enabled him to make a name for himself in the Dáil and he was regarded as one of the leading members of Fine Gael when de Valera called an election in 1954.

Fine Gael made another dramatic improvement in that election increasing its share of the vote by another 6% and gaining an extra ten seats to bring its total to 50. John A. Costello returned to power to form the second Inter-Party Government although this time it was composed of three parties, Fine Gael, Labour and Clann na Talmhan and was not as unwieldy as the first one.

By 1954 Cosgrave's appeal to the electorate was such that *The Leader* commented in a profile on the fact that he 'has been returned with majorities which could only be compared with those secured by the Taoiseach or Mr Lemass.' The profile went on:

'In Opposition he was assiduous in his attention to the needs of his constituents, in office to the duties of the department to which he was attached. If he is anything he is cautious. But if he has not yet done all that some hoped and still expect he has not disappointed. He has a great detestation of what he would call "codology" and he is not impressed by oratorical flourish or by sweeping, if attractive, generalisations. He has a sense of humour which is hard and yet never uncharitable; some would wish that he would let himself go more in his public appearance. He has been, if anything, over modest; there has never been the slightest trace of arrogance, of false humility or of flamboyance about him.'

That was the reputation he had in political circles when he was was given the senior post of Minister for External Affairs. Strangely enough Costello first offered the post to Sean MacBride who declined to join the Government because his party strength was so low. Instead MacBride decided to support it from outside.

During his term as Minister for External Affairs Cosgrave participated in trade discussions and was elected chairman of the Committee of Ministers of the Council of Europe in 1955. Far more importantly, during his term as Minister Ireland won admittance to the United Nations and Cosgrave led the first Irish delegation to a meeting of the general assembly in the autumn of 1956 and delivered an important address which defined Irish foreign policy for a long time to come.

That address followed two major international upheavals, the Russian invasion of Hungary and the British and French invasion of Suez. Cosgrave had no compunction about denouncing both sets of imperialists and the speech went down very well in Ireland. Conor Cruise O'Brien, at that time an Irish diplomat at the UN, who later served Cosgrave as a Minister between 1973–77, described in his book *To Katanga and Back* the impression Cosgrave made on professional diplomats at the UN:

'An independent, "Swedish", line was what we hoped for. Knowing the unfortunate tendency of many of our countrymen to talk big and act small, what we expected to get was something different. The result, even initially, was considerably better than most of us had expected. Mr Cosgrave, who headed our delegation on our entry in 1956, delivered a dignified and felicitous statement which considerably impressed the Assembly.'

Dr O'Brien added, however, that though the speech was an immeasurable improvement on expected form it was hardly conclusive proof of an independent Irish foreign policy.

'Suez and Hungary were sitters from the point of view of Irish public opinion. It was right at the time to demand the withdrawal of the

Anglo-French force from Suez and to condemn the Russian attack on Hungary. But, whatever about France, to criticise England is never entirely unpopular in Ireland and as for the Russians, a ringing denunciation in the circumstances was absolutely mandatory on any Irish politician who hoped to get re-elected. In short, the right positions were also the popular ones; and when the right and domestically popular courses were also those advocated by the United States no inward struggle was required to know what to do.'

This was written in the liberal 1960s when Western liberal intellectuals looked indulgently on the Soviet Union but with the hindsight of the 1990s it is clear that Cosgrave has little apology to make for his trenchant anti-Soviet policy. O'Brien subsequently served as a Minister in Cosgrave's Cabinet and has an enduring regard for him.

Even writing in the 1960s before he became a close political ally of Cosgrave's, O'Brien wrote:

'Mr Liam Cosgrave was a cautious and rather gentle conservative personality who was known to dislike the school of oratory which he called "dying for Ireland" and known therefore to have been made unhappy by the international antics of the first Inter-Party Government. Mr Cosgrave valued the advice on international matters of Mr F.H. Boland, the very astute and experienced secretary of the Department of External Affairs.'

The actual foreign policy adopted by Cosgrave became known as 'The Three Principles' and it was the foundation stone of Irish diplomacy until Ireland joined the European Community. Cosgrave outlined the three principles in the Dáil in June 1956. They were:

'1. - Scrupulous fidelity to the principles of the UN charter.

2. - The adoption of an independent line on all issues of foreign policy and non-association with any of the power blocks.

3. - To do whatever we can as a member of the UN to preserve the Christian civilisation of which we are a part and with that end in view to support whenever possible those powers principally responsible for the defence of the free world in their resistance to the spread of communist power and influence.'

Cosgrave visited the Vatican twice while Minister for External Affairs, attending Marian Year ceremonies as a representative of the Irish Government in 1954 and again in 1956 when he attended ceremonies to mark the 80th birthday and anniversary of the pontificate of Pope Pius XII. He was accompanied by his father and mother and they had a private audience with the Pope, bringing back memories of their meeting with the previous Pope in 1934.

In a broadcast on Vatican Radio on St Patrick's Day Cosgrave described Catholicism as synonymous with the struggle for political independence adding:

> '"As you are Christian so be you likewise Roman" was an injunction received from our Apostle, St Patrick, and to this injunction Ireland has ever remained true.'

Cosgrave did well as Minister for External Affairs. Professor Patrick Keatinge in his assessment of former Foreign Ministers writes:

> 'He was prepared to comment on world events and even to try and relate them to what was of necessity an isolated Ireland. This was a marked contrast to the parliamentary style of his predecessor and successor, Mr Aiken.'

As well as being Minister for External Affairs Cosgrave was acting Minister for Defence for long periods because of the illness of Sean MacEoin. His own time in the Army had given him an enormous respect and affection for the defence forces. One of his initiatives in that department was the establishment of the Army Apprentice School in Naas to provide trades and skills which would be of advantage to men while in the Army or, more importantly, after they left it.

During the 1954–57 Government Cosgrave's relationship with the Taoiseach, John A. Costello, was good and their styles suited each other.

> 'Mr Costello never interfered in any way with me in the department. He left the decisions to me but I kept him and the Government fully informed of all major matters.'

It was a style of running the cabinet which appealed to Cosgrave and which he in turn was to operate when his own turn came.

It was also his second experience of coalition government and he learned valuable lessons from it about the way such governments can be made to work. 'I thought and still think, given the circumstances, these governments were quite successful,' he once stated. It was during this period that Cosgrave renewed his acquaintance with Brendan Corish, who was Minister for Labour.

Cosgrave also made friends on the Opposition side. He knew and liked Seán Lemass and they had a common bond in their love of horse racing.

In 1954 *The Leader* remarked:

> '... He [Cosgrave] is not unaware of the artificialities necessarily created by the party system; and in his most confidential moments

might be expected to prefer the company and views of Mr Lemass to some of his colleagues in the Inter-Party Government.'

His friendship with Lemass led to speculation at one stage in the 1950s that the two of them would leave their respective parties to form a new political movement but there was never any basis for this rumour. The Government's major problem was a stagnant economy. Gerard Sweetman, the bright but abrasive Minister for Finance, took some valuable initiatives and promoted T.K. Whitaker, to be secretary of the Department of Finance. Before his more imaginative policies had a chance to work Northern Ireland brought the second Inter-Party Government to an end. The IRA campaign which began in 1956 provoked a hostile response from Costello who did his best to use the courts system to prosecute key IRA men. Intimidation of juries and ambivalence on the part of some jurors resulted in a number of prosecutions falling through but the Government, while resisting the temptation to invoke special powers, tried to keep up the pressure on the IRA. This was too much for Sean MacBride who put down a motion of no confidence in the Government. The motion was carried and the country was pitched into a new general election.

In that election Fianna Fáil under an ageing de Valera came roaring back to office winning an extra 13 seats to secure an overall majority in the Dáil for the first time since 1944. Fine Gael lost ten seats and slipped back below 30% of the vote but the party was still in a relatively healthy condition, compared to its near moribund state ten years earlier. 'The few genuinely professional politicians in Fine Gael had cause to be bitterly disappointed at the blighting of the bright hopes of 1954. Fine Gael had then pulled to within 15 seats of Fianna Fáil. Now it lagged 38 seats behind,' according to Joe Lee. There is a famous story told by Paddy Lindsay of the drive to Áras an Uachtaráin to hand in their seals of office which demonstrates a certain remoteness from Irish life which has always characterised Fine Gael. Lindsay shared the same car as Costello and Dillon and, on their way down the Quays, they passed the old Irish House pub and the conversation turned to pubs. 'You know I was never in a public house in my life except in my own in Ballaghaderreen,' said Dillon. Costello remarked that he had only ever been in a pub once as well. Lindsay exploded. 'I now know why we are going in this direction today and why we are out of touch with the people.'

Liam Cosgrave, though, was in closer touch than most of his colleagues with the concerns of ordinary people and was not as unfamiliar with the inside of a pub as some of his colleagues. Like his father he had a passion for horses and racing and this was his favourite form of relaxation. With a young family to rear Liam moved into Beechpark in the mid-1950s while his parents moved to a smaller house.

W.T. kept in touch with his old friend Gogarty who had been living for some time in the United States. In November 1956, W.T. wrote:

'With your permission I should like to make a comment on your declared intention of retiring. Don't! Everyone who does steps over a canyon making it impossible to retrace, then they find it lonesome and are prone to lose interest in men and things.'

Whether this reflected W.T.'s feelings about his own retirement is impossible to say.

W.T., the devout Catholic, wrote to Gogarty the following year with some practical advice on spiritual matters, reminding him in a friendly fashion that his age warranted doing something about the state of his soul.

Later that year Gogarty died and both W.T. and Liam travelled to the funeral near Renvyle in Co. Galway. Ulick O'Connor recalled the scene:

'At the funeral we stood on a hill over a small lake, with the Connemara mountains green and blue in the distance, the long incredible distance of the West, where the eye can see for many miles, yet there are never clear outlines, but forms blurred by bright colours. To the left of the grave a white ash tree stretched crooked and bent, silver against the lake's blue. A priest said the Latin prayers as the coffin was lowered into the grave. William Cosgrave, first president of the Irish Free State, stood nearby.'

Two years later W.T.'s wife, Louisa, died and he moved back into Beechpark to live with Liam and his family. He remained there until his death six years later.

As the generation who founded the State began to die off their successors were gradually coming into their own. De Valera finally stepped down and was replaced by Lemass who, though he was another veteran of the independence struggle, had a much more modern vision and promoted young men to cabinet positions around him. In Fine Gael the selfless Mulcahy retired in 1959 and Cosgrave made a daring bid at the age of 39 to become leader of the party.

7

THE JUST SOCIETY

WHEN Mulcahy retired as leader of Fine Gael in October 1959, it was widely assumed that John A. Costello would take over as party leader. However, despite the fact that he was 68-years-old, Costello wanted to continue his law practice and was only prepared to lead the party in a part-time capacity. While the issue was being considered Costello approached Cosgrave and asked him to take over as his 'managing director' in the Dáil if he took the titular leadership of the party. Cosgrave turned down the offer believing that Fine Gael needed a full time leader to rid itself of its image as a party of part-time politicians whose main interest was in the Law Library.

The hard-nosed Gerard Sweetman also opposed the notion of a part-time leader. Vincent Browne claims that Costello's hand was forced by Sweetman who began to orchestrate the candidature of James Dillon. 'Costello first heard of the moves against him at a cocktail party in the Canadian Embassy and decided there and then to throw in the towel, even though he calculated that he could win in a leadership contest against Dillon, who was Sweetman's protégé,' according to Browne.

With Costello out of the race Cosgrave then stepped in to challenge Dillon. The challenge surprised many people because at 39 Cosgrave was very young to consider going for the leadership, despite his family and political pedigree. Some senior figures deeply resented Cosgrave's presumption in putting himself forward at this stage. Cosgrave himself says that the challenge came because the alternative was James Dillon, son of the last leader of the Irish Parliamentary Party, John Dillon.

'Some members of the party thought that the old Sinn Féin tradition should lead the party rather than James Dillon, who was from the old Irish Parliamentary Party,' said Cosgrave. 'Neither then or subsequently did I ever ask anyone to support me but I agreed that the Sinn Féin tradition was more appropriate in the circumstances and so allowed my name to go forward.'

Liam Cosgrave would not have been human if he had not remembered that Dillon on his first day in the Dáil in 1932 had seconded the nomination of Eamon de Valera to take over the reins of power from his father. Dillon subsequently joined Fine Gael, left it during the War and returned to it during the first Inter-Party Government where he had been serving as an Independent cabinet Minister. A popular and colourful figure Dillon is remembered as probably the best ever orator to serve in Dáil Éireann and had a wonderful, rolling speaking voice. Stories of his wit are legendary but his political weakness was that he came from the Parliamentary Party tradition rather than the dominant Sinn Féin strain of Fine Gael and was always slightly outside the mainstream.

Cosgrave remembers that it was Kilkenny TD, Paddy Crotty, and Victor Carton from Dublin, who approached him and suggested that he stand for the leadership against Dillon. 'Gerard Sweetman strongly supported James Dillon and said so at party meetings. Paddy Donegan and Oliver Flanagan informed me prior to the party meeting to select a new leader that they were voting for James Dillon. Richie Ryan, who was elected in the summer of 1959 declared publicly at the party meeting that he was voting for Dillon,' recalls Cosgrave keenly aware of the irony that Donegan, Flanagan and Ryan would all become staunch supporters of his in time.

Ryan, who had just been elected to the Dáil as a brash young Dublin TD, confirms Cosgrave's memory:

'On the question of the election of the successor to Mulcahy I was, I suppose, very presumptuous as a young fellow in expressing a view. The discussion was taking place at the party meeting and I stood up and I said, "With all due respects to the former leadership, I think the party needs a dash of colour and James Dillon rather than Liam Cosgrave can provide that." So I declared my hand and I didn't regret it although eventually Cosgrave took over from Dillon in 1965.'

Donegal TD, Paddy Harte, who was not elected to the Dáil until 1961, recalls the mood in the Fine Gael organisation and the atmosphere following Mulcahy's resignation. 'James Dillon was the

popular choice for leadership rather than Liam Cosgrave.' Others
remember that Cosgrave was a somewhat isolated and lonely figure in
the party at this stage and his decision to run was something of a
surprise. 'Liam was very alone in the Fine Gael party at that time,'
recalled one party senior figure. 'He didn't seem to have any close
allies.' The Dillon campaign was supported by many of the longest
serving Fine Gael deputies, much to the horror of people like Tony
Barry, father of Peter, who regarded himself as the inheritor of the old
Sinn Féin tradition. Barry told colleagues how he had been canvassed
by Sean MacEoin. 'Here came this pipe-smoking myth from the Irish
Independence movement. He came in and started to talk to me asking
me to vote for the son of John Dillon against the son of W.T. Cosgrave.
I was horrified,' he remarked to a friend.

Despite his senior status in the party many TDs just didn't know
Liam very well. 'Liam is shy. There was a tremendous contrast between
Liam in his constituency and Liam in Leinster House,' said one
activist. This shyness or aloofness counted against him in 1959 but it is
impossible to gauge the size of his defeat. Because of a peculiar Fine
Gael tradition, which has survived until today, the voting strengths of
the candidates were never revealed. There were some suggestions at
the time that the margin was just a single vote but that has never been
established. Dillon took over the party at a difficult time because
Fianna Fáil under Seán Lemass were revitalised and in a position to
take advantage of the boom years of the 1960s.

Nonetheless in the 1961 general election Fianna Fáil lost eight seats
while Fine Gael gained seven. It was a good performance by the main
Opposition party but a majority of the Independents, who held the
balance of power, decided to support a continuation of the Lemass
Government because Fine Gael and Labour had both set their faces
against coalition at this time.

Languishing in Opposition Fine Gael began an internal struggle
that was to leave its mark on the party for two decades. The impetus
for a new departure came from John A. Costello's son, Declan, who
had been a TD since 1951 and who wanted to move Fine Gael
decisively to the left. Cosgrave by comparison was regarded as a dull
figure by younger and more radical TDs like Paddy Harte:

> 'Liam was a very private person. He didn't play a prominent role in
> the party between 1961, when I was first elected and 1965 when he was
> elected leader. He didn't catch the imagination of young deputies like
> myself.'

Costello was the attractive alternative for the younger generation but although he made numerous speeches in the Dáil calling for radical reform of Irish society he got very little support from the Fine Gael front bench. By 1964 he was becoming so disillusioned at the lack of internal support for his ideas that he made up his mind to resign if things did not change. In one last attempt to bring the party around to his views Costello drafted a set of eight principles which were to form the basis of a policy called the 'Just Society'. The thrust of the policy was higher state spending on health and social welfare linked to a greater role for the State in the economy through economic planning and more taxation.

'Sweetman was, of course, the main opponent of the Costello proposals,' wrote Vincent Browne a decade later. 'He particularly opposed the proposed shift from indirect to direct taxation, greater state intervention in industry, extensive economic planning and more control of the banks.' Sweetman was clearly out of tune with the economic fashions of the 1960s and 70s but time would justify some of his scepticism about higher state spending and increased taxes on labour as the panacea for the country's ills.

In the event, Costello presented his radical principles to the Fine Gael front bench and bluntly demanded the establishment of a policy committee to prepare a policy document for presentation to the Oireachtas party within three months. He half expected the front bench to reject his ultimatum. Garret FitzGerald who was contemplating joining Fine Gael at this time recalls meeting Costello for lunch in the Unicorn restaurant in Dublin to discuss the future of the party.

> 'He told me that he was at a critical point in his own relationship with Fine Gael. He had recently almost abandoned hope that it might become a progressive party but his father had said to him that before leaving it and joining Labour he should at least give Fine Gael a chance to decide where it stood by putting to the party the issues that he wanted them to adopt as policy so that they could make a clear decision for or against.'

Instead of rejecting Costello's eight principles, however, the Fine Gael leader, James Dillon, who was very lukewarm about the plan, agreed to set up a policy sub-committee on the subject and he asked Liam Cosgrave to chair it. Costello says that Cosgrave was appointed to this position because he was by 1964 a senior figure in the party who would not take an extreme or radical position on the principles but, more importantly, he was considered a fair and just person.

While the party was still considering the Costello plan Cosgrave made a speech to the Fine Gael Árd Fheis which indicated his support for the 'Just Society' and a shift to the left. He told the delegates in the Mansion House:

> 'It is a well-known political maxim that for a party to secure and retain public support should be slightly left of centre. This does not mean any doctrinaire socialistic approach to the problem of our time. I believe we must be ever alive to the need for seeking new approaches and new means to solve our problems. In this way we can show ourselves as an alert, active and assertive organisation capable of playing in the future a creative and positive part in the forward march of the Irish nation. In this way we can still forever the haunting spectre of a Tory ghost which is at times attributed to some who make up the party but is in fact unrepresentative of the vast majority.'

The positive attitude of Cosgrave to the 'Just Society' proposals came as a surprise to some of the conservatives in the party and his endorsement at the Árd Fheis helped to bring many doubtful ordinary party members along behind the scheme. A week later the outline proposals, with a number of changes worked out in the policy sub-committee, were adopted unanimously by the parliamentary party and Costello was given the task of fleshing out the principles through a number of sub-committees dealing with different policy areas. Cosgrave's support for the eight-point plan was as much pragmatic as anything else. He knew the party needed to grasp a big idea to generate the excitement and energy without which Opposition parties languish in the doldrums. He had no ideological hang-ups about the left-of-centre plan but his enthusiasm for it was based on the fact that it was the only plan the party had going for it.

Paddy Harte says that while Cosgrave was the chairman of the Just Society committee he came to very few meetings.

> 'Essentially the committees were set up to find a compromise between what Costello was proposing and what Gerry Sweetman would accept and the party was at a point of serious division and even of breaking up. There was talk of a Social Democrat party emerging. Costello at one stage almost joined the Labour Party and frightened the daylights out of the Fine Gael establishment.'

Garret FitzGerald's recollection of the background is that on 26 May 1964, 'Fine Gael fearful of Declan Costello's departure from the party announced its acceptance of his eight principles and authorised him to produce a policy statement fleshing them out.'

The document was just completed when the 1965 election was called by Lemass. It was widely believed at the time that the Fianna Fáil Taoiseach called the election because he feared the activity within Fine Gael might mark a resurgence of the Opposition party. When the election was called Fine Gael immediately adopted the 'Just Society' as its manifesto. Costello was delighted but remained sceptical about the commitment of senior figures to it.

In the election itself Fine Gael improved its vote marginally but failed to win any extra seats. Fianna Fáil put on 4% but gained only two seats while Labour gained six seats to bring its total to 22, a performance the party did not surpass until 1992. The net result was that Lemass continued to lead with another minority administration and Labour adopted an increasingly anti-coalition position in the belief that it could replace Fine Gael as the second party in the state. Cosgrave as usual performed strongly, topping the poll in Dun Laoghaire–Rathdown, as he had done at every general election since the constituency was established in 1948.

Following the disappointment of the 1965 election result Fine Gael leader, James Dillon, resigned immediately after the Dáil had elected Seán Lemass as Taoiseach on 22 April. The suddenness of Dillon's departure caught some of his colleagues by surprise and ever since there have been allegations in some quarters of a ready-up to deprive Costello of the leadership, although Costello himself rejects this theory.

According to Costello there was a violent and unfair press campaign against Dillon during the 1965 campaign and this intensified after the election. In the light of this Dillon decided to resign immediately, rather than wait for a few months and be seen to be reacting to a media campaign. Costello also says that in any case he was not interested in the leadership in 1965 or at any other time.

Paddy Harte vividly remembers the day Dillon resigned and Cosgrave became party leader.

'When he announced his resignation at the party there was shock and the party was stunned. I was the only one who begged him to reconsider his position and I begged him three times until he quoted the words of US President Ulysses Grant and said "If nominated I will not accept; if elected I will not serve. I want this party to select a new leader before the meeting ends this evening." Liam Cosgrave's name was proposed by I think Gerry Sweetman and seconded by Tom O'Higgins. The strange thing is that from 1957 to 1965 to the best of my knowledge Gerry Sweetman and Liam Cosgrave did not speak, because Cosgrave blamed Sweetman for being too harsh in his 1957 Budget which made the Government unpopular. It is said that Cosgrave told Sweetman the day of people living in big houses at the end of long avenues, with a Mercedes car sitting outside the door and a horsebox hitched on to the rear of it, ruling Fine Gael was over.'

Another story about the rift between Cosgrave and Sweetman is more personal. 'The reason they were not friendly was that old W.T. Cosgrave was chairman of the Racing Board when Sweetman was Minister for Finance during the second Inter-Party Government. There was a question that the Racing Board was looking for something in the Budget and Sweetman made W.T. come in to him while everybody else, including the Labour leader, Bill Norton, who had any business with W.T. Cosgrave, went out to the house. To Liam that was unforgivable,' recalls a former member of the parliamentary party.

He also remembers the surprise felt by most people when Sweetman proposed Liam Cosgrave.

'The interesting thing is that Sweetman got up and I was thinking. Who the hell is Sweetman going to propose? At this time Gerry and Liam were not by any means friendly. I looked around and the only person I could see whom he might possibly propose was John Grattan Esmonde. Those were the days that Liam was going along with the Just Society ideas as the way forward. I was amazed when Gerry Sweetman proposed Liam at that time.'

Sweetman, who was a TD for Kildare, was an upper-class, tough-talking conservative politician who at various times wielded great influence in Fine Gael. A very forceful personality he didn't suffer fools gladly and terrified many of his party colleagues. Born in Dublin into a wealthy family in 1908 he was educated at Beaumont College in England and Trinity College and spoke with a plummy west British accent.

Asked once why he didn't go for the leadership of Fine Gael himself he remarked 'What, with my fucking temper and my fucking accent.' A story is told about some members of the Kildare constituency executive who called to see him about party business one night. Sweetman was up in his study and his wife called up the stairs: 'Gerard, some peasants to see you.'

'Sweetman was a very strong, very hard working, demanding person,' says Richie Ryan. 'Unlike Cosgrave he didn't mind if you rang him any hour of the day or night because he was likely to ring you any hour of the day or night demanding some unreasonable thing, but he was even more unreasonable on himself. A very, very tough fellow.'

Sweetman is widely credited with pushing through Cosgrave's nomination to ensure Costello would not get the leadership. 'He (Costello) calculated that it would be about six months or so before Dillon would retire and by then he hoped that he would have built up a sufficient power base within the party to challenge all-comers,' says Vincent Browne.

Garret FitzGerald's version of what happened is similar.

'A week or so after the 1965 general election, which Fianna Fáil won by the narrowest of margins, we were dining in a restaurant with Alexis FitzGerald and his wife, Grace [Declan Costello's sister]. During dinner the phone rang; it was Declan calling from Leinster House to say that James Dillon had just announced his resignation as party leader at successive front bench and parliamentary party meetings and that Liam Cosgrave had immediately been elected in his place. We were all taken aback; insofar as James Dillon's retirement had been anticipated — and most of us had not, I think, seriously expected it so soon after the election — it had been assumed that an interval would follow before the election of a successor, in order to give time for candidates for the leadership to emerge, and that in those circumstances Declan would have had a good chance of being elected by the parliamentary party.'

Costello, however, has always maintained that he was not interested in the leadership and he also said that relations between himself and Cosgrave were never strained; if anything the two of them got on well on a personal level. He accepted that there was a difference of opinion on political issues but even on this level, he maintained that they never exchanged a cross word. The difference between them, he said, was that he believed Cosgrave moved too slowly and not far enough while he imagined that Cosgrave, in turn, felt the reverse about him.

Cosgrave's own recollection is similar and as regards the actual election as leader he recalls:

'Michael O'Higgins said to me that he would propose my name at the party meeting for leadership. Sweetman later came to me and said that as he had been publicly identified as a supporter of James Dillon that it would make clear that the party was united if he proposed me. I said to him "settle that with Michael O'Higgins". This was done and Sweetman proposed and Michael O'Higgins seconded the proposal which was carried unanimously.'

On the night of his election Cosgrave made no bones about the fact that he intended to lead on his own terms. He told the parliamentary party that 'he had not changed his views on proportional representation and that the party should not be under any illusion about these views.' This was a reference to the fact that he believed the Irish multi-seat PR system needed to be changed. He had kept a low profile during the 1959 referendum on the issue when a Fianna Fáil bid to change the system was opposed by Fine Gael and Labour and rejected by the electorate.

8

PARTY LEADER

So at the age of 45 Cosgrave followed in his father's footsteps and became leader of Fine Gael. He immediately moved to stamp his authority on the party by dispensing with the tradition whereby the front bench was elected by the parliamentary party. He made a number of interesting appointments. Gerard Sweetman, far from being rewarded for proposing him for the leadership, was switched from his dominant position in Finance and made spokesman on Agriculture.

'I subsequently got to know that Liam Cosgrave initially refused to put Sweetman on to the front bench,' recalls Paddy Harte. 'He was persuaded by people like Tom O'Higgins. who said it was impossible to keep a man like Sweetman off. He then offered him one of the smallest portfolios like Defence or Lands and Sweetman refused to accept it. Of course Sweetman was capable of being spokesman on one of the major portfolios like Finance or Industry and Commerce. Agriculture was the one of the big portfolio that Sweetman was least qualified to speak on but that was the one he was given, the one he had least interest in and the least knowledge of.'

Sweetman at 56 was the oldest and most domineering member of the front bench although he was chastened for a period. Tom O'Higgins was appointed deputy leader and spokesman on Finance while Declan Costello was appointed to Health and Social Welfare. Both their fathers had served in W.T. Cosgrave's governments in the 1920s so they had impeccable party credentials. Both were on the liberal wing of the party, although Costello was the more radical, and they represented a new generation in charge of Fine Gael. 'The new men represent almost a complete takeover by the new generation; the front bench does not contain a single representative of the Civil War days or the old conflicts. In fact, Mr Cosgrave has done a Lemass on Fine Gael and even gone one better,' said *The Irish Times*.

Paddy Harte was astonished to find himself offered a front-bench portfolio but he irritated Cosgrave when he said he might not be ready for it. 'Are you going to accept or refuse?' he was asked curtly and unsurprisingly he said 'yes'.

Cosgrave expanded his front bench in an unorthodox way by inviting three up-and-coming senators to join it as well. The newly-elected Garret FitzGerald, another rising star with a good Fine Gael pedigree, was asked to join along with Jim Dooge, who had been elected in 1961 and the party leader in the Seanad, Ben O'Quigley. FitzGerald, who confessed in 1996 that he actually voted for Fianna Fáil in 1961, plunged himself into intense political activity on his election as a senator.

'Cosgrave had a practical and expedient attitude to policy development and was prepared to be progressive if that is what he believed the electorate wanted. His attitude to the 'Just Society' plan was based on this approach. He was quite willing to adopt the plan but he had a keen nose for the conservative tendencies of the Irish electorate, particularly the Fine Gael voters,' says one former politician who loyally served both Cosgrave and Garret FitzGerald. Immediately after his election as party leader Cosgrave committed himself to the 'Just Society' programme. In fact he told a press conference the day after his election that it was on issues like social progress and its importance that Fine Gael differed from Fianna Fáil. 'A bird never flew on one wing' was a famous comment of his when questioned about the growing left-wing in the party. His central objective was to maintain party unity and that meant giving both the liberal and the conservative elements something to hold on to.

'Cosgrave was a very cunning man,' says Harte. 'He was a very underrated man; he didn't say much but he thought a lot. At times people thought he wasn't observing what was happening but he was watching every move. As soon as he got you into a position where he could catch you he snapped a trap. He once coined a famous phrase about "mongrel foxes" but he was no mongrel fox. He was game to do anything but he waited his time. As leader of the party in Opposition he didn't excel but he did excel as Taoiseach and was an excellent chairman of the cabinet. A safe man, a cautious operator rather than conservative.'

W.T. Cosgrave died in November 1965, just a few months after his son took over the Fine Gael leadership. In his old age he had given counsel not just to his son but, remarkably, to the Fianna Fáil Taoiseach, Seán Lemass, who consulted him on a number of important issues.

In the Dáil Lemass paid a moving and generous tribute to the man he had fought to overthrow by force of arms in the Civil War:

'Although William T. Cosgrave has left us the work he has done for Ireland endures. The generosity of his youthful response to the call to serve Ireland, the privations and the sacrifices which he endured so that national freedom might be ours, the capacity he displayed in presiding over the administration while responsibility was his, the grace with which he handed over responsibility when the people so willed, the dignity with which he carried out his duties as leader of the Opposition and later as a private member of this House, the generosity of spirit with which he lent his hand to the defence of the State in a time of national danger, the readiness with which, even in retirement from active public life, he gave of his counsel in the sphere of national development which was dear to him and, finally, the exemplary character of his long life, these are elements of a legacy which we in Ireland and indeed people who value freedom and democracy everywhere will forever cherish.'

There were also tributes from John A. Costello, who had served in office with W.T., and from Labour leader, Brendan Corish. Liam Cosgrave then expressed his thanks for the tributes.

'He would have deeply appreciated this expression of esteem and recognition of his work, marked in such a singular manner. I and the rest of his family appreciate it.'

W.T. was given a State funeral by the Government and the national Army, which he had helped create, accompanied his coffin to the family grave at Golden Bridge cemetery.

Apart from the sadness of his father's death Liam Cosgrave's first year of leadership went reasonably well and he kept both wings of the party happy. After that things gradually began to turn sour and he had to endure sustained pressure against his authority and sometimes open rebellion during his period as leader of the Opposition. Garret FitzGerald and Declan Costello were the leaders of the opposition to him within the party and they had the support of many young Fine Gaelers who became known as the 'Young Tigers.' In the early summer of 1965 Costello resigned from the front bench due to a combination of health problems and unhappiness with what he perceived to be an inadequate commitment among his colleagues to his 'Just Society' policy. On the advice of his family he decided to devote himself to his legal career rather than politics.

Dick Burke who joined Fine Gael in 1966 recalls the atmosphere in those days and the effect of the 'Just Society' document.

> 'It had the effect of positing Declan as a modern, articulate, thinker on policy issues. That would have been fine but the Seanad elections of 1965 had thrown up an excellent man called Garret FitzGerald. Then there developed an anti-Cosgravite strain in Fine Gael. I don't mean to make that sound too negative because from these kind of tensions there are always positive things. But I do not think it was so much Declan himself, who opted out of politics in 1967 in his famous Top Hat speech in Dun Laoghaire. But it was Garret now who was beginning to push at the edges. This is where Tom O'Higgins comes into it because Tom, being a character of broad appeal, was courted by these people as a means of putting pressure on Liam.'

In the first flush of leadership, though, Cosgrave and FitzGerald got along well, with the party leader supporting the younger man in his bid to get elected to the Seanad in 1965. FitzGerald was elected to the Upper House and Cosgrave appointed him to the front bench. 'I found the party leader, Liam Cosgrave, open to some of my ideas and before long I was working closely and harmoniously with him and with progressive elements among the senior members of the party,' according to FitzGerald.

The presidential election campaign of 1966 represented a shot in the arm for Fine Gael but conversely it encouraged divisions in the party. The candidate, Tom O'Higgins, contesting the election against Eamon de Valera spoke for a new generation and ran Dev to within 10,000 votes on polling day. The performance of O'Higgins reflected the huge changes that were then taking place in Ireland. Instead of being a backwater cut off from developments in the rest of the western world Ireland in the 1960s suddenly changed gear. The economic boom and the foreign investment promoted by Seán Lemass, Vatican II, the opening of RTE television and the youth culture of the 1960s all combined to change Ireland. It was a time when Ireland was, in the words of writer Heinrich Böll 'beginning to leap over a century and a half and catch up with another five'.

According to Garret FitzGerald the presidential election strengthened the progressive wing of the party and added a liberal element to the younger people already attracted by Costello's social concern. It also marked the beginning of a struggle for the soul of

Fine Gael which continued for 30 years. From 1966 until he became
Taoiseach in 1973 Liam Cosgrave's position as leader was never secure
as the liberals used a series of issues to mount challenges to his
authority.

The good relationship between Cosgrave and FitzGerald
deteriorated after the presidential election and while an open breach
was avoided it got progressively worse in the years that followed as
FitzGerald recalls.

'One theory prevalent within the party has been that in the aftermath
of the presidential election — during the summer of 1966 —
something of a vacuum developed within the top level of Fine Gael.
Tom O'Higgins took a well-deserved holiday. At the same time my
close relationship with Liam Cosgrave seemed to alter. There has
been speculation that this may have been due to the invention by a
political columnist *Backbencher* [John Healy] in *The Irish Times* — then
approaching the height of his fame as a commentator on the political
scene — of the term FitzCosgrave to describe my relationship with the
party leader. Into this temporary vacuum, so the conventional wisdom
in Fine Gael runs, stepped a forceful character: Michael Sweetman's
cousin, Gerard Sweetman. His relationship with Liam Cosgrave had
been clouded because of some disagreement about his treatment of
Cosgrave's father, W.T. Cosgrave, when Minister for Finance a decade
earlier. But now, in the summer of 1966, whatever coolness had
existed between the two men seemed to evaporate. Certainly by the
autumn Sweetman was firmly installed as organiser of the party, a
position for which his forceful personality well fitted him.'

Harte confirms this development. 'There had been a battle
between Sweetman and Cosgrave until the presidential election of
1966 when Tom O'Higgins asked Sweetman to be his director of
elections. The surprisingly good performance of O'Higgins rubbed
off on Sweetman and within a few weeks he became Liam Cosgrave's
right-hand man. From starting off almost not speaking to him he was
now in control of the party and appointed national director of
organisation.'

Vincent Browne, who at this time was becoming actively involved in
Fine Gael describes Sweetman as a 'devious right-winger' but
FitzGerald is more measured:

'He was not an ideological right-winger but rather a politician with a
business orientation and a practical interest in winning power for his
party. He was tough and had little instinctive sympathy with the
younger generation, least of all with the liberal youth of the 1960s. He

had no malice in him and did not bear grudges but in what he conceived to be the interests of the party he could be quite ruthless.'

Another leading Fine Gael figure says Sweetman's personality was a large part of the problem.

'He was combative to say the least and he believed there were elements in the party that were trying to undermine it by shifting it from the centre ground over to the left. He would have identified Garret FitzGerald as one of these but others as well. His obsession with control and with combating people led to a bad atmosphere and there was in turn not a little plotting by the anti-Sweetman group and that soured the atmosphere in the party right up to the time of Gerard Sweetman's tragic death. It is sad to say it but the atmosphere changed quite dramatically after that. While undoubtedly there was the normal political rivalry between various people, Garret and Liam, it didn't have the sort of edge in the period 1970 to 1973 that had existed 1967 and 1970.'

Both the conservatives and the liberals in Fine Gael took the presidential election result as a sign that the party was on the verge of power. With Lemass standing down as Taoiseach, and being replaced by Jack Lynch in late 1966, they believed the next election would provide the opportunity for a Fine Gael return to government. The question was whether the party should try to go it alone or whether they should woo Labour in advance of the election. Sweetman and the conservatives believed that if the party held its nerve it had a chance of replacing Fianna Fáil on its own and anyway they doubted whether Labour was interested in coalition at this stage. The Labour leader, Brendan Corish, in a speech in Tullamore in 1961 had ruled out coalition as an option.

The left wing, FitzGerald, O'Higgins and Costello, believed that Fine Gael's only chance of power lay in a coalition with Labour and urged the necessity of a deal. Costello even believed that a Fine Gael Government on its own would not be progressive enough and he wanted to coalesce with Labour to counteract the more conservative elements in his own party.

FitzGerald shared this view and began to orchestrate a range of contacts and private meetings with Labour. The contacts took place during 1967 and 1968 with the referendum on the PR system providing an excuse for teasing out a common approach. This initiative soured relations within Fine Gael quite badly because Cosgrave believed things were going on behind his back. The Fine

Gael liberals were also terribly naïve because Labour at this time was set on a left-wing anti-coalition course in any case.

'Corish's opposition to coalition with Fine Gael at this time was based on his experience in the 1954–57 coalition and in particular his experience of Sweetman as someone who was extremely hostile,' says Brendan Halligan, who became general secretary of the Labour Party in 1967. 'It was unusual for Corish to get on badly with anybody on a personal level but politically he couldn't abide Sweetman. Sweetman had behaved like a boor at cabinet and Corish was on the receiving end in Social Welfare.' Apart from Corish's personal experience Halligan adds that there was a general attitude in Labour that the time was ripe to drive Fianna Fáil and Fine Gael together.

> 'Going into the 1969 election there was simply no question whatsoever, as far as Corish was concerned, that the party was going to go on a coalition line. Now it has to be said that there was still a very substantial minority in the Labour Party which disagreed with that, which historians have ignored. Corish in fact had to make a very powerful speech at the 1969 conference where he used the famous expression. "We will not give the kiss of life to Fine Gael." That was summing up a debate on coalition. Sitting on the platform I thought the vote could go either way.'

FitzGerald's recollection of that period is that Labour's problem with Fine Gael lay in Cosgrave's leadership.

> 'My personal relationship with Liam Cosgrave seemed to me to disimprove further after an incident in 1967. Brendan Halligan of the Labour Party had told me about growing support in that party for coalition with Fine Gael, but said that Labour would not serve under Cosgrave as Taoiseach. Loyalty to my party leader seemed to require that he be made aware of this assessment, which could reasonably influence his thinking about any relationship with Labour. I naturally disliked being the messenger with bad tidings, however, and it was only after consulting James Dillon — and acting on his advice — that I told Cosgrave what I had heard. I doubt that it helped our relationship.'

FitzGerald, O'Higgins, and Costello, now found themselves out of favour with Cosgrave because of these developments.

'Liam Cosgrave was a quiet man but inside him was a ring of steel that never showed itself fully. At front-bench meetings I began to notice a certain linguistic interplay among three or four of its members. It was probably due to my country instinct that I came to the conclusion that a plot of some kind was underway,' wrote the late

Patrick Lindsay who was a member of the Fine Gael front bench at this period.

'My doubts centered around Garret FitzGerald, Tom O'Higgins and Declan Costello,' added Lindsay who saw evidence of the plot in the fact that at one front-bench meeting O'Higgins proposed that an economic advisor be appointed to the party, immediately adding that an ideal one was available. 'He further said that this person was prepared to resign his seat in the Dáil and take on the job full-time. He named him as none other than the then deputy for Dublin North-West, Declan Costello, who happened to be absent on that day. That proposal did not have any seconder and very quickly Mark Clinton rose and spoke vehemently against it.' Lindsay backed Clinton in quashing the proposal but he was convinced that it marked the first move in a conspiracy to oust the party leader.

John Bruton has a graphic memory of this period:

'Liam Cosgrave wasn't a good communicator, although he could be brilliant on the major set piece occasions at an event like an Árd Fheis. He wasn't somebody who easily communicated to people what he was trying to do and where he saw things going. He tended to be silent and then speak only when he had something important to say. A lot of people felt the Fine Gael message was not being articulated; they felt he wasn't listening because he wasn't telling them he was listening, but that didn't actually mean he wasn't. People also felt that he was not connecting with the electorate and all the other things that leaders of the Opposition are often felt not to be doing. There was a huge influx of young people into the party with very high expectations and then there was the advanced social thinking of the Just Society which people felt wasn't being communicated adequately. All of those combined created an impatience with Liam Cosgrave's leadership which events proved to be unjustified.'

Against this discontent with his leadership Cosgrave relied increasingly on Sweetman whose knowledge of Dáil procedure, his intelligence and his energy made him the party leader's most valued ally. At the 1968 Fine Gael Árd Fheis Sweetman as chairman managed to head-off an attempt by the liberals to change the name of the party to 'Fine Gael — Social Democratic Party.' Although most of the delegates appeared to favour the change Sweetman forcefully pushed through a procedural manoeuvre to have the issue referred to a postal ballot of party members. This resulted in an emphatic rejection of the name change by 653 votes to 81. In early 1969 Costello again announced his decision to quit politics and made it clear he would not be a candidate at the next election.

The fact that his enemies were so keen on coalition with Labour made it appear at the time as if Cosgrave had something against the idea in principle but his approach was at all times purely pragmatic. He insists that he was in favour of coalition if the Labour Party was interested but his judgement at the time, rightly as it turned out, was that Labour was hell bent on a go-it-alone policy. Cosgrave resisted Fine Gael being put in the position of going cap-in-hand to a scornful Labour Party but he was not opposed to coalition *per se*. In May 1968 he authorised Michael O'Higgins to make a speech calling on Fine Gael and Labour to form a united front based on the Just Society principles. The following day Corish bluntly rejected the O'Higgins proposal.

This Labour snub came after a period of hectic contacts between the two parties in late 1967, in the face of a common threat when Fianna Fáil again proposed a change in the electoral system to abolish multi-seat proportional representation. Fianna Fáil under de Valera had gone to the people with this proposal in 1959 and were narrowly rejected. This time around there was determination in Fianna Fáil to force the issue through. Cosgrave appointed FitzGerald to an electoral strategy committee in October 1967 along with Jim Dooge and they began to work out the effects of the Fianna Fáil proposal to change the electoral system. They found that Fianna Fáil would get 96 seats out of 144 under a straight vote system and 80 under single-seat PR.

Cosgrave agreed that talks should be opened with Labour on how to confront the threat and Garret discussed the matter with Brendan Halligan. FitzGerald has his own memoir of these contacts which he says resulted in an abortive plan for a merger of Fine Gael and Labour, in the context of a new electoral system, and he has included a detailed account of them in his autobiography. However, it should be pointed out that neither Cosgrave nor any of the surviving Labour figures of the time can remember any merger proposal. FitzGerald recalls one crucial meeting with Halligan:

'He [Halligan] said a short term link would certainly be of no interest; only a long-term or permanent link — perhaps even a merger — would have any chance. Those in Labour favouring an alliance or merger, according to Halligan, were Barry Desmond, Noel Browne, Sean Dunne, Stevie Coughlan and Michael Pat Murphy with Micky Mullen perhaps persuadable. Michael O'Leary was thought to be hostile, for tactical reasons until after the next election. Jimmy Tully too was hostile but his attitude could change in the event of a referendum on PR.'

Garret writes that he subsequently had discussions with Halligan and Barry Desmond at which Halligan repeated that a merger between the two parties was a much more likely option than a Coalition. 'On 3 January 1968 the Fine Gael front bench considered the issue from 11 a.m. until 5 p.m. Mark Clinton suggested such a merger, although he knew nothing of Labour views. Jim Dooge and Tom O'Higgins supported the idea of exploring the prospect, Sweetman opposed it and three others expressed reservations but only Maurice Dockrell demurred at the proposed talks, seeing them as dangerous.'

According to FitzGerald he received a phone call from Cosgrave the following Tuesday to say that he had raised the possibility of a merger with Corish who was not encouraging but sought a proposal in writing. However, a few minutes later Corish rang to withdraw his request, saying he was making a speech that night which would cut across the proposal for an arrangement between the two parties.

'I rang Halligan and at his suggestion went to see Corish in Leinster House. He was discouraging, fearing word of talks would get out and would damage Labour. He would be glad to see people like Declan Costello, Tom O'Higgins, Paddy Harte, Oliver Flanagan and myself in Labour but a merger of the two parties would be difficult. However, he would put it to his front bench the following day and would ring me afterwards. He did so the following afternoon saying "Nothing doing" adding that he hoped there would be no more approaches from us, as in that event they would have to issue a denial. Subsequently Jim Downey of *The Irish Times* told me that the proposal had been defeated by a small majority but I never got confirmation of this.'

Cosgrave's memory is that the question of coalition was raised at this time but not in the form of a merger proposal.

'In 1968 the PR referendum was held. Corish approached me and suggested a common approach by Fine Gael and Labour to oppose the referendum. I said "Yes" but only if Labour will agree to a coalition with Fine Gael. He said "No" and I said: "Well then each party will operate separately".'

The question of relations with Labour was only one of the problems confronting Cosgrave at this time. He was faced with a serious choice on the central issue which isolated him from many of his colleagues on both wings of the party. Back in 1959 Cosgrave had not opposed the plan to abolish multi-seat PR and he saw no reason to change his mind just because he was leader of the Opposition. He was particularly interested in the possibility of single-seat constituencies with a PR system of voting. He asked FitzGerald to carry out a private sounding of the Fine Gael front bench to see where everybody stood on the issue of single-seat PR. Garret found ten people in favour of retaining PR, although two not strongly convinced and eight in favour of single-seat PR, including Cosgrave.

Looking back Cosgrave has no qualms about his position:

'We had fought three general elections without success and as the Labour Party had adopted a go-it-alone policy it seemed to me that there was no alternative but to seek a majority for Fine Gael. I think also that single-seat constituencies avoid competition of an unnecessary and undesirable kind between elected representatives.'

Cosgrave had come to the view that whatever the short-term advantage to Fianna Fáil of abolishing multi-seat PR, in the long term single seat constituencies, even under the straight-vote system, offered Fine Gael the best chance of getting into power on its own. His father had shared a similar view and it was also strongly held by Gerry Sweetman. Fianna Fáil, keenly aware of Cosgrave's attitude and the potential that existed for a split in Fine Gael, toyed with the idea of proposing single-seat PR. Ultimately, though, the Government went for the straight vote hoping to get the most effective electoral system from Fianna Fáil's point of view with the added bonus of provoking a rift in Fine Gael.

A critical meeting of the Fine Gael parliamentary party took place in February 1968. Cosgrave threw everything into an impassioned speech in favour of some form of change in multi-seat PR. He clearly expected to carry the party with him but after a long debate that went on into the early hours of the morning he was solidly defeated by his own TDs and senators. He was shattered by the defeat which was widely regarded as a vital test of his leadership. Although a motion of confidence in him was immediately passed by the meeting there was no disguising the blow. 'The leader might be placed in a position where resignation has to be considered,' reported *The Irish Times*. Coming out of the meeting Sweetman remarked to Cosgrave, according to Vincent Browne, that they had been defeated by 'a combination of careerists and alcoholics'.

Following the party decision Cosgrave spoke in the Dáil against the Fianna Fáil Bill to change the electoral system. He argued that as the people had expressed their support for the existing system in 1959 there was no point asking them again and there were far more important issues to attend to than changing the method of voting.

During the referendum campaign itself the most decisive incident was a famous television programme in which Basil Chubb and David Thornley of Trinity College did an exercise with the figures. They showed that under the new system being proposed by Fianna Fáil the party would win a comfortable Dáil majority with as little as 40% of the vote and if they polled in their normal mid-40% range would win 100 out of the 166 seats in the Dáil.

With the straight vote the only issue Fine Gael and Labour fought a hard campaign against the Government proposal and it was defeated by wide margin with over 60% of the electorate rejecting the proposal.

The referendum campaign was not a happy period for Cosgrave because of his ambiguity on the PR issue. There were mutterings in the party with the liberals agitating furiously against him. The nervous atmosphere of that period is recalled by Dick Burke:

'I got caught up in this as well, a bit. Before I went into the Dáil, around the middle of 1968 there were attempts made to get a heave going against Liam. I remember being called at very short notice to a meeting of the Dun Laoghaire constituency where he made a speech and I remember the words. "I am the leader of the Fine Gael party and I intend so to remain."'

In the aftermath of the PR campaign there were rumblings from the Fine Gael dissidents but Cosgrave's leadership was not seriously threatened at this time. In the run-up to the 1969 election the Labour Party went on a firmly anti-coalition line in the belief that 'the Seventies would be Socialist.' With a dynamic general secretary in Halligan and the tide of public opinion appearing to move in Labour's favour the party was convinced it would make the decisive breakthrough. Big name figures like Conor Cruise O'Brien, David Thornley and Justin Keating joined and were nominated as candidates for the election.

Labour entered the 1969 election campaign in a highly optimistic mood with an undiluted socialist programme. The party was buoyed up by the belief that it was about to change the course of Irish politics and overtake Fine Gael as the second party in the state. Fianna Fáil countered with 'red scare' tactics which undermined a number of traditional rural Labour TDs. Cosgrave made no secret of his irritation with Labour and its go-it-alone socialist policies. 'They are none of them for 1969. The Labour programme is for 1984,' he said describing the party policies as 'far too doctrinaire and unrealistic.'

By comparison with Labour, Fine Gael appeared unfashionable although Garret FitzGerald and John Kelly represented new blood with intellectual muscle. The 'Young Tigers' had made some impact with their support for the 'Just Society' and Cosgrave campaigned hard during the election. He was up against Jack Lynch who had taken over from Lemass as Taoiseach in 1966. Lynch gave the deceptive appearance of being weak, particularly after the loss of the PR referendum. In reality the placid pipe-smoking Jack was shrewd and tough and he was a marvellous campaigner with an instinctive sympathy for the concerns of ordinary people.

With the two Opposition parties fighting each other as well as Fianna Fáil the result was predictable. Because Fine Gael and Labour were pursuing totally individual campaigns the vote transfer pattern was very poor and neither party achieved its potential. Fianna Fáil by contrast bounced back from the near miss of the presidential election campaign and the defeat on PR to register a solid 45% and win an overall majority. The redrawing of the constituencies by Kevin Boland helped Fianna Fáil to maximise its numbers but the principal reason for the party's fourth win in a row was the disarray on the Opposition side.

The biggest shock was for Labour who won a respectable 17% of the vote, its highest ever percentage until 1992, but that only translated into 18 seats, a net loss of four seats since the previous election. While the new Labour big names were all comfortably elected a number of traditional Labour rural seats vanished as a result of Fianna Fáil's red scare campaign. The crucial factor in the loss of seats was the collapse of Fine Gael transfers due to Labour's anti-coalition attitude.

Fine Gael did better, holding its own and increasing its number of seats by three to 50. This rudely put paid to the notion prevalent in liberal circles and sections of the media that Labour was going to replace it as the second party in the state. Nonetheless, the disappointment for Cosgrave was bitter and his enemies within the party began to circle in for the kill.

9

A DIVIDED PARTY

THE MOOD on the Opposition benches was grim after the 1969 defeat and the atmosphere wasn't helped by an outbreak of squabbling on the Fine Gael benches. The tensions between the two wings of the party erupted into open conflict when TDs returned from their summer holidays still licking their wounds. In the election campaign one young liberal candidate, Maurice O'Connell, who had been selected by his constituency convention to run with Richie Ryan in Dublin South Central, was dropped by the party's standing committee and the late John Kelly was imposed in his place. O'Connell then ran as an Independent and scuppered Kelly's chances. After the election Sweetman initiated disciplinary action against O'Connell and five of his leading supporters. They included Vincent Browne, then the editor of a Fine Gael youth magazine, and Henry Kelly who later became a well-known journalist and television presenter.

FitzGerald recounts his shock at news that his friends had been expelled from the party. He took legal advice before sending a letter to the Fine Gael trustees calling on them to reject the decision on the basis of procedural irregularities. The trustees accepted the argument and before the end of September Cosgrave proposed to the standing committee that the decision should be reversed.

The two factions were well represented on Cosgrave's new front bench. FitzGerald was given Education, Ryan got Foreign Affairs and Sweetman Finance. Although he was a new TD, FitzGerald quickly made his mark in the Dáil and with the media through his frenetic activity in the House. He spoke on a range of issues and wandered far from his own brief. Behind the bumbling academic image, which fooled some people into underestimating him, FitzGerald had an acute political brain and from the beginning his ambition was to become leader of Fine Gael so that he could use the party as a vehicle to implement his liberal vision of Irish society. Ryan had his own ambitions but he was fiercely loyal to Cosgrave. He resented FitzGerald as a presumptuous newcomer who wanted to take over the party. Ryan, a peppery and combative operator, did not shirk conflict with FitzGerald and the liberal faction.

In December 1969, tensions surfaced again when Cosgrave and Sweetman asked FitzGerald if he would take Maurice O'Connell into his constituency and he agreed. FitzGerald writes:

> 'Richie reacted to the news of the transfer by denouncing what he called "an anti-party group" which, he said, was trying to destroy Fine Gael; the Irish people were not going to abandon their property to revolutionaries who wanted to bring doctrines into Ireland that had been rejected by most other countries.'

He adds that while the row eventually blew over, relations within the party were damaged and a belief grew up that Cosgrave was surrounding himself with a clique of loyal supporters. 'It seems to me in retrospect that this would not have been in character. But the fact that he did not appear to deal with the Richie Ryan outburst, together with vocal declarations of loyalty to him by a number of his colleagues during the aftermath, gave the impression that he had sided unfairly with one group in the party; and party unity suffered,' according to FitzGerald.

Ryan remembers the incident differently.

> 'It developed because I gave utterance about groups within the party that were disloyal to the leadership. I was interviewed on the Sunday radio programme which added fuel to the fire. I think I mentioned that Tom O'Higgins was being used as a stooge. I had no doubt that there were efforts to mobilise people against Liam. O'Higgins was part of it and he would have been willing to take over the leadership then, if it had fallen his way. But he was not the instigator, it was Garret, looking for friends through the O'Higgins connections.'

Ryan's view is still a matter of contention and friends of Tom O'Higgins are adamant that he was never interested in taking over the leadership. One individual recalls a meeting of the liberal faction at which O'Higgins reacted with horror to the suggestion that he should try for the leadership, saying that for a start he couldn't afford to take it as it would severely curtail his extensive legal practice.

Ryan recalls a front-bench meeting in the aftermath of his attack at which Tom's brother, Michael O'Higgins, proposed that the whip should be withdrawn from Richie. 'Michael and I were great pals, and still are, but they were incensed that I should have mentioned the O'Higgins name.' Ryan says that he responded to the move at the front bench by saying:

'"I was elected a Fine Gael TD, I will never stay a day in Leinster House, except as a Fine Gael TD. If the whip is removed from me I will resign and you can have a by-election in which I will not stand."

'That put them off. Liam, of course kept his poker face but I could see a smirk across the face of Gerry Sweetman who was very loyal to Liam and loyal to every leader. The meeting had to adjourn then to consider what to do and Denis Jones came to me. Denis was a man who commanded great respect and he said it could all end if I withdrew my allegations. I said there were serious efforts to destabilise the party and that I wasn't willing to withdraw because too many people knew it was going on. He said "Ah, think of the loneliness of Griffith and Collins signing the Treaty. Think of what they had to do." When it was put like that what could I do but withdraw?'

As these battles were going on newer Fine Gael deputies were being sucked into the fray. The newly elected TD for Dublin South, Dick Burke, was asked by Cosgrave to be chief whip, a tall order for a new TD. Burke asked Sweetman how to handle the job. 'Sit tight, keep your mouth shut and listen,' he was told.

'I did that for a month. One of the first things I did was to get helpers and as there was no such position as assistant whip I lit on another new TD, a young fellow called Bruton and asked him to help out. He became assistant whip and we had a great time together.'

Apart from internal wrangles both Fine Gael and Labour found it difficult to come to terms with the fact that they had allowed Fianna Fáil to win power for the fourth time in a row in 1969. Initially there was a lot of hostility between the two Opposition parties with recriminations over the result. Immediately after the election Tom O'Higgins delivered a sarcastic attack on Labour's new intellectual TDs describing them as 'the horny-handed sons of toil' who had helped Fianna Fáil back to power. This came as a surprise to the moderates in the Labour Party who regarded O'Higgins as a potential ally with whom they could do business.

The Labour leadership knew immediately after the election that they would have to change tack on coalition if they were to ever have any chance of breaking the total Fianna Fáil dominance of Irish public life. 'I certainly changed my mind about coalition,' says Brendan Halligan. 'I changed it in the television studios looking at seats tumbling down all around me.' A few days later Halligan went down to Wexford to meet Corish. 'While we didn't reach any decisions our minds had certainly been profoundly changed by the experience. We had been humbled and humiliated by it and the primary concern became sustaining the party and keeping it going as a meaningful force in politics.'

Leaving aside the Boland constituency review, which drew new constituencies up in a blatant attempt to favour Fianna Fáil, Fine Gael and Labour strategists could see that both parties had thrown away an opportunity to win extra seats due to the absence of transfers. 'We finally realised that if we were in an STV system we might as well accept the logic of it,' says Halligan.

Two by-elections in Kildare (due to the death of Sweetman) and Longford–Westmeath in April 1970, showed that both Fine Gael and Labour had learned the lessons of the 1969 election. The parties asked their supporters to give their number two's to the other and the result showed what a good transfer arrangement could achieve. In Kildare Patrick Malone of Fine Gael was elected while in Longford–Westmeath, Pat Cooney won easily. In both constituencies over 64% of Labour transfers went to Fine Gael.

In early May 1970, the political system was plunged into a crisis which appeared at the time to threaten the foundations of the State. The arms crisis saw the Taoiseach, Jack Lynch, firing his two most powerful Ministers, one of them a future Taoiseach, the resignation of two others because of a plot to import arms into the country.

Liam Cosgrave played a central role in the whole affair. He received two tip-offs about the plot a few days before the news burst on an unsuspecting public. One of the tip-offs came to him on Garda notepaper alleging that two Ministers, Charles Haughey and Neil Blaney, were involved.

Michael Mills, who was then political correspondent of the *Irish Press* confirms the tip to Cosgrave and the names on the list. The tip-off is believed to have come from Chief Superintendent Phil McMahon, a retired head of the Special Branch, who because of his extensive knowledge and contacts had been retained by the Garda authorities as an advisor on subversion.

Cosgrave was stunned by the note and he showed it to a journalist and trusted friend, Ned Murphy, political correspondent of the

Sunday Independent. Murphy made a copy and brought it to the editor of the *Sunday Independent,* Hector Legge. After some consideration a decision was taken not to run with the story because of the difficulties in confirming the information and because Legge decided it would not be in the national interest.

When the Dáil next met on Tuesday, 5 May, neither Jack Lynch or the Ministers involved had any idea that Cosgrave was in possession of the crucial information. Lynch took TDs by surprise by announcing to the Chamber at the beginning of the day's business that Michael Moran, the Minister for Justice, who had no connection with the plot, had resigned. Cosgrave was on his feet immediately to ask:

'Can the Taoiseach say if this is the only Ministerial resignation we can expect?'

'I do not know what the deputy is referring to,' replied Lynch to which Cosgrave responded.

'Is it only the tip of the iceberg?'

Cosgrave went on to make the cryptic comment that the Taoiseach could deal with the situation and he added that smiles were very noticeable by their absence on the Government benches. Most TDs and journalists had no idea what Cosgrave was talking about and Lynch still didn't get the message that Cosgrave knew what was going on. When nothing further had happened by that night Cosgrave wasn't sure what was happening and he began to wonder whether the tip-offs he had received were designed to trap.

He decided to consult a few of his closest colleagues that evening and ask their advice. Those present were Tom O'Higgins, Michael O'Higgins, Mark Clinton, Denis Jones and Jim Dooge.

Cosgrave told his colleagues there was something important he wanted to tell them. He said he had received a tip-off about a plot to import arms.

'I want your advice. What should I do? Is this a plant? Is someone trying to plant this on me to make me go over the top?' he asked his colleagues.

'We argued first of all as to whether he could take it as being something he could act on, because he feared the danger of just being hoist on a petard. And we came to the conclusion that yeh, on balance, we had to act.' Having agreed on this Cosgrave said he had a second question about the form of action he should take. 'What do I do? Do I bring it up in the Dáil? Do I go to the newspapers? Do I go to the Taoiseach?' he asked.

Mark Clinton was the first one who spoke and he said:

'I think this is of such national importance the only thing is go to the Taoiseach and go to him tonight.' The others present agreed.

'And Liam went off and rang Jack Lynch's office and established that Jack was still in Leinster House. The Dáil had risen and Liam went off for a while and we all sat around wondering what was happening and he came back and I always remember it, he sort of stood in the door and closed the door behind him and then he looked up and looked at us and said "It's all true". I will always remember that. And then he called a front-bench meeting for the following morning,' said one of the people present that night.

Following Cosgrave's visit Lynch spoke personally to Blaney and phoned Haughey. He asked both men to resign but they refused. He then went home to consult his wife, Mairin, and at 2 a.m. he instructed the head of the Government Information Service, Eoin Neeson, to issue a statement that Haughey and Blaney had been fired.

Lynch took action that night as a direct response to Cosgrave's intervention. The Peter Berry diaries, published in Magill in 1980 show that the Taoiseach had decided a week earlier to bury the whole incident and even during the Dáil exchanges on 5 May Lynch does not appear to have grasped that Cosgrave knew of the whole affair. It was only when the Fine Gael leader went to him that night that he was catapulted into action.

Fine Gael's Peter Barry recalls speaking in the Dáil that evening on a financial resolution.

'It was about 6.30 or 7 p.m. on a Tuesday evening, the only time a back-bencher can get a slot. I was less than a year in the Dáil and it was one of my early speeches. The next thing the Taoiseach, Jack Lynch, comes in pushes Johnny Geoghegan aside and starts interrupting me. "How do you justify that? Where did you get that figure?" So it wasn't on his mind at 7 o'clock that he had any problems.'

The Dáil record for that evening bears out Peter Barry's memory; he was heckled three times by the Taoiseach during his speech shortly before 7 p.m.

When the Dáil met at 11.30 a.m. on 6 May the sensational news of the dismissal of the two Ministers, Haughey and Blaney, had convulsed the country. A third, Kevin Boland, resigned in protest along with parliamentary secretary, Paudge Brennan. Lynch proposed to a stunned Dáil that the day's sitting be postponed until 10 p.m. that night to give his parliamentary party an opportunity to discuss the

issue. Cosgrave reluctantly agreed while making the point that a
Fianna Fáil party meeting should not take precedence over the
business of the country.

Dáil deputies of all parties were shell-shocked and few believed that
Lynch could survive. There was a widespread view that Lynch couldn't
carry the party with him against Haughey, Blaney and Boland.

'The atmosphere in Leinster House for those few days was
incredible, the most incredible of my life,' says Brendan Halligan.
'Nobody went to bed, for the first time RTE put an outside broadcast
unit at the Dáil and was running a commentary non-stop ... There
were all sorts of rumours sweeping the place and people, as you saw
with the fall of the last government in 1992, were prepared to believe
anything. Except in this case the issues were very serious, they were
talking about the Gardaí they were talking about the Army, they were
talking about the role of parliament itself.'

Lynch's first priority was to survive the Fianna Fáil parliamentary
party meeting and after that to win the confidence of the Dáil. Despite
the strength of forces arrayed against him Lynch, by deft political
footwork showed that it is well nigh impossible to shift a Fianna Fáil
leader against his will; a lesson well learned by Charles Haughey.

The tactics adopted by his supporters at the party meeting was to
get the debate on to the issue of whether the Taoiseach had the power
to dismiss his own Ministers. Once that was the issue the deputies had
no option but to accept the constitutional position that indeed the
Taoiseach has such power. With the debate constrained in this way
Lynch managed to bring his parliamentary colleagues with him.

'Lynch chose to seek vindication for his own actions by a very clever
resolution at his parliamentary party which was the prerogatives of the
Taoiseach. He didn't say I did right or wrong, you should or should
not be helping Nationalists in the north of Ireland. He said "It's the
Taoiseach who has the prerogative to exercise the powers under the
constitutions to appoint or dismiss Ministers." It was very clever, but
Lynch was right. It wasn't just tactical to do that, it was also focusing on
the real issues,' says Halligan.

'I have no doubt from my own contacts in the political system at
that time that Liam Cosgrave and Jack Lynch headed off a grave
situation which could have embroiled the security forces of the State
in the Northern Ireland situation. This was his finest contribution,'
says Barry Desmond who was elected as a Labour TD for Dun
Laoghaire in 1969.

When the Dáil met at 10 p.m. on the night of 6 May the motion before the House was simply for the appointment of Des O'Malley as Minister for Justice in place of Michael Ó Moráin but Lynch made it clear that he was prepared during the week to debate all the issues involved in the arms crisis and to nominate other new Ministers in the course of the debate. He told the Dáil that he had asked Haughey and Blaney to resign a week earlier because he had information which purported to connect them with an alleged attempt to unlawfully import arms. They had asked for time and to consider their positions and he agreed but had again asked for their resignations the previous evening. When they refused he had terminated their appointments.

> 'I may say that on the question of suspicion Deputy Cosgrave came to me yesterday evening to say he had some information from an anonymous source connecting the two Ministers with this alleged attempt at unlawful importation.

Cosgrave then rose to speak.

> 'Last night at approximately 8 p.m. I considered it my duty in the national interest to inform the Taoiseach of information I had received and which indicates a situation of such gravity for the nation that it is without parallel in this country since the foundation of the State. By approximately 10 p.m. two Ministers had been dismissed and a third had resigned ... Yesterday when I received a copy of a document on official Garda notepaper which supported the information already at my disposal and which also included some additional names, I decided to put the facts in my possession before the Taoiseach.'

Cosgrave went on to refer to his 'modest statement' of the day before when he had referred to the resignation of Ó Moráin as 'only the tip of the iceberg'. He added that for a considerable time the Opposition had been commenting on the activities of certain Ministers which made them unfit for public office but it now emerged that not only were they unfit to be Ministers they were engaging in activity which undermined national security and recklessly endangered the lives of people in the North.

> 'So far as this situation is concerned these are criminal activities but worse than that, the gravity of the national situation is now emphasised by the fact that the Taoiseach and the Ministers who are left are prepared to cling to power with the support of people whom the Taoiseach considers unfit to hold Ministerial office. This is a situation that those whom we commemorated at Arbour Hill today could never have visualised would have happened. I am privileged to

speak from a family tradition that as far back as '98 gave lives in defence of the rights of the Irish people to govern themselves. This party asserted and defended and vindicated the people's rights to ensure that this sovereign authority and it alone would act and work and discharge its responsibility. We are prepared to resume that historic assignment and there is an inescapable obligation on the Taoiseach and his colleagues to resign and to give this country an opportunity of electing a government of integrity, of honesty, of patriotism, in whom the people and the world can have confidence.'

In a short and emotional debate which lasted until almost 3 a.m. on the morning of 7 May Conor Cruise O'Brien warned of the impending national tragedy which was building:

'Now the people have heard that the Taoiseach, who at Tralee last year made a very sensible statement, expelled from his government people who were playing with violence, only when those people were exposed by the leader of the Opposition, Deputy Cosgrave. They would not have been exposed had not Deputy Cosgrave done it. I do not think that in all matters I would agree with Deputy Cosgrave but he has rendered a public service.'

When the vote was taken on the appointment of Des O'Malley the Government won by 72 votes to 65. The sacked Neil Blaney, and Kevin Boland who had resigned in solidarity with him voted for Lynch's motion. Haughey was in hospital as a result of a mysterious accident at his home in Kinsealy.

When the Dáil met again at 10.30 a.m. on Friday 8 May the issue was the appointment of three new Ministers to replace Haughey, Blaney and Boland. The new appointees were Gerry Collins, Bobby Molloy and Gerry Cronin. This time the debate continued day and night for 36-and-a-half hours until 11 p.m. on Saturday night.

Cosgrave repeated his account of going to Lynch the previous Tuesday night and continued:

'This is the greatest scandal that has hit this State since we won independence. I am not given to verbal exaggeration. In fact, some of my friends in the press have probably thought that I have been unduly mild in my remarks during my political career.

'It was not until I presented the situation as I knew it that the Taoiseach and those of his Ministers who were left with him knew that the game was up and they could no longer conceal the true facts of the situation from the people ... No one can accept, nobody can believe, a single statement by any Fianna Fáil Minister. I regret having to say that because I agree with Deputy O'Higgins that there are many decent men in the Fianna Fáil party, there are some decent Ministers in the Fianna Fáil party but they have not been able to come to the surface. This is not merely a serious question for the Fianna Fáil party, what is serious is that it reflects on the whole fabric and the whole character of the nation. I want to assure not those merely in this part of the country but in the six counties of the North as well, that people need not be unduly concerned. They have here a realistic and capable and patriotic alternative government composed of men of integrity, composed of people who, totally disregarding self-interest, are prepared to serve the nation.'

Winding up his speech Cosgrave reverted to his bedrock principles about the institutions of the State:

'For the second time in the past half-century, in our long and chequered history, this country and our people may thank God that they have this party to maintain and defend and assert the people's rights. Only for this party there would be a real danger of civil war, civil war of the worst kind, of a religious character. This Taoiseach and this government must now resign and dissolve this Dáil and let the people elect a government in whom they can have confidence and who will guarantee their lives and liberties, their homes and hearths and show to the world that this country, this State established by Griffith and Collins, is fit to, and will, govern itself.'

The effect of the arms crisis was to put the internal dissension in Fine Gael on the back burner for some time but it had a more significant effect. It encouraged all the key people in Fine Gael and Labour to begin to edge closer to the notion of coalition. 'The events of May 1970, had a profound effect on Corish. He came to the conclusion that for the sake of Irish democracy there would have to be an alternative to Fianna Fáil and the only alternative was a coalition with Fine Gael. He very reluctantly came to that decision,' says Halligan.

Conor Cruise O'Brien believes that it was necessity rather than the arms crisis which forced the change in Labour's attitude.

'I would like to think it was the arms crisis but I think it really stemmed from Labour's need to get off the hook of its own stupid commitment to no-coalition. Halligan and O'Leary got us on to that one and talked Corish into it. They made him give hostages to fortune by delivering strong anti-coalition declarations as if this was an eternal principle. And they had to get rid of this bilge and I think the arms crisis was a good excuse, frankly. I think I was the only one of the Labour people who felt particularly strongly about the arms trial business and my opposition to coalition would never have been very serious. I suppose the arms trial would have made it seem to me more urgent than it would otherwise have been to get rid of this lot.'

After Charles Haughey's acquittal in the arms trial in late 1970 Fine Gael put down a motion of no confidence in the Minister for Agriculture, Jim Gibbons, to test the loyalty of Fianna Fáil colleagues to each other. There was a widespread expectation that Haughey would not be able to vote confidence in Gibbons and that the Government could fall.

With this a possibility the Labour leadership panicked and convened a special conference to overturn the no-coalition commitment. It was a traumatic conference for Labour in Cork in December 1970 but the conference reversed the party's anti-coalition stance and Noel Browne led a walkout of disgruntled left-wing delegates.

Fine Gael and Labour were already coming closer even before the Labour conference. In December in the Dublin South by-election caused by the resignation of Kevin Boland from the Dáil, Fine Gael's Larry McMahon made it three victories in a row with the help of Labour transfers. The death in a car crash of Labour's *bête noire*, Gerry Sweetman early in 1970, also made it easier for the two parties to gradually move closer together.

It was by no means a sure thing, however, because of the hostility of the Labour left and the splits and divisions within Fine Gael. Despite the problems contacts gradually developed between the two parties. Due to the tensions within Fine Gael, however, those most favourable to coalition had bad relations with Cosgrave and it was not clear what his views on the issue were.

Garret FitzGerald, Tom O'Higgins and Jim Dooge were the crucial contact group. All three were regarded as being on the social democratic wing of Fine Gael and they were strongly in favour of a coalition arrangement with Labour. 'During the course of 1971 there were unofficial, informal contacts. These would have consisted on the Fine Gael side of Garret, Declan Costello, Alexis FitzGerald and Tom O'Higgins and on the Labour Party side, Justin Keating, Conor Cruise O'Brien, Mick O'Leary and myself,' says Halligan. 'Now this was not a cabal or a conspiracy. We were seeing if it was possible to come to some kind of an understanding. If you like these were feasibility talks.

'As regards the heaves inside Fine Gael about Cosgrave, certainly they existed. We had nothing to do with it. There was a feeling that I and other people in Labour had that the removal of Cosgrave as Fine

Gael leader would make the prospects of coalition easier but I didn't know Cosgrave good, bad or indifferent, I was just representing a view within the Labour Party,' says Halligan.

Dick Burke recalls the fevered atmosphere of the time.

'Garret came into my place as chief whip one day and said: "We must get rid of Liam. We must get rid of Liam, you know. Brendan has asked for it." I think he was inciting the Labour Party to press for Cosgrave's removal. I remember saying "Garrret, there will be no coalition without Liam in charge". He couldn't shift us. It was a pity some people in Fine Gael were so hostile to Liam because in later years the relationship between the Labour crowd and Cosgrave was perfect. All through those years there was this heave, heave, heave. It didn't mean that we slavishly had to agree with everything Cosgrave said but, on the essential question of who was going to lead the party into a coalition, I was never going to accept a situation like that of poor old Mulcahy who was forced to stand aside.'

Ryan says that as part of that plot FitzGerald tried to undermine early efforts at a coalition deal with Labour.

'I am sorry to say I think Garret would have been making it difficult for the Labour Party because he would have been picturing the impossibility of a coalition and supporting the Labour people in their view that they needed to have a socialist leader of Fine Gael like himself.'

Cosgrave himself bided his time on coalition. He remembered that before the 1969 election he made some overtures but had been rebuffed and he refused to be rushed by more enthusiastic members of his front bench.

In the meantime tension continued to simmer away on the Fine Gael front bench. FitzGerald, who in 1971 was made party spokesman on Finance, took a deep interest in Northern Ireland affairs, to the irritation of Ryan, the party's Foreign Affairs spokesman. FitzGerald visited the North on a number of occasions and wrote memos to Cosgrave but in October 1971 he became very concerned when Ryan proposed in the Dáil that Northern Ireland should be constituted as an international protectorate and Cosgrave himself called for a phased withdrawal of British troops. Garret and John Kelly expressed concern at these two speeches at the next front-bench meeting:

'Cosgrave's reaction was instantaneous and, to say the least, vigorous. He told the front bench with evident anger that I had been engaged over a period in discussions in the North about the situation there without his knowledge and that I had produced and given to people

two documents, the second of which I had brought to the North
before he had seen it,'

wrote FitzGerald who responded by producing a detailed account of
everything he had been involved in plus his letters to the party leader.

'In retrospect it seems to me that while on the one hand Liam
Cosgrave had not been prepared to instruct me to stop what I was
doing — he was perhaps more inhibited about confronting me than I,
never the most sensitive of people realised — this very restraint,
combined with some pressure from an aggrieved shadow Minister for
Foreign Affairs, Richie Ryan, must have built up in him a head of
frustration. And, as was to happen on several other occasions during
those years, this had eventually exploded.'

Ryan has an entirely different perspective on these events and has
evidence of what was regarded by Cosgrave's supporters of a plot by
FitzGerald to depose the party leader. The existence of a plot puts
Cosgrave's outburst into a very different perspective. 'From day one
Garret wanted to be leader of the party. No matter who was leader he
would have wanted to push him aside,' says Ryan.

'I have in my possession a list made in late 1971 as to how the party
would divide if there was a challenge to Liam's leadership. And it is
Garret FitzGerald's list. He visualised there would be three
candidates, Cosgrave, O'Higgins and FitzGerald. And in that list he
saw that on the first count it would be Cosgrave ahead, FitzGerald
second and O'Higgins third. O'Higgins would then be eliminated
and on the second count FitzGerald would have a majority. And he
has amendments made in his own handwriting, changing one or two
people. I should say it is a photocopy I have, someone else has the
original. What happened was Garret was at a meeting and had a huge
big bundle of papers. He left the meeting in his usual hurry and lifted
all the papers except this one, which was left on the table. So we knew
he was plotting in 1971 to take over the leadership.'

Flare-ups continued on other issues such as the American bombing
of North Vietnam. FitzGerald, Tom O'Higgins and Jim Dooge tried to
get a statement from Fine Gael condemning the bombing but a
majority on the front bench declined to back it. FitzGerald
subsequently aired his views at the Fine Gael Árd Fheis and Cosgrave
responded by referring obliquely to his enemies as 'people who allow
their humanitarian instincts to lead them to become communist
dupes'.

One issue that drove a wedge between Fine Gael and Labour was
the referendum on joining the European Community which took

place in April 1972. Fine Gael, like Fianna Fáil, was enthusiastically in favour of Ireland joining but the Labour Party was opposed. While some senior Labour figures were half-hearted in their opposition and some were privately in favour the fact that the two parties were on opposite sides in the campaign helped the Labour left to argue that they should stick to their anti-coalition policy and try and drive the two big parties together.

'One issue that was very pertinent at the time was that the two parties were divided on the question of EEC membership,' says Halligan. 'I remember that during the course of one of the informal discussions on coalition, which usually took place in the evenings in somebody's house, we got word that the referendum date had been announced. We said look, that's it — we can no longer meet, and we simply stopped meeting because we had to disagree on that particular matter.'

It was not until June 1972 that the real breakthrough came when Brendan Corish made a carefully considered speech arguing the case for coalition. He said that it would be 'an act of irresponsibility' not to give the electorate the opportunity of electing an alternative government. 'I had been given a copy of the speech beforehand by Brendan Halligan, with Corish's knowledge,' recalls Cosgrave. The media immediately pressed him for a comment and his cryptic response was typical:

'Politics is the art of the possible, the possible looks more probable now.'

Shortly afterwards the Fine Gael and Labour General Secretaries, Sanfey and Halligan, arranged for a meeting between their two leaders. The crucial meeting took place in Sanfey's house in Terenure. Cosgrave and Corish sat in easy chairs at either ends of the living room while Halligan and Sanfey sat facing each other across the room. Cosgrave opened the meeting by saying baldly. 'Brendan, you and I are getting old and there's not much time left,' recalls Halligan.

The two party leaders did most of the talking after that and they agreed to go back and report to their parliamentary colleagues on the fact that conversations had taken place. They then put the talks on a more formal footing and their respective deputy leaders, Tom O'Higgins and Jim Tully, were included. However, the talks never got down to detail and the reporting back to Fine Gael and Labour was vague.

'What was more important was that they were establishing good working relations between people and the ethos was being established whereby eventually the two sides were to collaborate and work together in the 1973 election as if they were one team,' says Halligan.

With stirrings of coalition in the air Fine Gael looked forward with great confidence to the Mid-Cork by-election which took place in August 1972. Labour had a strong candidate in former TD, Eileen Desmond and there were hopes that a good transfer to Fine Gael would win the seat for the Opposition. In the event the result was a bitter disappointment for Cosgrave as the Fianna Fáil candidate, Gene Fitzgerald, easily romped home. It was a blow to Cosgrave's leadership and his critics within the party became more vocal. His failure to tie up a coalition deal fuelled their anger and his enemies began to circle ominously for the kill.

10

MONGREL FOXES

SHORTLY before 10 p.m. on the evening of 1 December 1972, the lights were burning late in the Dáil and Liam Cosgrave's enemies in Fine Gael had him cornered. He was almost completely isolated with only Paddy Donegan ready to stand by him whatever the consequences. Virtually all his TDs and senators were in the process of walking out of the Fine Gael party room in disgust at their leader's determination to vote with Fianna Fáil in support of emergency security legislation. Suddenly a loud thud was heard and the windows of Leinster House vibrated. The first Loyalist bombs had gone off in Dublin. They killed two people and saved Cosgrave's political life.

The heave against Cosgrave was the culmination of tensions that had been building at the top of the party all through 1972 as senior figures like FitzGerald and O'Higgins became increasingly distant from their leader. Now, a quarter of a century later some of the leading protagonists, including Cosgrave, are inclined to play down their animosities but those not so directly involved vividly remember the deepening fissure between the party leader and his chief lieutenants.

At the Fine Gael Árd Fheis of May 1972 Cosgrave's resentment at his opponents in the party exploded in an unscripted remark during his leader's address:

> 'I don't know whether some of you do any hunting or not but some of these commentators and critics are now like mongrel foxes, they are gone to ground and I'll dig them out and the pack will chop them when they get them.'

Much of his audience and the wider public were puzzled by the reference but its intended targets, sitting beside Cosgrave on the platform in the City Hall in Cork, got the shock of their lives.

'The tone of this unscripted attack was disconcerting, especially for those of us who were seen as its targets; for a moment indeed, I wondered whether I should leave the platform, as I believe several others considered doing but discretion outran valour,' wrote FitzGerald. He came off the platform fuming at what he regarded as a direct attack on him and his allies by their party leader.

It was quite out of character for Cosgrave to lash his critics in public but Cork TD, Liam Burke, puts the remarks in context:

'I was put in charge of Liam for the weekend and was to second the vote of thanks to him after the speech. My job was to look after Liam so I took him across the road into the Black Swan bar across from the City Hall. We had a room upstairs and Ned Murphy the journalist was there and of course he and Liam were great buddies. I went over anyway and said to the boss what are you having and he said "I'll have an Irish and soda". So I poured him out a very big measure of whiskey and I could see the ould lips puckering after it, but himself and Ned kept chatting away. He was to go in around 3 o'clock and at about a quarter to three I said "will you have another one?" and he said "just a little one" so I gave him another *teascáin* anyway, and I'd say it was even bigger than the first one. And the next thing he was over in City Hall delivering the speech and that's when he came out with the mongrel foxes remark.'

The mongrel foxes did not forgive Cosgrave for his attack and tension mounted within the party. In early November the strained relations between Cosgrave and Tom O'Higgins, his deputy leader, became visible at a party meeting, according to FitzGerald:

'This led to a very full, and unusually frank, discussion at front-bench meetings on 8 and 14 November. Many speakers at these meetings questioned openly for the first time, aspects of Cosgrave's leadership, and in particular expressed concern at what his critics perceived as a withdrawal of confidence on his part from some members of the front bench during the immediately preceding years, together with what was seen as undue reliance on a small group of "loyalists" on the front bench.

'At the end of the front-bench meeting of 14 November Cosgrave asked for 24 hours to consider his position. But when the front bench resumed 24 hours later, he ignored the discussion of the previous day and proceeded as if it had never happened. If this was intended to disconcert those who had initiated this discussion it certainly succeeded.'

News of the internal dissension did not get out immediately but on 18 November the political correspondent of *The Irish Times*, Michael McInerney, reported:

> 'Something of a slow-burning but persistent and rising discontent has become evident in Fine Gael over the past fortnight about the present position of the party in the country and the degree of responsibility of the leader, Mr Liam Cosgrave, for what is considered to be the failure of the party and its leader to be seen as the credible alternative to the Taoiseach, Mr Jack Lynch.

> 'The burst of criticism first broke out last week at a meeting of the front bench when one deputy said quietly that prominent members of the national council were not alone in believing that Mr Cosgrave — in spite of his many qualities — did not measure up to the ideal of national leadership.'

McInerney reported that a heated discussion developed from the remarks of the unnamed front-bencher and was followed by an apology the next day. Nonetheless, he said that the apology did not stop the discussion in the party and he added: 'It is accepted generally that front-benchers like Deputy Tom O'Higgins and Deputy Garret FitzGerald are in the field for the leadership, whether they would admit it or not.' He added that O'Higgins was more likely to succeed than Garret, although Cosgrave would win if he stayed and fought.

Towards the end of November political tension rose to fever pitch. IRA leader Sean McStiofain was on hunger strike in Dublin; the Government sacked the RTE Authority for allowing an interview with McStiofain to be broadcast in breach of the law. In the middle of it all the Minister for Justice, Des O'Malley, published legislation to tackle the IRA threat more effectively. The Offences Against the State Bill 1972, abolished jury trials for terrorist offences and provided that a person could be convicted of IRA membership on the word of a Garda superintendent.

A huge public controversy immediately developed with the media, civil liberties groups and the Labour Party denouncing the Government's crackdown on the IRA. It was Fine Gael, though, which was thrown into most disarray. Liam Cosgrave's initial instinct, in line with his father's legacy, was to support Jack Lynch's Government against the forces which were trying to wreck the State, particularly as there was a chance of the measure being defeated in the Dáil with the ex-Fianna Fáil TDs threatening to vote against Lynch.

Most of his colleagues in Fine Gael saw things differently from Cosgrave. Whatever their views on law and order they simply regarded the issue as an opportunity to defeat the Government. Some in Fine Gael also supported the civil liberties argument and others saw it as the opening they had been waiting for to undermine Cosgrave's leadership. When the Fine Gael front bench met to consider the issue on Monday, 27 November, it became clear that differences on the matter ran very deep. Eventually it was decided to refer a decision to the parliamentary party the following day, without a recommendation from the front bench.

Paddy Harte vividly remembers driving to Dublin fully intending to back Cosgrave and the emergency legislation but when he walked into the pressure cooker atmosphere of Leinster House he allowed himself to be swayed against his better judgement:

'When I came into the house I was stopped by three senior deputies; my full intention was to throw my bag and my briefcase into the office and go immediately to Liam Cosgrave's office and tell him that he was right and I was backing him. But I was buttonholed at the lifts and three deputies, who are no longer members of the House, knowing what my feelings were, stopped me and argued so strenuously that I decided not to go to Cosgrave's office.

'Looking back on it I was sucked into Fianna Fáil–Fine Gael politics, by the three people who buttonholed me. It was one of the things I always regretted because when the bombs went off two days later we knew how necessary it was to provide absolute law and order.'

Garret FitzGerald recalls the parliamentary party meeting to which Paddy Harte had rushed from Donegal as follows:

'When the parliamentary party met, Cosgrave favoured the legislation whereas a majority wanted to oppose on the second stage because they took exception to some of its clauses on civil liberties grounds, including the provision regarding a chief superintendent's evidence. Eventually, late that night, after a discussion in the course of which twice as many members spoke against the Bill as for it — including a number normally strongly supportive of Liam Cosgrave, such as Richie Ryan, Mark Clinton and Oliver Flanagan — he most reluctantly agreed to go along with a proposal to oppose the Bill on the basis of a reasoned amendment to be proposed by the shadow Minister for Justice, Pat Cooney, and seconded by the party leader himself. It was after midnight when the meeting adjourned. Cosgrave was reported to be distressed at the party's decision but, the press said, would nevertheless vote as the party had decided; there was no threat to resign.'

When the Dáil debate began on Wednesday, 29 November, Pat
Cooney responded to the introduction of the Bill by Minister for
Justice, Desmond O'Malley, by arguing that the Government had
failed to use the powers that were already available. It was Cosgrave's
speech seconding Cooney's amendment, however, that grabbed
attention. According to Garret the speech disturbed many of his
colleagues because it stressed the willingness of Fine Gael to give the
Government power to deal with subversives remorselessly.
'Communists and their fellow travellers and soft-headed liberals are
always talking about repression,' he said, also referring to anti-
apartheid marches which 'degenerated into a rabble and were a
disgrace to all associated with them.'

FitzGerald continues, 'Press reaction was that Cosgrave had
hijacked his own front bench, shot down the reputations of his own
top men and ended prospects of a coalition with Labour.' This
assessment is taken from a piece by John Healy on the front page of
The Irish Times but it is very selective. Healy did write:

> 'It was a political bloody Wednesday as far as his front bench was
> concerned — or that portion of it which favours coalition. And when
> he had finished not only had he shot the reputations of some of his
> key men; he had left any hopes for a coalition arrangement lying
> mortally wounded on the floor of the Chamber.'

But he went on:

> 'Cosgrave was not merely pulling the party back from an untenable
> political situation ... he was also reminding his deputies that it was the
> ancestors of Fine Gael who had established law and order in the
> country and they were not now going to give Fianna Fáil the moral
> position of taking that from them. He made nonsense of Dick Burke's
> posturing on RTE and of Garret FitzGerald. Garret came dashing in
> halfway through his speech to sit beside a sober Paddy Cooney who
> knew just how closely his leader was supporting him in his seconding
> speech.'

Michael McInerney in the lead story of *The Irish Times* described
Cosgrave's contribution as 'one of the best speeches of his life.' He
added, though, that the expectation was that Cosgrave would vote with
the majority of his colleagues, as he had done on proportional
representation in 1959 and 1968.

The Fine Gael parliamentary party met again that night, after the
leader's speech. The issue of how the party would vote at the end of
second stage was debated all over again but there was still a clear
majority against the Bill. On Thursday rumours swept the Dáil that

Lynch would call a general election and go to the country on the law and order issue if the Bill was defeated. In *The Irish Times* Healy denounced the cynicism of all the Fianna Fáil republicans who were now cloaking themselves as advocates of law and order. 'Fine Gael, instead of taking the proposed legislation as a serious piece of legislation, instead — as Liam Cosgrave did — of identifying it as an election set-up and treating it as such has allowed itself to be outflanked on the law and order issue.'

By Friday, as the debate continued in the Dáil, there was concern, according to Garret, that Cosgrave might vote against his own party and an approach was made to Fianna Fáil to try and get agreement on amendments. Fianna Fáil scenting blood rejected any compromise.

> 'When word of this was received at 4.30 p.m. Cosgrave called yet a further party meeting in the hope of persuading his colleagues to reverse their twice-taken decision. This proved too much for the members, who, just before eight o'clock, after several hours debate in the party room and with Tom O'Higgins already on his feet in the Dáil for half an hour waiting to hear what line he was to take, voted 38 to 8 to oppose the Bill. Six of the eight opponents of the Bill immediately rallied to the majority, leaving Liam Cosgrave and Paddy Donegan alone in their dissent. As some members tried to persuade an unyielding Cosgrave to change his mind and vote with his party, I went down to the House to put Tom O'Higgins out of his agony,'

wrote FitzGerald.

Paddy Harte too recalls that Cosgrave was totally isolated that evening:

> 'The entire party, including myself, were on our feet ready to walk out of the room. Paddy Donegan and Sir Anthony Esmonde were the only two who didn't get up to walk away. I think the reason they didn't was only because they were sitting so close to Cosgrave and they felt sorry for him; then we were walking out the bombs went off. The windows vibrated violently. Within seconds we discovered that bombs had gone off in Dublin and the motion that the party had tabled before the Dáil was withdrawn. Rather than opposing the Offences Against the State we agreed to support it. It was very dramatic.'

In the Dáil chamber Tom O'Higgins was attacking Fianna Fáil for its arrogance in refusing a compromise on the Bill when word reached the chamber that bombs had just gone off in Dublin.

> 'I think I whispered this news to Tom O'Higgins just as a Fianna Fáil deputy, Noel Davern, interrupted to ask him if he supported the

bombings. Tom replied to Davern that he was aware of them and told him not to be a bloody ass.

'I went upstairs to our party corridor and found a large number of our deputies engaged in heated discussions on the landing outside the party room. After a few minutes there was general agreement, albeit with some dissenting voices, that in view of the bombings ... we should reverse our stand and agree to support the Bill. I returned to the House, where Tom O'Higgins had concluded — inconclusively — and had gone to look for Liam Cosgrave to tell him what had happened.'

John Bruton remembers that night when, as a young TD, he sided with the majority of the party against his leader:

'I graphically remember the bombs going off. I was actually in the lobby getting ready to vote and if my memory serves me it was decided in the lobby in a series of huddles that we would back the party leader's line after all. It was as late as that, it was within minutes of the vote that the party cohered again around the leader rather than split. It was a very rare parliamentary event.'

After the huddles in the lobby and consultation with the Government Pat Cooney intervened in the debate at 9.45 p.m. to withdraw the Fine Gael amendment and the second stage was passed two hours later with just two Fine Gael TDs, Oliver J. Flanagan and Eddie Collins voting against, along with the Labour party and Independents. The committee stage of the Bill began close to midnight and continued until 4 a.m. on Saturday morning.

When the House then adjourned many in Fine Gael, including supporters of Liam Cosgrave, left for home believing that he would be replaced as leader the following week. But unknown to most deputies he had during the course of the evening appeared on television to great effect and by Saturday morning he was widely seen as the hero of the hour; the man who had stood firm and had been proved right.

Dick Burke has a vivid memory of that television performance.

'Ted Nealon was presenting *Seven Days* at the time. They went around the Dáil before the bombs went off asking practically everybody in Fine Gael but they wouldn't go on. I said I would because I had a plan to do something dramatic. I got up from my seat in the middle of the interview and said "I am not the right person to have on here at all. I think you should ask Liam Cosgrave to come on. I will try and find him for you", and I got up and left the studio.

'This was rather dramatic on television. I went out and of course Liam wouldn't go on but I said the vacant chair was there. By this time the bombs had gone off and the possibility was there of Jack Lynch calling an election. You couldn't tell what would happen. I thought that the man who had come out best out of all of this was Liam Cosgrave so I kept after him and stood at the back of the Dáil with Liam and listened to the end of the debate and Cooney winding up.

'I said to Liam: "Look, I have told the people of Ireland I am going to try and get you to come on." He said "What will I say?". I told him "go in and say this is your finest hour". I physically had to push him into the studio and into a chair. They kept the programme going for a few minutes past the deadline and there was Liam. Of course everybody in the country could see now that he was right. It was the highest audience of all time.'

In fact there were many in the media who had felt Cosgrave was right all along. It was mainly his opponents on the liberal wing of his own party who had cast him in the wrong on the issue, so when the tide turned in his favour it should have been no surprise that the media presented him as a man vindicated.

Richie Ryan has no doubts about the source of the dissension within the party. 'I imagine the move would never have happened was it not for Garret's unbridled ambition. The party substantially remained loyal to Cosgrave but there were understandably loyal people who thought we would never make it under Cosgrave. He lacked that dynamism. People on the Dáil gallery always enjoyed Cosgrave's asides and witticisms. He could always in any speech throw in these wonderful asides, but by the end of 1972 some decent people thought we needed a new leader.'

Paddy Harte's memory of the dramatic events of December 1972, are made even more rueful because of what happened shortly afterwards:

'Needless to say there was a general election two or three months later and those three people who had persuaded me to oppose him were in Cosgrave's Cabinet. Now I often wonder what would have happened if I had gone to Cosgrave's office and said to Liam "I am backing you and I am going to go through hell and hot water to support what you are saying" because that is the way I was feeling. I was angry because I felt we should have hand consensus and be backing the Government. There were members of our party who only wanted to play party politics. And then of course Cosgrave didn't enamour himself to a number of deputies who were disappointed with him and this was their chance to get rid of him. Until the day I die I will be wondering what my political future would have been had I gone to Liam

Cosgrave that day and said "Liam, you are right and I am backing you".'

Vincent Browne in an account of the incident written in 1975 takes the FitzGerald view of the week's events and claims that Cosgrave vacillated right through the crisis and actually adopted five different positions in the course of it. His account of the week is identical to FitzGerald and he quotes Garret as saying at a party meeting the week after the crisis that Cosgrave 'neither led nor followed'.

Cosgrave completely rejects this version of events:

'My attitude was constant. The Bill was necessary and its passage had to be facilitated. I was always in favour of the Bill and determined that it would pass. In a matter of such gravity the nation must come before party. In retrospect even those who were opposed to its terms realised that it was necessary and indeed in certain circumstances hardly strong enough.'

What is crystal clear is that from the beginning Cosgrave wanted to support the Bill and firmly believed that the liberal wing of his own party had got it completely wrong. Of course he twisted and turned to try and sustain his position as party leader on the one hand while bringing his TDs around to his own minority point of view on the other. In the end circumstances worked in his favour but there is no doubt that on an issue of fundamental principle he was prepared to vote against his own party, lose his position and abandon all hopes of ever being Taoiseach.

FitzGerald generously admitted in his autobiography that in retrospect Cosgrave was proved right.

'Our emotional opposition to this Act was not subsequently justified by the use actually made of it ... Moreover, in political terms Cosgrave was also right: had we opposed the Bill we would, I believe, have been severely defeated in a post-Christmas law-and-order election.'

Bruton agrees:

'Cosgrave showed tremendous courage, really, and was right and virtually all the rest of us, including myself, were wrong. I have to say I didn't see the issue first and foremost as a question of trying to topple Liam Cosgrave. I think that we considered he wanted us to take a mistaken line on the Bill itself. But I think in retrospect whatever about the legalities of it he certainly had the politics of it right. The rest of the party, apart from the few who supported him, had it wrong.'

Even in the weeks that followed Cosgrave's enemies couldn't come to terms with the fact that he had reinforced rather than undermined his position by the stance he took during the crisis. During the Christmas holidays approaches were made to him by senior people in the party, including his deputy leader, Tom O'Higgins, to ask if he would consider running as Fine Gael's presidential election candidate in 1973. The approach was clearly designed as a way of easing him out of the leadership and Cosgrave flatly refused to consider it. O'Higgins, who had done so well in the 1966 election against Eamon de Valera, was then left with no option but to let his name go forward again as the Fine Gael candidate for the office.

11

ELECTION SHOWDOWN

WITH Fine Gael still licking its wounds during the long Christmas Dáil recess which followed the bruising Offences Against the State Act debate Lynch suddenly decided to pounce. On 5 February 1973, the day before TDs were due back in Leinster House after the Christmas recess, he dissolved the Dáil and called a general election for 28 February.

The timing caused consternation in the Opposition ranks because the coalition talks had not come to any kind of conclusion and if anything Fine Gael and Labour appeared deadlocked. The two parties had expected Lynch to go for an election if he had been defeated in the Dáil two months earlier but they were totally unprepared for a February campaign.

One senior Fine Gael figure recalls that shortly before Lynch dropped his bombshell Liam Cosgrave had come to a Fine Gael party meeting to review the progress of the talks and said in exasperation 'these talks are getting nowhere. We might as well end them'. Just days after that remark Lynch dissolved the Dáil. 'Liam's comment leaked to him and he decided to do it. He thought he would catch us on the hop.'

In fact many people in Fine Gael were convinced that they had been caught completely off guard and senior party figures were in despair on the day the election was called. 'The day the general election was announced in 1973 they couldn't find Liam,' recalls Richie Ryan. 'Jack Lynch was looking for him to tell him he was going to the country. It is a courtesy that all Taoiseach's have observed in telling the leader of the Opposition. They couldn't find Liam and his secretary got me at home and told me the press were looking for Liam and the next thing RTE rang me and asked me to go on the 1.30 news. And I told them a white

lie because they asked me what was going to happen in the election and
I said "Oh, of course we'll win" but if they saw me, I was in my study
looking in the mirror and I was white as a ghost as I said it.'

Peter Barry recalls a similar sense of shock: 'Our morale was very low
at that stage. Jack Lynch definitely decided that Fine Gael was tottering,
with big divisions in the party, low morale, and poor organisation and
he decided during the Christmas recess to dissolve the Dáil.'

The gloomy mood didn't last long because the announcement of an
election jolted Cosgrave and Corish into action. The two men,
accompanied by their deputy leaders and general secretaries, met in
Cosgrave's office the day after the election was called and agreed within
minutes to offer the electorate an alternative government by fighting
the campaign on a common platform. It was understood that Cosgrave
would be Taoiseach and Corish Tánaiste in the event of victory but
there was no discussion of the number of cabinet posts for each party.

'We drew up the 14-point plan with Labour in no time,' says Peter
Barry. 'The plan was agreed without any problem. The smell of power
you see. Power is the aphrodisiac.'

Brendan Halligan gives a flavour of the meeting to devise a joint
election manifesto.

'What was obvious to me was that Cosgrave and Corish got on
extremely well with each other. They were very much at ease with each
other and that was evident from the moment we walked into the room
and the conversations began. If you like, the agreement to go into
coalition was done within the first two minutes. It makes the point
that when two people are in agreement with each other you don't
have to go through tortuous negotiations lasting three or four weeks,
writing everything down in fine detail and having it verified and
notarised and all the rest of it.'

Having agreed on the principle of coalition Cosgrave and Corish
decided to bring others into the discussion on the contents of the
election manifesto to be put to the Irish people.

That group gathered in Cosgrave's office later in the afternoon.
Cosgrave was accompanied by Tom and Michael O'Higgins, Richie
Ryan, Jim Dooge and Jim Sanfey. On the Labour side were Corish, Tully,
Michael O'Leary, party General Secretary, Halligan, and party
chairman, Roddy Connolly. By the time the group met Halligan had
prepared a draft of the manifesto and Cosgrave made no objection to
using the Labour document as the working draft. The meeting was a
cordial one and people present recall the eagerness of all to reach an
agreement.

'More progress was made in a few hours between Fine Gael and Labour than in all the time between the Inchicore speech and the declaration of the election,' is how Cosgrave remembers that eventful day. Everybody at the meeting knew there was no time for haggling and both Fine Gael and Labour negotiators quickly moved on to common ground and made no attempt to pitch their demands at an unacceptably high level for the other. By contrast to the complex, inordinately long and tortuous coalition negotiations which have now become commonplace after elections, Fine Gael and Labour in 1973 produced a short, solid and attractive manifesto which let the electorate know just what they would do if elected to government.

Fine Gael got commitments on law and order, Europe, a peaceful solution to the Northern problem, the removal of compulsory Irish and the abolition of death duties. Labour laid stress on the removal of VAT from food, social reform, increasing house building to 25,000 a year and controlling prices. Garret FitzGerald inserted a clause promising a tax on wealth to replace death duties. There was also a private agreement, not included in the document, that farmers would be brought into the tax net. When the main outlines of the programme were agreed after a couple of hours Cosgrave decided to let the negotiators hammer out the detail and he decided to go home. Before he left, however, he laid down the law on one point. Brendan Halligan recalls the scene.

'Basically Cosgrave's approach to the whole thing, which it was never put expressedly, was as follows: "You know where I stand on various issues. I don't have to spell them out to you. I will accept the fact that you will not abuse where I stand. Therefore you go away and negotiate and I will agree to anything you agree upon, because I know that you will not exceed your understanding of where I am at. But I want to make it clear that there is absolutely no way I will agree to anything which weakens my position on law and order."

'When we got to the night the election was called, documents had been exchanged between Fine Gael and Labour coming up to this point, in effect the guts of the 14-point plan. I had drafted most of it and it had gone through the Labour parliamentary party. We had presented that to Fine Gael and they had given us back something very light, to be honest. But as soon as the election was called we got together two teams of negotiators led by Cosgrave and Brendan. And Cosgrave left at something like 10 or 11 o'clock at night to go home saying "I am leaving it all in your very good hands but remember what I said, you can put anything in as long as you don't give a commitment to get rid of that Act [Offences Against the State]. It stays." When he went out of the room I asked if he really meant it and the reply was "Oh he really means it" and I said, "In that case forget it. We will just have to sell that to the Labour Party."'

The incident is a revealing insight into Cosgrave's character. On one level it shows that he was a pragmatist, prepared to negotiate and strike a deal on nearly all issues with people of a very different political persuasion. On the real fundamentals, however, like protecting the institutions of the State he was inflexible, regardless of the consequences.

The story reveals that Labour were also very flexible. The party had fought tooth and nail against the Offences Against the State Act only two months earlier but in the light of Cosgrave's views they backed off, knowing that was the only way into government. Like Halligan, Fine Gael people recall the speed with which the coalition arrangement was agreed the day after Lynch called the election. Jim Dooge recalls:

'We met the night when the election was called. Two and a half hours later we had a programme for government. Labour had produced a document and we went through that as a working paper and then came out with a final version. It is interesting that the one point that came up at the Fine Gael parliamentary party meeting the following day was that we shouldn't call it a coalition, that it had always been an inter-party government. I intervened to say that was the only way to do it otherwise we would spend half the campaign arguing with Fianna Fáil as to whether it was a coalition.'

With agreement on using the term coalition rather than inter-party government the parties decided to call the arrangement the national coalition. *The Irish Times* political correspondent, Michael McInerney, jumped the gun by calling it the 'People's coalition', a description some Labour people liked, but the Eastern European socialist connotations did not appeal to Fine Gael.

Tom O'Higgins says that the adjective before coalition was put to one side and a blank left during the negotiations on the programme.

'I remember when we finished at half two or three in the morning it was raining and I went out to get into my car and Brendan Corish was there and Richie Ryan was going to get the final draft typed for a meeting of the two parties the following day. He was getting into his car and he shouted over "We never filled in the blank" and I said "Brendan, what about National?"'

By this stage Cosgrave was long at home in his bed. It is hard to think of any other senior political figure who would have left his subordinates to conduct the detailed negotiations but it was typical of the man. His capacity to delegate responsibility was always a feature of his leadership and one that was perceived by all his colleagues as a strength rather than a weakness while he was in government. There was also a side to his character which found the nitty gritty of negotiations tedious in the extreme; he had no interest in arguing over the meaning of words or the placing of commas in the text, activities that some politicians find compulsive.

The following morning Cosgrave was back in his office and the haggard negotiators discovered there were important things which they had left out. A paragraph on broadcasting was inserted and another one on fisheries hastily cobbled together for the programme.

The statement of intent, as the draft manifesto was now called, was put to the Fine Gael and Labour parties later that day. It was first approved by the Labour Party administrative council, with just one dissenting voice while at the Labour parliamentary party meeting there was also just only dissenter, Noel Browne who didn't stand in the 1973 election. David Thornley, who had been reluctant, signed a pledge supporting the manifesto.

On the Fine Gael side Cosgrave asked Richie Ryan to read out the manifesto to the party's TDs and senators. It was greeted with loud applause and a standing ovation and there was little discussion of its contents. 'I think I raised a question about the idea that we were going to provide old age pensions for everybody without a means test which was one of the things that was suggested,' says John Bruton who adds with a laugh. 'My latent fiscal rectitude was already rearing its ugly head in 1973.'

Brendan Halligan takes up the story: 'The next morning it was all put to bed. Bits were added in at the last minute. It was a very easy atmosphere.' Dooge remembers:

'The next day that document was through Fine Gael without amendment and through the Labour Party with one amendment by Conor Cruise O'Brien in regard to Northern policy, toning it down to say we would attempt to do something rather than do it.'

Following the agreement of the two parties to the manifesto a press conference was called for Leinster House on 7 February when it was unveiled to the public. The political scene was transformed because for the first time since the 1950s the voters were clearly being offered an alternative government. The 1973 campaign was the only time in Irish political history that Opposition parties came together on a joint programme and waged a joint election campaign, giving the voters a real choice rather than the pot luck they were offered in the 1980s and 1990s.

The central features of the manifesto were economic ones. The reduction in rates, through the removal of health charges, the removal of VAT from food, the abolition of death duties, the introduction of price control and a pledge to control wages. Commitments to move towards the elimination of poverty, an end to discrimination against women, the building of more houses, pledges to control rents and taxes, reform of local democracy and education were all elements of the manifesto. Reflecting Cosgrave's own concerns there was also a firm commitment to protect the democratic institutions of the State and to work for peace and justice in Northern Ireland.

The package was an attractive one for the voters because it combined economic self-interest with the offer of an alternative government after 16-years of Fianna Fáil. The timing of the election before the publication of the new electoral register in April disenfranchised many young people who were keenly looking forward to voting, following the referendum to lower the voting age to 18. This became an important issue in the campaign. Pat Rabbitte, then president of the Union of Students in Ireland issued a hard-hitting statement saying he was sickened by 'the cynical announcement' of the election which he said disenfranchised about 200,000 voters.

Rabbitte remembers that the USI produced a clever poster with a distorted image of Lynch's face and various anti-Fianna Fáil slogans on it.

'We had no money to produce the poster so I called to Labour Party headquarters to see if they would contribute. Who did I find there only Garret FitzGerald furiously typing away on an old typewriter. There didn't seem to be anybody else about but eventually Brendan Halligan wandered into the room. When I asked about money Halligan told me they didn't have any to spare. Garret told me to go up and see Liam Cosgrave as Fine Gael had more money than Labour. I remember being ushered into Cosgrave's office in Leinster House and I stated my business. I was a long-haired radical student at the time and he looked at me, twiddled his little moustache and said absolutely nothing. Then he shouted "Richie" and Ryan who was in the next room came in. Cosgrave told me to repeat my story to Richie and he left the room. Eventually Richie gave me a note for Col. Jim Sanfey and I got a brown paper bag with £100 or something like that, in it.'

The coalition campaign got off to a flying start because of the unified approach of the two parties involved. 'The style of the campaign was set from the very beginning because we called a joint press conference. This was seen by everybody and particularly the media, who pick up mood, as being very positive. Here were two guys at the top who were easy with each other and were running a joint campaign. That was most unusual. During the campaign we effectively ran an integrated election committee which would be chaired alternatively by Cosgrave and Corish, simply subject to their availability,' says Halligan who became the *de facto* press officer of the joint campaign.

Halligan remembers telling Cosgrave and Corish at the beginning:

'We don't need any 14-Point Plan or election manifesto. All that is needed is for the two of you to walk down the centre of the street of any town or village or any part of Dublin together. Don't say anything about politics just talk to each other. The two of you exude reassurance. You are both somewhat conservative but reassurance is what the people need at this time.'

In his speeches Cosgrave gave details about how the election promises would be funded but he also reiterated traditional themes. In Roscommon on 11 February he said that Fine Gael was asking for support 'to provide a government pledged to uphold the democratic institutions of the State. The outgoing government had failed in this primary duty which would be Fine Gael's first concern.'

The security issue and the recent internal problems in Fine Gael didn't feature much during the campaign. John Healy in his Backbencher column in *The Irish Times* was the only journalist to give prominence to it. Healy wrote:

'Cosgrave's leadership has been threatened at times because he insisted on putting nation before party. It was Cosgrave's known attitude and the knowledge that he would not budge from that basic position which led the mongrel foxes to try and take him on the head of the Offences Against the State Act. They are sadder and wiser men today and must be chastened and they are terribly glad now to shelter behind his new stature. As glad indeed as Mr Brendan Corish and his party. For if the dissident Fine Gael deputies scuttled back behind Liam on the night of the bombs and were thankful to have him, Brendan Corish and his party were no less thankful to scuttle in behind Cosgrave and Fine Gael when Jack Lynch put a bomb under the nineteenth Dáil.'

It was economics, though, which featured as the main issue. Fianna

Fáil tried to get the debate on to the North, on which they felt they were more in tune with public opinion than Fine Gael, but the electorate was not greatly interested. The Government lost the initiative in the early stages and struggled to regain it as Cosgrave and Corish barnstormed around the country and Garret FitzGerald blitzed George Colley in television debates.

The coalition parties had one secret weapon which is still a matter of great sensitivity. They had a spy at a very senior level in Fianna Fáil who gave them information about the Government's strategy during the campaign. Brendan Halligan confirmed in 1996 that Labour and Fine Gael benefited from inside information in February 1973 but he refused to disclose the identity of the mole. He did confirm that the coalition parties knew in advance of major Fianna Fáil announcements and were in a position to take counter measures. The Fianna Fáil volte-face on rates was one key issue where the coalition parties were forewarned and in a position to react calmly.

The Fianna Fáil proposal on rates emerged after a lot of internal wrangling among Government Ministers about their response to the coalition campaign. The feedback from Fianna Fáil canvassers left the party leadership in no doubt that things were not going well and morale began to slip. Martin O'Donoghue then came up with a plan for the spending of over £30 million a year which would be saved on agricultural subsidies by Ireland's accession to the EEC. Initially the package was rejected on the advice of Minister for Finance, George Colley, but in the light of the poor campaign Lynch decided to go ahead with it anyway. The coalition parties were alerted in advance by their Fianna Fáil saboteur that the package was coming and a speech was prepared for Cosgrave to be delivered in Rathmines on 21 February. In this speech he outlined how the coalition would spend the £30 million saved through EEC membership. This pre-emptive strike threw the Fianna Fáil campaign into some confusion but they decided to go ahead by emphasising a small number of items from what had originally been a detailed package. The item they picked on to highlight was the complete abolition of rates on domestic dwellings. The announcement by Lynch of the plan to abolish rates on the morning of 22 February, less than a week before polling, clearly posed a major problem for the coalition parties.

'The defining moment of the campaign was when Lynch capitulated on the question of rates and he called a press conference that morning at which he changed the party policy,' recalls Halligan.

'Cosgrave immediately tried to contact Corish who was then in Kerry driving to North Tipperary. Nowadays you just ring a mobile phone number but things were different in 1973. Corish had to be stopped somewhere around Newcastle West by the Gardaí. They were waiting for him and flagged him down and he went into the station and took the call from Cosgrave. I was sitting beside Cosgrave and the conversation took place for no more than two minutes and it was very simple. Cosgrave was very low-key about it, and said "we don't do anything, we don't react, we don't change". I couldn't hear the other end of the conversation but it was very clear that Brendan Corish was saying exactly the same thing. So they both agreed.'

Cosgrave called a press conference for that afternoon in Leinster House. Senior Labour and Fine Gael figures gathered in his office. 'His authority was automatically accepted, he didn't have to exert authority. I mean everybody sat around him. It is very important the way people position themselves in a room. Literally they sat around his desk in a big semi-circle and he was the meeting and he laid down the line,' recalls Halligan.

There was agreement on the line propounded by Cosgrave and then Halligan interrupted to say it was time for the press conference across the corridor in the Fine Gael rooms. Everybody started to stand up but Cosgrave paused and said:

'Do you know what happened last night when I was coming back home, driving through the Phoenix Park? There we were in the dark and we caught something in the headlights, running across our track and do you know what it was? — a mongrel fox.'

'Now what a wonderful bloody thing to say,' says Halligan. 'It was self-deprecatory, it was a perfect political joke and it simply and absolutely broke the tension. We were all laughing as we walked into the press conference and that made a striking impression on the journalists. I remember Michael Mills saying to me that this made a huge impact on him. These people are coming in here laughing, they are so confident, this is going very well for them. And because of the way in which Cosgrave led us in we had no problem at the press conference and in fact turned it around to our advantage. Fianna Fáil were panicking and we were holding steady. That is the side of his personality that the public never saw and it made an enormous impact on me.'

Cosgrave simply told the press conference:

'There is obviously a gale blowing in our direction but we are refusing to join the auction.'

The *Irish Press* reported him as adding: 'Our proposals had been dismissed by the Government as pie in the sky but now in a last minute effort to buy votes from the electorate they are agreeing with them.'

On the last weekend before the vote *Backbencher* wrote:

'There is now a reasonable chance that Liam Cosgrave will be the next Taoiseach. Astonishingly Cosgrave has forced Lynch off his ground and on to Cosgrave's. This is his first victory and it is a considerable one. Secondly he has forced Lynch into establishing Cosgrave's credibility as a tactician and leader.'

In an interview with Michael Mills of the *Irish Press* Cosgrave responded vigorously when asked if he foresaw any difficulties being in government with Labour.

'No, I think we never had any difficulty with Labour Ministers before and I wouldn't anticipate any difficulties again. The difficulties in the past were with other elements but Labour are, on the whole, experienced politicians and they have committed themselves in advance to this programme and worked out policies that I believe offers a reasonable hope of stability.'

Asked by Mills if he was confident of victory Cosgrave's reply was typically modest. 'At this stage it is very hard to say. I think there is a fair chance that the majority are in favour of a new government.'

In posters and advertisements during the campaign the Fine Gael slogan was 'Cosgrave puts the Nation First,' while Fianna Fáil's message was 'Progress with Stability'. On the day before the election the Fine Gael newspaper advertisements stated simply. 'Don't Blame the Government. Change it Tomorrow — Vote Fine Gael.'

Cosgrave tried to reassure traditional Fine Gael supporters by emphasising the reforming rather than radical nature of the coalition. 'We must resolutely defend and protect our great Christian heritage and this can only be done if we continue to improve rather than alter the present system,' he said in Tullamore on 20 February.

The Fine Gael campaign was run with a skeleton staff. Michael O'Higgins was director of elections and Jim Dooge his assistant. Alexis FitzGerald and Dooge handled a team of speech writers who came in each day around 5 p.m. and wrote speeches which were then checked before being allocated to speakers. Unless the initials of either FitzGerald or Dooge appeared on the bottom the speeches were not issued to the press. People involved in the campaign remember having great trouble with one speech writer who kept trying to sneak in the phrase 'ex-occupants of the dock' when referring to Haughey and other leading members of Fianna Fáil. The offending speech writer was none other than a youthful Michael McDowell.

Overall the coalition got a good press during the campaign. The *Irish Independent* was sympathetic to Fine Gael while *The Irish Times* was strongly anti-Fianna Fáil and pro-Labour. The *Irish Press* backed Fianna Fáil but the coalition parties got extensive and fair coverage and the paper's political correspondent, Michael Mills, conducted a long interview with Cosgrave on the eve of the election.

John Healy in *The Irish Times* on the eve of the election publicly declared he was voting for the national coalition. 'Starkly put, it offers more talent, man for man, and under the stern leadership of Liam Cosgrave will give this country good government and make for healthy democracy.'

As polling day drew near the omens were looking good for the coalition. At a final Fine Gael rally in the Mansion House Cosgrave delivered a hard-hitting speech and summoned over Declan Costello to speak to party workers, indicating that tensions with the 'mongrel foxes' were buried, for the campaign at least.

Polling took place on 28 February with the count the following day. As the results came in it became clear that there had been no landslide. Fianna Fáil actually increased its share of the first preference vote compared to 1969 but the coalition pact delivered crucial transfers between Fine Gael and Labour. The final result saw Fine Gael win 54 seats, a gain of four, Labour got 19, an increase of one, while Fianna Fáil dropped six to 69 seats. It was nothing like the landslide some of the leading coalition figures expected and resulted in an overall majority of just two. It was enough. Fianna Fáil were out of power for the first time in 16 years and Liam Cosgrave had achieved his life's ambition of becoming Taoiseach.

On the night of his victory Cosgrave didn't do the usual round of media interviews. 'When the 1973 general election results were available and it was clear he was going to be Taoiseach Liam disappeared,' says Richie Ryan. 'The media just couldn't find him and the media are very good at finding people. I know where he was but he had disappeared because he wanted to take his own counsel.'

It was an advance warning about his style of leadership in government.

12

TAOISEACH AT LAST

WITH the election won Cosgrave had to pick his cabinet and his very first move was one which cemented the loyalty of the Labour Party for the duration of the Government. The issue was the number of cabinet seats for each of the two coalition parties. On a proportional basis Fine Gael were entitled to eleven and Labour four but Brendan Corish decided to make a pitch for five cabinet positions.

'We were going to ask for five instead of four,' recalls Brendan Halligan. 'I had constructed about ten different mathematical formulas to prove the impossible before a meeting arranged between them [Corish and Cosgrave] on the Monday after the election. Corish had come up the previous day and we had spent Sunday evening working out the impossible. We went at it again the next morning and later we had lunch in Snaffles. I felt like a manager putting a boxer into the ring. Off he went and I went away to chew my fingers to the bone and expected to be waiting until five or six o'clock in the evening.'

Instead Corish came back half an hour later and retailed to an astonished Halligan how, before he had a chance to open his mouth, Cosgrave had said: 'Five seats Brendan and you can have the Department of Finance, but if you don't take it yourself we will have it.' With the numbers decided the question then arose as to which departments each party would get. The offer of Finance to Labour on condition that Corish himself took it was a big surprise to the junior coalition party. It had always been an article of faith with Labour that getting Finance was the ultimate goal of Labour in government but Corish simply refused to take it. Brendan Halligan and other senior Labour figures tried to persuade him but he was adamant.

'I tried to persuade him without great enthusiasm to take it but he rightly said "I am not a Minister for Finance. I am not having it." Of course we expected Garret FitzGerald to get it, as Garret did himself.'

With Corish's refusal Labour missed the opportunity, or given what was to happen, some might say the liability, of Finance. It was not until almost 22 years later with the formation of the rainbow coalition with John Bruton as Taoiseach that Labour obtained Finance for the first time in the history of the State.

With Finance ruled out Corish looked for Industry and Commerce, Posts and Telegraphs, Labour, Local Government and he asked that two other departments, Health and Social Welfare be amalgamated into one department which he wanted for himself. After some consideration Cosgrave agreed to merge the two departments and he conceded the other portfolios requested by Labour. Cosgrave himself wanted to keep the security Ministries of Justice and Defence for Fine Gael. He also wanted Agriculture because of the antipathy between Labour and the farmers and was equally wary of giving Labour Education because of the potential rows with the Catholic Church. As it happened the Fine Gael and Labour priorities were compatible and there was only one serious row about dividing up the cabinet positions. After the agreement was reached Cosgrave came under pressure from some of his own people not to give Industry and Commerce to Labour. Before they took office the British prime minister, Edward Heath, invited Cosgrave and Corish over to London for a briefing on Northern Ireland policy in advance of a White Paper to be published by the British side.

It was clearly understood by both coalition leaders that Cosgrave would pick the Fine Gael Ministers and Corish the Labour ones, even though the constitutional theory is that all Ministerial appointments are the prerogative of the Taoiseach. The two men went about their task in very different ways. Cosgrave, typically, adopted a quirky approach. Over a period of days he called senior party figures to his room and asked them if they were willing to serve, without specifying which department. When they said yes they were given no further information and none of them, with the exception of Richie Ryan, knew with certainty what portfolios they were getting until the Taoiseach read out their names and departments in the Dáil.

'I think I was possibly the only future Minister who was consulted beforehand,' recalls Ryan. Cosgrave called him to his office and said. 'I want to make you Minister for Finance.' Ryan's initial response was one of shock. 'Oh good lord, I haven't done economics since I was a student and everybody is expecting Garret to get Finance,' said an anxious Ryan.

'I can't see any reason why you would make me Minister for Finance,' he persisted. 'I am doing it because I respect your judgement,' was Cosgrave's reply. Ryan asked for 24 hours to think about it and went back to Cosgrave the following morning and repeated his reservations. 'You were very kind saying you respected my judgement but these there are a number of reasons why I should not be Minister for Finance,' said Ryan but Cosgrave was having none of it and eventually Richie Ryan accepted the position.

FitzGerald has written that the only inkling about his future came a week after the election when Cosgrave asked him, without prejudice, which Government post he would prefer.

'I said I would be happy to continue in Finance, which I had been understudying as shadow Minister, but was, of course, prepared to accept whatever he might propose. He responded by saying that it would either be Finance or another senior post, I asked which other senior post he was thinking of; he hesitated, and then said, perhaps understandably, that he would prefer to leave that over.'

It was not until the morning of 14 March, the day the Dáil was due to meet to elect Cosgrave Taoiseach, that FitzGerald got the first hint that he was getting Foreign Affairs and not Finance as he had expected.

'I was on my way to Leinster House when I passed a friend from the Department of Foreign Affairs, who said out of the corner of her mouth: "Welcome to Iveagh House". Shortly afterwards in the restaurant at lunchtime Brendan Corish, the Labour leader, called me over and told me not to be too disappointed if I were not appointed to Finance. "What's the alternative?" I asked him. "It could be Foreign Affairs," he replied.'

Only after Cosgrave's election as Taoiseach by the Dáil did the Fine Gael Ministers know for certain that they were in the cabinet. Cosgrave summoned all his team to his office at 5.30 p.m. FitzGerald remembers the scene: 'I waited in the corridor outside, expecting that we would be called in one by one, but at 5.35 p.m. I was asked to join others inside. As I entered, Liam Cosgrave stepped forward, shook my hand and said, "Foreign Affairs. Is that all right?" I assented.' FitzGerald's wife, Joan, burst into tears in the public gallery when the appointment was announced because she was afraid of flying and hated the idea of the travel her husband would have to undertake.

Pat Cooney was left in an even more uncertain position than FitzGerald. Cosgrave didn't even tell him he was going to be in the cabinet until the 5.30 p.m. meeting and he was in a fraught mood on the day of Cosgrave's election. Brendan Halligan recalls:

'Cosgrave's style came out very differently from Brendan's. Whereas Brendan told the other four that they were in the cabinet and the department they were going to get, Cosgrave just simply asked "Will you serve?" to which the answer was "yes." And then there was a grunt and the individual didn't know what it was he was getting. He told Paddy Cooney last and he kept Paddy Cooney waiting up to less than half an hour before going into the Chamber. I told Cooney. I said "Sit down for Christ's sake and just take it easy. You are the Minister for Justice," but Cooney just didn't believe it. Now there is a difference in style.'

FitzGerald has a similar recollection:

'Just three months earlier Pat Cooney, together with Tom O'Higgins, Jim Dooge and myself had led the opposition to the Offences Against the State (Amendment) Bill that had almost cost Liam Cosgrave the leadership of the party. Pat Cooney's description of that Bill as comparable only to repressive legislation in South Africa, and his stance at that time on liberal issues can scarcely have recommended him to his leader for this portfolio. True, in the years that followed Pat Cooney moved to the right, but that was hardly predictable in March 1973.'

The switching of FitzGerald and Ryan caused a lot of surprise in political circles and was much commented on by the media. Cosgrave has refused to be drawn on why he didn't appoint FitzGerald to Finance but it appears that he simply did not trust FitzGerald's judgement.

Cosgrave told Ursula Halligan he made his decision on the basis that Ryan had more experience of Finance and FitzGerald more experience of Foreign Affairs.

'He [FitzGerald] had no practical experience of financial matters although he had been a lecturer in university. His experience in the Dáil was much more limited than Richie Ryan's. He was only four years in the Dáil — in fact he wasn't even four. Before that he was a few years in the Seanad, whereas Richie Ryan had been in the Dáil since 1959. It's true that he had been shadow spokesman for Finance for a short time, but it's quite a different thing to be shadow spokesman and the real thing.'

What to do with Declan Costello was another problem for Cosgrave. Costello came back into the Dáil in 1973 having opted out of electoral politics in 1969 and he expected a place at cabinet. Cosgrave was reluctant to appoint him despite pleas on his behalf from senior party figures. One story at the time was that John A. Costello personally pleaded with Cosgrave to give Declan a cabinet position but the Taoiseach-elect simply refused. He eventually offered him the position of Attorney General but only after it had been turned down by Kevin Liston.

Costello's appointment as Attorney General was widely regarded on the liberal wing of Fine Gael as an attempt by Cosgrave to limit his power and influence. Costello admitted later that he would have liked a senior Ministry but maintains that he was pleased enough with his appointment. It was only afterwards when he learned in the job how limited his powers were that he became disillusioned.

Another striking feature of Costello's appointment is that when Cosgrave offered him the Attorney General's position he expressed the view that the Attorney should not continue his practice at the bar, as had been the norm, but should devote himself fulltime to his office. On being offered the job and informed of the conditions Costello requested time to come to a decision but a few days later accepted.

FitzGerald has an interesting observation on the portfolios eventually offered to himself and Costello:

'He could also have been influenced by memories of his father's Cumann na nGaedheal government of the 1920s, in which my father had served as Minister for External Affairs until 1927; in this connection it may be significant that Declan Costello, who had returned to politics in this election after a period of withdrawal for a combination of health and political reasons, was simultaneously appointed to the post of Attorney General, which his father, John A. Costello, held under W.T. Cosgrave in the latter period of that first government.'

Cosgrave's other rival in the party, who also held an historic Fine Gael name, was Tom O'Higgins but the 1973 election had come at the worst possible time for him. Already selected as the Fine Gael presidential candidate he decided that he could not credibly run for the Dáil in 1973 and as a result he forfeited a senior cabinet position and possibly the future leadership of the party as well.

Apart from FitzGerald and Costello the rest of the Fine Gael team was relatively easy to pick. With Richie Ryan in the key post of Finance other stalwarts like Mark Clinton and Paddy Donegan were slotted into Agriculture and Defence, respectively. Dick Burke got Education, which Cosgrave was adamant should go to Fine Gael. Tom Fitzpatrick was offered Justice but turned it down and eventually settled for Lands while relative newcomer, Peter Barry, was the surprise choice being elevated to Transport and Power. Tom O'Donnell was the final member of the Fine Gael team in the Department of the Gaeltacht. John Kelly was appointed chief whip.

On the Labour side Corish took Health and Social Welfare and appointed Conor Cruise O'Brien to Posts and Telegraphs, Keating to Industry and Commerce, Michael O'Leary to Labour and Jimmy Tully to Local Government. An extra responsibility that was given to Cruise O'Brien was responsibility for the Government Information Service. Richie Ryan recalls: 'The fact that the Cruiser was chosen for that job always intrigued me because I wouldn't have blamed Cosgrave if he felt that a slant might have been put on things by the Cruiser but the Cruiser was extremely loyal and always said what was agreed to be said.'

Cosgrave says that there were a number of factors which influenced his selection with competence and experience playing a large part as well as geographical location.

'It was a mixture of all three; you look for a competent person with experience for instance someone like Richie Ryan who was a long time in the Dáil and was a competent performer with a lot of experience at home and abroad. Then you select people whom you know have sound judgement, I'm thinking of a person offhand like Mark Clinton who again had vast experience. Then you have to consider regional distribution because it is important that a region not only is represented but feels itself represented. Again you must make it a mixture of competence, a man like Peter Barry in Cork, a very experienced businessman who also represents Cork and the people from the west like Henry Kenny, who again was an exceptionally able person but wasn't recognised as such until he got the position.'

Cosgrave claims that the personal loyalty to himself of those chosen was not a major issue affecting his selection. Support for him during the heaves against his leadership was not of itself a guarantee of a position unless the person also had the necessary qualities for the job.

'Commentators who have written on this matter either did not know or ignored the facts. I worked with the members of the party irrespective of whether they voted for me or not. The records will show that deputies were appointed to the front bench and eventually appointed to Ministerial positions on the same basis.'

Like virtually all Taoisigh of modern times, with the exception of Albert Reynolds, Cosgrave picked his Fine Gael cabinet team in such a way that both wings of the party were represented. Like most wise politicians he knew that the party as a whole had to be satisfied with the selection and if that meant appointing some people he did not like or necessarily agree with that was politics.

Cosgrave exercised the Taoiseach's prerogative of selecting his cabinet without prior consultation with anyone and he is still happy that he picked the best team available.

'From memory, I asked deputies whom I considered suitable for appointment as Ministers to call and see me in my room. No one offered a position refused or demurred to the position offered.'

He also said that some of the appointments that caused most surprise in the media did so only because journalists were not aware of their experience and abilities.

'I was working with the lot of them for years. A lot of people probably had reservations about some of the appointments because they didn't know them. They weren't conspicuous in the comment of the media or the press but, in fact, well I take again a person like Mark Clinton, everybody recognises he was an outstanding Minister for Agriculture. When he was selected a lot of people would have had great doubts about him mainly because they didn't know he was involved in running a very huge outfit in Peamount and on top of that had been for a long time on the Dublin County Council and the Hospital boards. I think he turned out very well.'

Cosgrave took his time about putting his cabinet team together but by the morning of 14 March, when the Dáil was due to meet to elect a new Taoiseach, all the Ministers, with the exception of Cooney, knew at least that they were in the cabinet, even if they did not know what post they were getting.

Peter Barry recalls how he was offered a post.

'I guessed I would be offered a job and Liam rings up and says simply "Hello. Are you available?" Naturally I told him I was and said I would like something on the economic side of things, if that were possible. I didn't find out until the day that I was getting Transport and Power. They were the days that everybody including Labour, accepted that

Fine Gael had to have Justice, Defence and Finance. That was an unwritten but accepted law.

'I was in the Dáil with my supporters having a drink and the ushers were flying around and one of them came to me and told me the Taoiseach wanted me and to go up immediately. So I went up anyway and he asked me to do Transport and Power and he told me I was involved. He said "it is going to be very busy for you because I won't be able to give you a parliamentary secretary. You will have to do it on your own." It was a big department covering areas like tourism, transport, aviation and energy. I said "thank you very much Mr Cosgrave that is fine" but I didn't even know where the department was so I went out and had some more drink, naturally enough.'

Barry remembers going up to the department the following morning and making a pleasant and surprising discovery. 'Up over the door of the department is a woman's face, representing the face of Ireland. I found out that my own mother was the model for that back in the 1930s. It was built by Boyd Barrett of Cork and the sculptor used my mother as a model so she was up there on the top of that building and I was now the Minister.'

When the Dáil met that afternoon Brendan Corish proposed Liam Cosgrave for Taoiseach and the nomination was seconded by Maurice Dockrell. Cosgrave was elected by 72 votes to 70 after Lynch was defeated by 73 to 69. Blaney voted no to both nominations.

Cosgrave said little in the Dáil immediately after his appointment but Lynch made a point about the election.

'It is fair to say that on this occasion the people had an alternative. At least the people knew in advance that an alternative coalition government was available. Now they have given that coalition a majority, small thought it may be. They have also given them a mandate.'

The Dáil adjourned for a few hours, Cosgrave summoned his cabinet and they headed for Áras an Uachtaráin to get their seals of office from the President. Garret FitzGerald recalled that because of the uncertainty about when they were leaving none of the new Ministers had anything to eat all day before leaving for the Park.

'I was in the last car with Pat Cooney. Along the quays we saw a sweet shop; we stopped the car and I dashed in to buy several bars of chocolate from an astonished shopkeeper. We were still dining off them when we arrived at the Áras. After the formal proceedings we held, in accordance with custom, our first cabinet meeting at a table in the Áras, which had been that of the first government of which my father had been a member.'

After coming back from the Park Cosgrave announced his Ministerial team to the Dáil. Typically, Jack Lynch spoke for twice as long in opposing the new Government as Cosgrave did in defending it. Lynch quoted a famous phrase from Lemass in 1948 who told Costello on the formation of the first Inter-Party Government. 'We are leaving you this country in good shape ... Make sure that you hand it back that way.' Cosgrave, who was there for the original comment in 1948, immediately hit back. 'I think the real reason why the country is all right is that it has got rid of a Fianna Fáil government.'

The new Taoiseach then went on to outline his priorities.

> 'This Government was founded in a spirit of cooperation and I believe that spirit of cooperation will influence their work and guide their activities.'

He went on to add that they would seek the cooperation of the trade unions, the employers, the farmers and vocational interests with a view to greater industrial harmony and higher living standards.

Turning to Northern Ireland Cosgrave then enunciated two principles which are still the basis for this state's approach to the north.

> 'There must be justice for the minority in the Six Counties and this means the establishment of institutions which through the operation of power-sharing will obtain and will be accepted. There must be direction by peaceful means for a genuine union of the Irish people. There must be co-operation through a Council of Ireland of the two parts of the island for the social, economic and political betterment of all our people ... We must also recognise that Ireland has a European and a British dimension. God has interlocked these two Western islands and they are now set on a new career of progress and development in the context of Europe.'

He also had a cut at Fianna Fáil for some of the Republican rhetoric it had come out with during the election campaign.

> 'I believe one of the clear decisions of the electorate in this election, whether they voted for the present government or the outgoing government, was that a majority of the people, irrespective of party, rejected voices from the past counselling extremism, doctrinaire solutions and violent ways as a method of solving the problems of the present or the future.'

On the calibre of his government Cosgrave was proud and sardonic at the same time.

'This Government has been described as one of many talents and commentators and informed writers have been unanimous in their speculation on at least a minority of the members who would form the team. They all agree that it is a talented team, I need hardly say that I am glad to have got a place on it.'

The Dáil adjourned for two weeks and when it met again the names of the seven parliamentary secretaries were announced. There were five Fine Gael and two Labour junior Ministers. One of the Fine Gael appointments was the 25-year-old Young Tiger, John Bruton.

In his first full Dáil day as Taoiseach on 28 March Cosgrave handled the order of business and questions with the crispness and brevity which were his trade marks. He never used two words where one would do and he only used one if it was absolutely necessary.

His attitude to coalition was aptly demonstrated at a press conference at the beginning of the election campaign. He was asked what he would do if there was a serious row between Fine Gael and Labour. Refusing to contemplate such a prospect, he asked the assembled political correspondents. 'Do you remember Boss Croker's definition of an honest man? A man who when he is bought stays bought.' As far as he was concerned a deal had been done and it would stick.

13

COSGRAVE THE MAN

THE MAN who occupied the Taoiseach's office often appeared to the public as a cold and remote character. He hated appearing on television and was usually uncomfortable with the media. Yet Liam Cosgrave inspired intense loyalty not only among die-hard Fine Gael supporters but also among the Labour Ministers who served him. Everybody who worked with him in government — Ministers, deputies and civil servants — still remark on his personal kindness and courtesy.

'He was an exceptionally decent man, very nice to work for with tremendous concern for his staff,' says Ted Nealon who served as Government press secretary from 1975 to 1977. 'One good example of that in those days, when it was a great perk to go on a foreign trip, was that he would always bring a different member of staff from his own private office so that everybody would get a turn.'

Brendan Halligan echoes this view:

'Cosgrave was an intensely courteous man in personal relationships. For example he would always be most assiduous in knowing about your family and inquiring about them in a way you knew was genuine. Phyllis Corish liked him very much which mattered a great deal. A politician's spouse is very important and has enormous influence. She liked Cosgrave and trusted him.'

One of his own TDs, Liam Burke, also remarked on Cosgrave's courtesy:

'Cosgrave was a marvelous man. A man of great honesty, great integrity. I don't think he knew what it was to tell a lie. While I have great respect for the present Fine Gael leader, John Bruton, I would have to say that Liam was the leader of our party who impressed me most. I think he was the most humane man I ever met in public life.'

John Bruton had his own experiences of great personal kindness. He was a junior Minister in Education as well as Industry and Commerce and on one occasion had to take a stream of Dáil questions when both his senior Ministers were away.

'A lot of questions were on subjects I knew nothing about because as junior Minister I wasn't *au fait* with the whole range of issues. Of course Fianna Fáil were quite indignant that neither Minister was there and were anxious to make little of my efforts. I got into trouble on a few occasions when I wasn't able to answer questions and I got a bit tongue tied at one point. Apart from coming out of the House in a cold sweat, I remember the following day John Healy who used to write a very penetrating, and sometimes slightly unkind, column on the front page of *The Irish Times* said this was my worst performance ever and he went on to say that I wasn't the brightest.

'I was in my office the following morning when I read this. I was feeling really down in the dumps when the phone rang and I was told the Taoiseach was on the line. I assumed that he had been reading *The Irish Times* too and had decided that he needed brighter people than me in his Government. So I was somewhat hesitant lifting up the phone. But Liam Cosgrave said, "Don't worry about that stuff in the papers. You are doing a good job so keep at it and forget about the papers." Now what really struck me about that was the kindness the Taoiseach would show to a very junior person like me who didn't count for much in the ordinary things in government. It was really very touching because it wasn't as if he was ringing me up every morning. I probably hadn't spoken to him for three or four months before that.'

Politicians who didn't always agree with him still respected Cosgrave on a personal level. His Labour constituency colleague Barry Desmond says:

'On some crucial moral and social issues Liam Cosgrave and myself stood at quite different ends of the argument. Liam accepted without question the Pope's teaching on issues such as contraception and divorce. On social questions like equality legislation he was equally conservative. On those issues his Catholic beliefs took absolute precedence and on other important developments such as the establishment of multi-denominational education in Dun Laoghaire we also parted company. And yet, unlike Noel Browne, for example, he was never personally offensive about our deeply-held different views.'

'Again, through the years, people who met Cosgrave on a man-to-man basis were always quite surprised to find such a gentle, humorous, kind person. He wasn't the cold fish that he often appeared,' says Richie Ryan. 'Television didn't suit Liam. He didn't like television and he would admit that. I remember on one occasion preparing for a party political broadcast and, knowing Liam's detestation of television, I took him to lunch in the Montrose Hotel and gave him a few good stiff whiskeys to relax before we went into RTE. After the lunch Liam was in great form, and we went up to Montrose to do the party political broadcast feeling very relaxed. Well the day went off fine and this smiling confident man was a different Liam Cosgrave to the one people usually saw. But some gremlins got into the system towards the end of the recording and the whole thing had to be scratched and done again. By the third re-run the beneficial effect of the whiskey had worn off. And he came over as a terribly fierce man.'

Whiskey was always Cosgrave's drink. Even with a meal he preferred whiskey to wine and rarely touched any other form of alcoholic drink. In contrast to many politicians who develop unhealthy life-styles and bad eating habits because of their long and unsocial working hours Cosgrave was always careful about what he ate and drank. 'He was a most frugal eater and looked after himself extremely well,' says Peter Barry. 'He was very fit and never smoked. I remember as a Minister having lunch and he would come in and have a plate of fruit. It was a pleasure to have him to dinner, chambers of commerce used to say, because he would be gone at a quarter to 11 and you didn't have to look after him to 2 o'clock in the morning. Yet he was great crack after a couple of half ones.'

Despite his enormous responsibilities Cosgrave never became obsessed by politics like so many of his colleagues then, and now, who allow the business to consume their entire lives. While he was Taoiseach he went home to have lunch with his wife, Vera, in Beechpark virtually every day. He left Government Buildings at 12.45 p.m. and returned shortly after 2 p.m. That time was sacrosanct and nobody could contact him unless the business was extremely urgent.

In fact he protected his privacy to such an extraordinary extent that none of his cabinet Ministers were given his home telephone number. If they wished to contact Cosgrave at home they had to ring Dermot Nally, the assistant secretary of the Taoiseach's Department and if Nally decided the matter was of sufficient urgency he would ring the Taoiseach.

'He was a man who got up in the morning and did his day's work and went to bed at night and got up in the morning again. His view would be that you had obligations and you didn't want to be theorising too much. Your job was to run the country so you ran it. Your first duty was to secure the State against threats to its security. These were not simplistic but were very basic principles,' says Peter Barry.

'Liam was a very quiet man,' says Richie Ryan. 'I had no more access to Liam's home than other Ministers. We didn't have Liam's home number. The cabinet sincerely believed that I was the only one who had the number but it wasn't true. The only one who did have it was Comdt. Jim Sanfey. He lived on Templeogue Road near me and Liam knew that I could reach him through Jim if the matter was urgent. I did have Liam's private number before and after we were in government but Liam liked his private life and he liked to cut off. He went home for lunch as well.'

'He believed in preserving his privacy and believed other people were entitled to the same privacy. When I was working there he had to be contacted through his private secretary, Frank Murray, or through Dermot Nally, the assistant secretary,' recalls Ted Nealon.

A striking feature of his personality was that he was a man of few words. 'He didn't make speeches in cabinet. In fact he didn't care much for speeches at all, even in the Dáil,' says Cruise O'Brien. 'He had a horror of rhetoric. Indeed the first time I ever heard him say anything was when I was an official during his time in External Affairs in the 1950s. Our estimate was being debated in the Dáil and Cosgrave came out into the curved corridor where officials wait. The senior official from the department asked "And who is talking now?" "So and so of Fianna Fáil," replied Cosgrave. "What is he saying?" "Oh, dying for Ireland, as usual," remarked Cosgrave. A lot of the man is in that little vignette. I took rather a liking to him from that time on.'

Even though he was politically close to Cosgrave, Barry did not often socialise with him. 'I don't know anybody who was ever in his house. Even his Ministers in the government didn't have his telephone number. You rang Dermot Nally if you wanted him at weekends. There was this book of numbers with a star opposite Cosgrave's name and you rang Dermot Nally and he decided it was important enough to contact the Taoiseach.'

He was a man of such few words that his opponents in the Dáil often found it difficult to get to grips with him. His classic answer to one convoluted parliamentary question was: 'Since the first part of the Deputy's question is in the negative the second part of the question doesn't arise.' His advice to his Ministers and those who worked for him was to say as little as possible.

'Despite his taciturn nature he is a man of extraordinary wit who really appreciated wit and was a very witty man himself,' says Nealon. 'He loved the old chat and that was totally different from the public perception of him. For instance I often thought that he would be happiest of all the day he wasn't mentioned in the papers at all. It is an amazing contrast to current politics where everybody is out for maximum exposure. He generated great loyalty and great respect from the people in both parties of the coalition at that time.'

He could take a joke as well as deliver it. His first Government press secretary, Muiris Mac Conghail, remembers being in his office on one occasion when Michael O'Leary, who was a great mimic, was imitating the Taoiseach. 'He was in full flight when Liam Cosgrave stuck his head around the door and stood there silently and smiled. He could take a joke and in some respects it was a government of fun even though they had enormous problems.'

Cosgrave's relations with Corish were the key to the successful operation of his Government. Despite their differences during the 1960s they trusted each other completely and that trust was the rock on which the coalition was built. 'Here was a man who wasn't an intellectual, who presided over a cabinet of intellectuals,' says Mac Conghail. 'Cosgrave was a man of practical politics who established a very close relationship with Brendan Corish. Those two actually formed the nature of that Government in many ways. They were practical people who weren't great intellectuals, who didn't have an awful lot to say and what they had to say they said to each other. Although it was a cabinet of all the talents those two guys were the ones in charge. What they had going for them was the shared experience of government 16 years earlier and the fact that they were not people who desperately wanted to be in office. They won office on the 14-point plan. And there was such a relief in the country generally that there had been a change of government after 16 years that they got an enormous grace from the public.'

Cosgrave's lack of airs and graces and his down-to-earth practicality were attractive and effective traits in a political leader. Mac Conghail remembers Cosgrave's first EEC summit in Denmark at which there was a row over whether the Arab nations would be allowed to address the meeting. Cosgrave's intervention was typical. 'With the lights

Liam Cosgrave as an Army officer in 1943.

W.T. and Liam at the Vatican in 1950 with J.J. Walsh.

Parliamentary Secretary, 1951.

Minister for External Affairs arriving home from New York at Shannon in 1956.

Addressing an election meeting outside the GPO in 1954.

At the first day of the Horse Show with children Mary and Liam Jr,
in the early 1960s.

At his father's grave in 1965 with his wife and children.
Also in the picture: the then Minister for Finance, Jack Lynch, and the
Minister for Industry and Commerce, Paddy Hillery.

Called to the Inner Bar.

The leader of the Opposition and the Taoiseach, Seán Lemass, at a Mass for the Civil War dead in 1966.

Fine Gael front bench, 1965. Back row, left to right: Declan Costello, Tom Fitzpatrick, Mark Clinton, Paddy Donegan, Michael O'Higgins, Pa O'Donnell, Paddy Lindsay and Gerry L'Estrange. Front row: Maurice Dockrell, Gerry Sweetman, Liam Cosgrave, Tom O'Higgins and Paddy Harte.

Dancing with wife Vera.

With Richie Ryan at the Árd Fheis, 1970.

*At the election count in Dun Laoghaire town hall with Labour's
Barry Desmond, 1973.*

Fine Gael front bench 1972. Back row from left: Michael Begley, Pat Cooney, Gerry L'Estrange, Peter Barry, Paddy Hagan, Dick Burke, Tom O'Donnell, Donal Creed, Eddie Collins, Godfrey Timmins and John Bruton. Front Row: Tom Fitzpatrick, Richie Ryan, Tom O'Higgins, Liam Cosgrave, Garret FitzGerald, Paddy Donegan and Mark Clinton.

1973 Cabinet – Fine Gael/Labour Coalition

Back Row (L/R) T.J. Fitzpatrick, Michael O'Leary, Tom O'Donnell, Garret FitzGerald, Conor Cruise O'Brien, Dick Burke, Peter Barry, Justin Keating, Paddy Cooney, Declan Costello.

Front Row (L/R): Jimmy Tully, Paddy Donegan, Liam Cosgrave, President Eamon de Valera, Brendan Corish, Richie Ryan, Mark Clinton.

President de Valera presents the seal of office to Liam Cosgrave in March 1973.

With Garret FitzGerald, Margaret Thatcher, leader of the Conservative Party, Brendan Corish and Conservative Northern Ireland spokesman, Airey Neave, in 1976. Airey Neave was later murdered by the INLA.

The Taoiseach and his family outside the Dáil. From left: Ciarain, Mary, Liam, Vera and Liam Jr.

Addressing a joint session of the US Congress on St Patrick's Day, 1976.

The Taoiseach gets a ride in an armoured car.

Meeting at Hillsborough of Irish Government Ministers and members of the Northern Ireland Executive, 1974.

Cosgrave meets Brian Faulkner at Baldonnell in 1974.

Sipping the stirrup cup at the South County Dublin Hunt with daughter Mary in 1974.

With British Prime Minister, Ted Heath, and the three Northern party leaders who headed the Executive, Oliver Napier, Brian Faulkner and Gerry Fitt.

At the launch of the late Paddy Lindsay's memoirs in 1992 with Lindsay and Jack Lynch.

Three generations. With son Liam Jr, his wife Joan and grandson, Barry.

going out all over western Europe surely we can meet these guys,' he said.

Mac Conghail developed a great regard for Cosgrave.

'He was a man of great practical common sense. He would never have seen himself as a great political philosopher. He wouldn't have seen himself in the role that Garret FitzGerald saw himself, as being somebody who wanted to make his mark. He saw himself as a man who had taken on a great task and it was a matter of honour to do it.

'This man was not an intellectual but he was a fine politician. He had wide contacts over a long period; he had a great training first as a parliamentary secretary and then as a Minister and he also had the wisdom his father passed on to him.'

One incident which is still recalled by politicians from the 1970s and political journalists who were around at the time is the day a scare developed in Leinster House about a cabinet crisis. 'The word went around after lunch after a tetchy cabinet meeting that Cosgrave and Corish had adjourned for a crisis session. They were together for so long in the Taoiseach's office that rumours began to circulate about the break-up of the coalition. All the political correspondents had convinced themselves there was a Government crisis,' recalls Halligan. 'Everybody was sure the game was up. The story suddenly swept the place. They had gone off together, nobody could get to them, it must be very serious and then of course you must find a justification for it. I walked into Leinster House in the middle of all this and I had guys jumping on me the minute I walked in the door. I went up and hammered away at the door of the Taoiseach's office and when I eventually got in I found the two boys were sitting there with a bottle of whiskey and looking at the horse racing from Cheltenham on the television. I eventually told them what everybody was saying and they were both just in fits of laughter. Now that sort of easy camaraderie was very important.'

Mac Conghail also remembers the bond between Taoiseach and Tánaiste and their similar approach to life.

'While Cosgrave was a man who had come to high office from a family which had experienced high office I think he saw himself as a servant carrying a grave burden. He tried to lighten that burden every now and then. Himself and Corish were interested in racing, they spent a lot of time together as friends and indeed that partnership between the pair of them, of two disinterested people in public office was very important.'

Racing has always been a passion for Liam Cosgrave, as it was for his father before him. Ministers recall that the racing page of the *Irish Independent* was the only element of the media that he really cared about. 'He had a way of folding up the racing page and marking it that was quite distinctive. He marked his cabinet papers in the same way and it was not unusual for him to come to a cabinet meeting with the racing page wedged in between the other documents. There were even occasions, when the discussion was getting tedious with Garret going on a bit, when he would slip out the racing page and study the form,' says a former colleague.

As well as being interested in horse racing he also kept horses and was a good rider. Dermot Mullane of RTE remembers going up to his house in Beechpark on the morning Cosgrave was due to be elected Taoiseach. Mullane expected to find the Taoiseach-to-be preparing his speech to the Dáil later in the day but instead he found him mucking out the stables. Liam Cosgrave saw no reason why his elevation to high office should distract himself from his everyday routine.

During his career Cosgrave received a mixed press and he was never the darling of the media. He was always polite to journalists but he didn't relax with them, rarely gave them a quotable quote and said as little as possible. 'I wrote plenty of critical stuff about his Government but he never, ever uttered a word of complaint when he met me,' recalls Dick Walsh. Michael Mills also recalls Cosgrave's courtesy and consideration. 'He would always inquire after any of our colleagues who was ill and I distinctly remember him asking after my wife Brid when she was in hospital. He did it in a way you knew was genuine.' *Irish Times* columnist John Healy was generally very critical of Cosgrave and came up with the dismissive nickname 'Little Liam' for him but Cosgrave showed no resentment. Generally, though he only talked to journalists when it was strictly necessary on occasions like Sunningdale or European summits. Ted Nealon recalls one summit in Rome.

> 'He loved Rome. Of all the places that he went to he had a tremendous knowledge of Rome because he had been in it many times. He was always in a hurry home from any capital he went to but he was never in a hurry home from Rome. What he wanted to do was share his pleasure in Rome with anyone in the party. One example of it was a summit meeting there. The political correspondents Chris Glennon, Michael Mills, Dick Walsh and Seán Duignan were there to cover it. Now naturally most politicians like to get the maximum publicity on a major visit like this. But of course he never had any

great interest in publicity. I remember him at a reception in the Irish Embassy in Rome the night before the summit started telling the political correspondents about the tremendous sights they should see and he suggested where they should go.

'Suddenly he looked at them and he says "what are you doing tomorrow?" And they said "well, we are covering the summit all day." He said "forget about that, there'll be nothing in it. I'll give you my car and you can go and see the sights instead." He paid no heed to the publicity he might lose as a result. He just wanted these people to share his pleasure in the sights of Rome.'

Cosgrave always remained close to his constituents and never forgot the fact that he was Taoiseach because he had been elected in the first place by the people of Dun Laoghaire. Long before Tip O'Neill coined the phrase he realised that all politics was local. Even as Taoiseach he would occasionally send official notices over to the political correspondents' room highlighting, not a matter of great national importance, but the fact that he had a school warden appointed for Rochestown Avenue or pedestrian traffic lights installed on the Kilmacud Road.

He did this, according to Mac Conghail, because he recognised that at the end of the day, his political strength came from the fact that he had served his own community and his constituency.

'I recall on one occasion being at the Elysée Palace at an important meeting when we were just about to take over the presidency of the European Community. It was a very long meeting and all the higher civil servants like myself were in the outer room, and all of our men were on their own. At the time a prolonged strike was going on in Blackrock Post Office and Cosgrave naturally took a great interest in this.

'Anyway after some hours a major-domo arrived out of the council room and summoned me over. "A message from your prime minister," he said handing me a note. As I opened it I was surrounded by other officials so I had to try and hide the contents but I need not have bothered. The note did not concern high European politics but simply read "Any news on the Blackrock post office strike?" On one level it was amusing but that was his strength, that he remembered where his mandate came from. Number one was Ireland of course but number two was his political base. His advice always to Ministers was to look after their constituencies because that was where they got their democratic mandate. He was very conscious of that and very proud of it.'

That awareness of his political base had another side which infuriated some of his liberal colleagues who believed Fine Gael should stand above the grubby business of political patronage.

Cosgrave believed in using the levers of power that were available to him and when it came to the employment of porters and other staff which are under the direct political patronage of the Taoiseach of the day, or appointments to state boards, Dun Laoghaire came first followed by Fine Gael.

Fianna Fáil had always distributed the spoils of office and Cosgrave was determined that during his term he would look after Fine Gael people who had been ignored for so long. A few years after he left office RTE wanted to do a documentary on Cosgrave and a researcher looking for subjects to interview contacted Alexis FitzGerald to ask who his friends were. 'They wouldn't be much use to you; they are all judges now,' FitzGerald is reputed to have replied.

Cosgrave's loyalty to those who served him in government, whether as Ministers, TDs or officials was a striking feature of the man. While even strong supporters of his believe that his loyalty might sometimes have been misplaced it was a central feature of his character.

'I remember in 1977 we lost office and I was quite young at that stage and again I had one of my rare conversations with him,' says John Bruton. 'He called me over and said "now you should look at all your options as far as your career is concerned. We mightn't be in office again for quite a while". His concern was personal, to ensure that everybody that he had anything to do with by bringing them into government wouldn't be at a loss or suffer for that. This was two weeks after he suffered his great defeat in 1977 and you might expect that his first concern would be brooding over the fact that the Fates had dealt him an unjust blow but, in fact, his concern was about others and what they were going to do.'

To this day people in politics recall his kindness to those who served with him in government long after 1977. He regularly visited Phyllis Corish in Wexford after her husband's death. He also called to see Frank Cluskey on a number of occasions during his final illness. 'Liam Cosgrave is a thorough gentleman and the kindest man you could meet,' says former Labour senator, Jack Harte.

'He was always very kind,' says Richie Ryan, who suffered a serious accident in 1995. 'When I was in hospital he was one of my best visitors. I think he never stayed more than ten minutes but I think he knew the importance of coming in and boosting the morale.'

Cosgrave's personal kindness has not always been reciprocated. 'When his son was defeated I sent Liam a note saying I was sorry,' says Ryan. 'I got a little note back thanking me and he said "you were one of the very few to express any thoughts on the matter".'

14

ALL THE TALENT

THE COSGRAVE coalition started office brightly and the 'Government of all the talents' got a very good press for the first few months. Its first Budget was hailed by *The Irish Times* as 'the greatest social welfare Budget of all time' and 'the most progressive budget yet'. Relations between the coalition parties were so good that in April at the Fine Gael Árd Fheis Oliver Flanagan was able to declare: 'Now the party of Arthur Griffith stands united with the party of James Connolly.'

The presidential election in May which pitted Tom O'Higgins against Erskine Childers also helped to bond the parties with Labour campaigning for the Fine Gael candidate. Despite this support O'Higgins failed to win and did not do nearly as well as he had against de Valera seven years earlier. The election result brought the Government down to earth. An event later in the year brought reality home in an even firmer fashion.

The Arab–Israeli war of October 1973 caused the first oil crisis. This led to massive inflation and unemployment right across the western world and it threw the Cosgrave Government's economic calculations out the window. Even before the oil crisis erupted on a complacent world inflation was becoming a big problem in Ireland with wage increases running at 20% by mid-1973. The oil crisis accelerated this trend and the result was a very sharp rise in prices.

'There was hardly any European Minister or government who survived at that time because of the totally new circumstances created by the oil crisis,' says Richie Ryan. 'A sudden sucking away of 20% of the economic activity and dynamism in the economy was an enormous shock and people didn't appreciate it. But if you look at the economic performance of OECD countries Ireland had the shortest duration of

economic turndown at that time. We did borrow because that was part
of the conventional economic wisdom of the OECD, World Bank and
the United Nations. They all said the western world shouldn't allow
their economies to suffer. At the same time every utterance of mine
and of the Government was that this was a short-term operation and
would only be continued until the economy started to turn up again.'

To cope with the crisis Ryan increased borrowing from 8% of GNP
in 1973 to 11% in 1974 and a massive 16% in 1975. However, in 1976
he hauled back to 11% and by 1977 it had been brought down to 9%.
One of the most difficult tasks the Government had was convincing
the trade unions to accept pay moderation at a time when inflation,
fuelled by wage increases, was proving the biggest problem in the
economy. The unions eventually agreed to a deal which saw wages
temporarily lagging behind inflation in return for food subsidies
which protected the worst off.

'I think in retrospect the economic policies of the Government
were in all the circumstances quite credible. The unprecedented oil
rise in 1973 hit this country, as it did most of the rest of the world, like
a whirlwind resulting in plans and assumptions already made having
to be drastically and quickly revised,' said Cosgrave. 'The moderate
wage agreement secured by the Government with the cooperation of
employers and unions was indeed remarkable. The maintenance to a
large extent of employment and the creating of many new jobs by the
IDA and others testify to the effectiveness of Government policy. At
the end of the period inflation was falling at a steady and continuing
rate and agriculture and industry were expanding. At the same time,
despite all the adverse effects of the oil price rise which permeated the
economy, over 100,000 new houses were constructed, an all-time
record for the State.'

The two coalition parties faced the oil crisis together and there was
just one moment of serious tension when Labour threatened to walk
out of Government over an attempt by the Department of Finance to
restrict Social Welfare increases. Conor Cruise O'Brien recalls that the
crisis developed in 1976 out of a statement by Richie Ryan that the
coalition Government should consider cutting children's allowances
and other social subsidies like school transport, food subsidies and
disability benefits. 'This was really pushing it. So Corish called on
Liam to summon an emergency meeting of the cabinet. It was the only
time he did this. Liam summoned it and Brendan announced on
behalf of the five of us Labour TDs that if this was decided on as

Government policy we were all going to resign. That was the only time the threat of resignation was used. It was used legitimately on a major issue of great importance for Labour. And Cosgrave said, "well in that case we won't abolish food subsidies". There was no cliffmanship.'

Brendan Halligan also remembers the incident but he believes the outcome displayed Cosgrave's skill as a government leader.

'For me that was the high point. It was a powerful piece of political management. Cosgrave did not give us everything we wanted but gave us enough that we could live with. From Richie's point of view Cosgrave made sure that while he did not get everything he wanted he still got something he could live with. Cosgrave had an instinctive understanding that we were coming to him because we were in real trouble and we wouldn't have come to him otherwise. This is the important point; when coalition works you don't go in every day complaining. You do it maybe once a year. You don't cry wolf so that when you do cry everybody knows that it is a wolf. Going in to him you knew you were going to be dealt with absolutely honestly and straightforwardly. I can't say anything more than that.'

In terms of protecting its social welfare constituency, Labour did very well during the Cosgrave coalition. Total welfare spending rose from £91.6 million in 1972–73 to £274.5 million four years later. Welfare expenditure as a percentage of gross national produce rose from 6.5 to 10.5%. Most benefits rose by 125%, well over the rate of increase in both wages and prices. The qualifying age for the old age pension was brought down from 70 to 66 and groups like unmarried mothers and prisoners wives received allowances for the first time. Cosgrave went on record after the start of the oil crisis to say that the poor were not going to bear the brunt of the problem and he was true to his word.

The political return to the coalition for all its concern for social welfare was absolutely zero. Richie Ryan recalls the tempestuous arguments he used to have with the late Frank Cluskey around the cabinet table over the scale of the welfare increases being sought by Labour. He chuckles at the memory of meeting Cluskey for the first time after the 1977 election debâcle. 'Jaysus Richie, you were right. You always said we'd get no fucking thanks for all the welfare increases,' was the Labour man's blunt assessment.

Another social achievement of the coalition was Jim Tully's determination to deliver a substantial increase in the number of new houses being built. The number jumped to an average of 25,000 new houses a year. In all 100,000 houses were built during the coalition's first four years, an increase of 50% in the public and private sectors. The removal of VAT from food in July 1975, was the fulfilment of another election promise. While it was widely welcomed at the time it didn't do much for the Government's long term popularity and in the long run helped to worsen the burden of tax on labour which was to become the millstone around the Irish economy's neck in the 1980s and 1990s.

Another superficially progressive move which ended up doing a lot of political damage to the coalition, particularly Fine Gael, was the introduction of a wealth tax. The notion of replacing the existing system of estate and death duties with some form of wealth tax was a pet project of Garret FitzGerald. He had unsuccessfully tried to have it incorporated in the 'Just Society' programme of 1965 and later failed to get it adopted by his Fine Gael front-bench colleagues in 1969. FitzGerald finally managed to get the idea incorporated into the Fine Gael–Labour election manifesto of 1973 and after the election the task of implementing it fell to Richie Ryan.

'What happened in relation to the wealth tax was that the promise in the 1973 manifesto was to abolish death duties and replace it with a wealth tax which would be paid on an annual basis,' says Ryan. 'Of course people conveniently forgot one half of the promise — that the death duties would be replaced by the wealth tax. Now when we had a look at the situation in government there were a few things that caused considerable concern to myself as Minister for Finance. One was that there was no example in the world of a wealth tax in a taxation system similar to Ireland. You had them in Germanic and Francophone countries but you didn't have any in countries like our own. So we had to start from the very beginning and see where we could go and how we would tackle it. The second point I had to consider was whether the introduction of it and talk about it would stimulate fears which would lead to a flow of money out of the country which obviously had to be of major concern. At the cabinet there were a number of Ministers who were very strongly against the wealth tax from the beginning but the majority were in favour of it.'

The economic sub-committee of the cabinet, set up in April 1973, set about examining the best way of implementing the measure. The committee, which was chaired by Ryan, also included FitzGerald, Clinton and Barry from Fine Gael and Keating and O'Leary from Labour. The deliberations of the sub-committee were dominated by a bitter wrangle between Ryan and FitzGerald which did nothing to improve their already sticky relationship.

'There were a number of meetings of the sub-committee and at the meetings the Department of Finance officials and the Revenue Commissioners pointed out the difficulties of introducing a wealth tax as proposed,' says Ryan. 'While not ruling out the prospects of a wealth tax, because the plus side was the abolition of death duties, I wanted to tie the two together. So I asked the department to prepare a memorandum which would indicate what the difficulties were. And I thought it appropriate to bring this to the notice of the Government so that we wouldn't rush into anything.

'There was another aspect of it. There were those in the cabinet who wanted the rate of tax to be at least 2.5% or even 3% but the indications from the Revenue Commissioners and the Department of Finance was that this was unrealistic. That it would in certain cases be a confiscatory tax as it wouldn't be paid out of income and it was at too high a level.'

FitzGerald viewed things differently. He says that the Department of Finance was vehemently opposed to the notion of reforming capital taxation and in effect made an extraordinary attempt to reverse Government policy by retaining inheritance tax and refusing to devise the kind of wealth tax promised by the coalition parties during the election campaign. Garret then prepared a draft report for the cabinet sub-committee in opposition to the views of Finance but Ryan expressed his disapproval of its contents. More particularly Richie took grave exception to a suggestion that Finance officials had acted without his approval in voicing reservations about the tax. FitzGerald modified his report but brought it along to a cabinet meeting and handed it around to his colleagues. This action was a clear breach of cabinet procedure which dictates that all memoranda have to be circulated in advance and have to go to Finance for observations about Budgetary implications.

Ryan was furious with FitzGerald. 'No paper can appear on a government agenda except under the name of the Minister who has responsibility and any proposal which involves cost has to have the view of the Minister for Finance attached,' he says. 'Now this document of Garret's contained allegations that the Department of Finance and the Revenue Commissioners were trying to frustrate the policies of the Government, a claim which I strongly rejected. I maintained that objective advice had been sought and was being given and if we were not manly and sensible enough to consider the pros and cons we were going to run ourselves into trouble.

'Then without any more ado or consultation with me Garret issued a circular to all Ministers before a Government meeting saying that the paper which was put down in my name had in fact been rejected by me at cabinet sub-committee and that I wasn't standing over it. And of course it wasn't even marked secret or confidential and it went around all departments. Here I was, according to Garret, rejecting or renouncing my own advisors. I was understandably annoyed at Garret saying that I wasn't standing over this thing. I circulated a note saying that there had been a serious breach of Government confidentiality by the Minister for Foreign Affairs who had made an allegation but that as I respected cabinet confidentiality I couldn't possibly say what did really happen at cabinet meetings.'

Cosgrave himself was neutral on the idea of a wealth tax but as the debate raged at the cabinet he came to the view that the measure might be counter-productive. He believed that needless public concern was being whipped up about an issue which would have no great impact on the exchequer one way or another and he privately favoured the option of replacing the wealth tax with a modified form of death duties which would not have the same emotive title but which would have got a contribution to the exchequer from the wealthiest people in the country. However, Garret FitzGerald and the Labour Ministers were adamant that they had to have their wealth tax and Cosgrave didn't raise any fundamental objection.

Eventually the Government agreed a White Paper on the wealth tax. Ryan recalls that this caused turmoil in business circles and says that within a few months the cabinet realised that the proposals were excessive. 'I did my best to have them watered down before the White Paper was published,' he says. 'I didn't succeed but later on the Government substantially modified the proposals and I announced them at a lunch. I believe the tax was fully justified but we introduced it in the middle of the oil crisis when there was enough deflation of confidence and there was a lot of fear that it wasn't the time to do it. I feared not only the electoral unpopularity but the economic effect it was going to have. The Central Bank set up a very careful monitoring operation at my request to watch the capital outflows and we were pleasantly surprised there wasn't any identifiable outflow which appeared to indicate that as introduced the business community accepted it. But it certainly created the impression that the

Government had a philosophy of "if it moves tax it and if it doesn't move tax it too".'

Halligan remembers the importance of the wealth tax to Labour:

'The debate was not with Cosgrave but with Richie Ryan. I think that here again it was Cosgrave's instinct that kept everybody on the rails. He understood very well that we in Labour had to have a wealth tax. That while it hadn't been agreed before the election, the internal dynamics of the Labour Party required a symbolic gesture. He also understood that he was in with a party which was not united on the matter of being in government. And he understood what certain key issues were symbolically as well as in reality and he understood that we had to have certain things. And if Cosgrave had said no to the wealth tax it wouldn't have happened.

'Now Richie Ryan fought the battle as Minister for Finance on the basis of Finance briefs as to why these taxes should not be introduced. But it also needs to be said that once the cabinet decided it was going ahead with the tax the ranks closed very rapidly and Ryan fought more manfully for these three bills than anybody else. He ended up being called "Red Richie" and "Richie Ruin". Of course Fianna Fáil fought so bitterly against the legislation it had to be guillotined through in the end. This had an interesting impact on the cabinet because it brought about greater coherence. Because our people said "Richie fought the fight he did against us in cabinet but look at the fight he fought outside." And Richie Ryan's stock went up enormously in the Labour Party.'

At a political and financial level the wealth tax was a disaster for the Government. Fianna Fáil's total opposition to the tax not only impressed the party's rich backers but perversely attracted popular support from an Irish electorate which has a pathological aversion to new forms of taxation, even if they don't have to pay it themselves. On the financial front the wealth tax brought in less revenue to the exchequer than the old estate duties. When Fianna Fáil returned to power after 1977 the wealth tax was abolished and the estate duties were not reimposed. The net effect was to further narrow the tax base and place a bigger burden on ordinary taxpayers.

Richie Ryan suffered politically as a result of the tight economic situation and became a target of Fianna Fáil criticism. Totally unaware of the battle that had gone on at cabinet over the wealth tax the media portrayed Ryan as the originator of the project and had no inkling of his reservations. 'When we were in government and the heat was turned on, particularly on me, Fianna Fáil had a poster saying "Get

Rid of Richie". It never upset me personally. I used to be amused oftentimes about the attacks.'

When the heat was at its worst Ryan spoke to Cosgrave and suggested a cabinet reshuffle. 'Look, the time has come when you should have a cabinet reshuffle. I don't want to be put out of cabinet but it might be worthwhile to shift me to another ministry, particularly as the economy is now recovering,' he told the Taoiseach. Cosgrave responded sharply. 'I won't do that. It would be unfair to you because you are being proved right.' Another factor with Cosgrave was that people would have expected FitzGerald to get Finance in any reshuffle and Cosgrave just didn't respect his judgement.

As well as being attacked by Fianna Fáil Ryan was pilloried on a satirical RTE television programme called *Hall's Pictorial Weekly*. The coalition as a whole took a drubbing on the programme but Ryan was singled out for special treatment. Remarkably Richie never saw it.

'I was invariably too busy but I heard plenty about it. And quite often when we would be assembling for a government meeting Ministers would be seething with anger at the Frank Hall programme which oftentimes was on the previous night. At the beginning of government meetings at the top of the agenda there is a run around the table to see if any Minister wants to raise a particular point. Again and again the issue would be Frank Hall's programme and how unfair it was and they would be demanding that Conor Cruise would intervene with RTE and get Frank Hall censured or curbed or dismissed. But Cosgrave and Conor would have no truck with that. They had the same view that you just didn't do that kind of thing. If you are in the kitchen you have to put up with the heat.'

Ryan is not bitter at his treatment by Frank Hall, even though the programme never made any attempt to treat the subsequent Fianna Fáil Government in like fashion, but he believes that ordinary people got a false impression of his character from the media generally. 'Meeting people for the first time I often got the same reaction as people often had to Cosgrave when they met him. I think people on a social basis were very surprised to find that I took a jar and could sing a song. Many people thought I didn't drink or smoke or could be in any way convivial.'

If Ryan was the *bête noire* on the Fine Gael side of the Government Cruise O'Brien occupied that role in the Labour half of the coalition. As well as being Minister for Posts and Telegraphs he was also head of the Government Information Service. Cosgrave's decision to give a Labour Minister responsibility for the Government's relations with the media demonstrated a level of trust in a coalition partner which would be unthinkable in the late 1990s but it demonstrated the level of trust the Taoiseach placed in all his Ministers.

'I think it says a lot for Cosgrave as much as for the Cruiser that Conor, who can write so liberally about so many things, has respected the confidentiality of that government and has not written about it as he could so easily have,' says Richie Ryan.

During the lifetime of the Government O'Brien was regularly involved in controversy about the North. He took a very strong anti-Republican line and tried to bring the electorate around to an understanding of the Unionist position, often inspiring a furious reaction not only from Fianna Fáil and the media but from many of his own colleagues in both Government parties. Michael Gallagher in his study of the Labour party says:

> 'Dr O'Brien's frequent criticisms of the media for allegedly portraying the IRA too favourably and his use of statutory powers to prohibit RTE from broadcasting interviews with members of the Provisional IRA, Provisional Sinn Féin or the Official IRA made him unpopular with many journalists.'

Whatever Cosgrave thought of O'Brien's views he never interfered and never asked him not to make the kind of controversial statements that became his trademark. As far as Cosgrave was concerned Cruise O'Brien was Labour Party spokesman on Northern Ireland and was entitled to express his views in that capacity.

15

FREE VOTE

LIAM COSGRAVE did many unothodox things during his political career but the most stunning was the way he voted in the Dáil against his own Government's contraceptive legislation in July 1974. It was one of the most remarkable episodes in Irish political history and it left many of his Government colleagues dazed for a long time afterwards.

Contraception was a serious political issue when the coalition took office. Under a 1935 act, the sale and importation of contraceptives was illegal but in 1973 the Supreme Court found that the ban on importation unconstitutional and there was a widespread demand for reform of the law. The matter was the responsibility of Minister for Justice, Pat Cooney, and he instructed his officials to draft a piece of legislation which was entitled the Control of Importation, Sale and Manufacture of Contraception Bill. This would have permitted contraceptives to be imported and sold to married people only, under licence by chemists.

FitzGerald remembers that when the issue came before the cabinet in the spring of 1974 Cosgrave stayed silent during the discussion on the terms of the Bill.

> 'This was not strictly a Government Bill but one introduced by the Minister for Justice, Pat Cooney, on his own account, a distinction that I am afraid was far too subtle for many people to grasp. Three times at the meeting Conor Cruise O'Brien endeavoured to extract from the Taoiseach a reaction to the proposed Bill but each time he failed. We left the meeting no wiser about his attitude.'

Cruise O'Brien remembers things a little differently.

'I had an idea that Cosgrave would vote against. And I pressed him on it in cabinet to tell us what way he was going to vote and all he would say was "a free vote, there must be a free vote. We are all free to vote whichever way we want." I was the only one who pressed him on it.'

The drafting of the Bill and its introduction into the Dáil took some time and it was not formally introduced for the second stage debate until July. By this time there were suggestions that a small number of Fine Gael and Labour TDs were unhappy about the legislation and might avail of the opportunity of the free vote to oppose it. On the Fine Gael side Oliver Flanagan and the Fine Gael leader in the Seanad, Michael O'Higgins, were known to be hostile while Labour's Dan Spring was another who had serious doubts about supporting the Bill.

Fianna Fáil, sensing an opportunity to embarrass the Government, had no hesitation in opposing the bill and imposing a whip to ensure that all the party TDs voted against it. It was a cynical manoeuvre by Fianna Fáil because while many of the party's TDs would have voted against the legislation a number of them had no problem with it. With the coalition parties allowing a free vote and Fianna Fáil opposing the Bill with all its might the writing should have been on the wall but the media and most Government supporters didn't see it that way at the time.

The Bill was introduced into the Dáil by Cooney on 4 July. He pointed out that the Criminal Law Amendment Act 1935, Section 17 provided that it was an offence to sell, import or advertise for sale contraceptives. The Supreme Court in the McGee case had decided that the ban on importation was unconstitutional but had made no finding about the issue of sale. 'We now have a rather anomalous situation that there is no restriction whatever on the importation of contraceptives but there is an absolute prohibition on their sale,' said Cooney who argued that the ban on sale could be successfully challenged in the courts by a married couple.

Cooney's proposals regulated the importation and provided that the sale of contraceptives be through chemists shops. The right to purchase being confined to married people. 'The provision in the Bill is quite simple and unambiguous; it makes it unlawful for an unmarried person to purchase a contraceptive.'

Fianna Fáil opposed the Bill with what in retrospect seems a parody of moral indignation. In terms more suitable for the pulpit than the

Dáil chamber, Desmond O'Malley, Fianna Fáil spokesman on Justice, spoke in trenchant terms.

'I feel that our duty as a legislature is, so far as we can within the confines of our Constitution, as interpreted for us by the Supreme Court, to deter fornication and promiscuity, to promote public morality and to prevent in so far as we can, there are of course clear limitations on the practicability of that, public immorality.'

John Kelly, Government chief whip and parliamentary secretary to the Taoiseach reflected on how a politician like Michael O'Higgins, leader of the Seanad, who was genuinely opposed to the Bill should be called upon to act.

'He would sooner, I believe, leave politics altogether than be driven like a sheep into a dipping pond by me or by the whip of the Seanad to support a point of view which he sincerely thinks in his heart is pernicious and damnable ... A man who genuinely believes this Bill is wrong and that it would not be just mistaken for him to support it but wicked for him to support it, should not, apart from the fact that he cannot be obliged to support it.'

The vote was taken on 16 July and the Bill was defeated by 75 votes to 61. The defeat was bad enough for the Government but the amazing thing about the Dáil division was that the Taoiseach voted against his own Government's Bill. He was joined in the 'no' lobby by Minister for Education, Dick Burke, and five other Fine Gael TDs. One Labour TD, Dan Spring, father of Dick, who was known to be opposed to the legislation did not travel to Dublin for the vote.

Cosgrave had not intended to influence any of his colleagues and had kept his opposition entirely to himself. He planned to vote last so that no-one else would be swayed by his decision. That strategy came unstuck, however, because the Government chief whip, John Kelly only discovered after the vote had been called that his Taoiseach was going to vote against the Bill.

Garret FitzGerald recalls the general mood in the cabinet.

'We had managed to convince ourselves that he would support the Bill when the time came ... the Chief whip, the late John Kelly, clearly had no qualms on the matter and was busy persuading the small number of anti-contraception Government TDs that they should vote for it, as, according to him, Liam Cosgrave was doing. What we did not realise was that John Kelly had no direct assurance from Liam Cosgrave but was, it seems, relying on an impression of his attitude gleaned from his private office, where the Taoiseach's position had apparently been misunderstood.

'TDs had already begun passing through the lobbies when John discovered his error. Appalled at having misled some conservatively minded deputies into voting for the Bill on a false premise, he immediately urged the Taoiseach to vote without delay — for, unaware of John Kelly's activities, Liam Cosgrave had loyally intended to wait until the end before casting his vote so as not to influence other members of the party. Once urged by John, he voted immediately against the Bill, and some who had not yet passed through the lobbies decided to follow him. By then, having voted, I was back on the front bench and, seeing what was happening, I said to Pat Cooney, "Wouldn't it be funny if he defeated the Government."'Not realising yet that this was what in fact had happened.'

Peter Barry says he had no inkling of Cosgrave's intentions.

'Maybe he told Richie or Mark Clinton. It was no problem for me at all. I knew it was a big problem for Liam. I knew it was part of cementing the Government to put this through. He insisted this was a free vote but I thought he was protecting some of the back-benchers who had a problem like Des Governey. Blow me pink when I saw him walking up the stairs. You could have knocked me down. First of all I went pale but then you couldn't help feeling "well, fair dues". He believes in something, he knows the price he may have to pay for doing it. But of course we had been warned on the Offences Against the State Act that he wouldn't go against his own conscience but we never took it on board you see. That was a warning. There was principle there and he was going to abide by his own conscience. I don't know how he would have dealt with divorce.'

Richie Ryan finds it amusing that people like Peter Barry still believe Cosgrave had told him what he was going to do.

'It was discussed in cabinet and the cabinet decided by a majority to support the Cooney bill. Then there was this proposal that there be a free vote. It was agreed and then Liam said "Remember, a free vote's a free vote", and he went on to the next topic. Several members of the cabinet asked me what I thought Liam was going to do and I said "I don't know really, I have my own ideas." And they said "Come on has he told you, will you ask him?" And I said "I won't ask him because he wouldn't tell me but I have my own ideas." I remember even as we were going into the Dáil to vote on it. Just outside the lift the lads wanted to know "what is the boss going to do?" "I don't know, I haven't spoken to him about it and he hasn't spoken to me." He went in and voted against and they then accused me of knowing all the time. I did have a hunch and I reminded them that Liam said "A free vote is a free vote". There was no point in his saying that unless you got the message from it. It was the kind of remark that if you had any wit at all you knew what it meant. It was example of Garret's poor judgement that he didn't get it.'

Conor Cruise O'Brien, was another who was not in the least surprised by Cosgrave's vote.

'Afterwards some of my colleagues, talking without attribution to the Press, said we were all stunned. I wasn't stunned, I was expecting it. I respected his decision. I was, of course, on the other side, but I couldn't say that he had led us in any way to believe that he would do anything else other than what he actually did. It might have been better if he had told us frankly "I have to vote against this" but you could see that was the way it was heading.'

O'Brien remembers an amusing incident the following day.

'The day after the vote two of my colleagues were discussing it in the early morning in Leinster House. They were talking about this with dismay and how extraordinary and inexplicable it was and one of the elderly cleaners listened to this stuff and just couldn't stick it and she veered back on her hunkers and she said: "What are ye all talking about; surprised at the way he voted! Sure that man was an altar boy until he was 24." And that was the whole story, he thought it was contrary to faith and morals.'

Other people in Government were shocked to the core. 'It took the heart out of that Government,' says one senior Fine Gael figure. 'I remember being quite shocked to see Liam Cosgrave, Tom Enright and Richard Burke voting against the Bill,' says John Bruton. 'There was a lot of surprise in the party. I don't think it was the right thing for Liam Cosgrave to do. I would be inclined to be favourably disposed towards most of the things he did but it was a mistake for a Taoiseach not to vote with his own Government. It was not collective responsibility.'

Brendan Halligan ruefully recalls:

'It was the Labour Party which had come up with the formula of a free vote. In fact I started the formula because I was stupidly trying to say to people we should have the culture that exists in other parliaments that on matters of conscience a free vote should be exercised without it being taken as no confidence in the Government. Of course it didn't run that way because Fianna Fáil imposed a three-line whip. So a free vote was only exercised on one side. Then it can't really work. In the days afterwards everybody and particularly John Kelly had' no

animosity to him at all because he had said it was going to be a free
vote.'

Halligan recalls Kelly saying 'the mistake we made was that we started
to behave towards our back-benchers as if there was a whip on'. Of
course it was a huge shock to the coalition but Halligan believes that it
did not have any long term repercussions.

> 'Cosgrave's view was that he was as entitled to a free vote as anybody
> else and it didn't occur to him that being Taoiseach made any
> difference to that. A side of his character which the public never
> understood was that he was an extraordinarily humble man. It
> wouldn't have occurred to him that as Taoiseach he had to behave
> differently to everybody else.'

Halligan also points out that if there had not been a free vote
Cosgrave would not have been able to accept the legislation. 'Then
you would have had a real crisis. As it was. It was a very good formula
for getting around it.' Cruise O'Brien has a similar view. 'In a way, on
the religious thing I think he had gone as far as he could be expected
to go in letting his cabinet produce a Bill and then insist on a free
vote.'

One issue on which there was a vote at cabinet and which did reveal
some of the tensions in Government arose because of the friendship
between Garret Fitzgerald and Justin Keating. Keating was not poplar
with most of his Labour colleagues in Government. Jim Tully, Conor
Cruise O'Brien and Michael O'Leary, all for various reasons, did not
get on well with Keating whereas FitzGerald did.

Unaware of the tensions FitzGerald, through his friendship with
Keating, presumed that he knew what Labour was thinking and often
sought to position himself on the same wavelength. The bond
between Keating and FitzGerald, both of whom were academics at
UCD, developed because as Minister for Industry and Commerce
Keating accompanied FitzGerald to European Council of Ministers
meetings when foreign trade was up for discussion. They also regularly
went on holidays to France together with their wives, and were
accompanied by other members of their set like Mary and Nick
Robinson.

The relationship between FitzGerald and Keating was so close that
the Fine Gael Minister campaigned to get the job of European
commissioner for Keating as Patrick Hillery's term approached its
close. While FitzGerald was pushing Keating's claims Dick Burke had
sought and secured the support of the Taoiseach and his Fine Gael

colleagues for the position. Nonetheless FitzGerald continued to back Keating on the basis that Burke 'did not seem to me to have the same intellectual capacity as his Labour colleague.' This campaign deeply annoyed both the Fine Gael and the Labour members of the cabinet. Fine Gael Ministers were annoyed at Garret breaking ranks to support a Labour man while Labour Ministers were annoyed at being pushed into the position of having to back Keating whom they did not feel like going out on a limb for. They would have preferred to leave the matter to Cosgrave's discretion as Fine Gael had the numbers to win if the issue came to a vote.

Dick Burke recalls:

> 'Garret lobbied for Justin Keating. Justin had an inside track in that he was standing in a lot for Garret on foreign trade issues. My desire for the job had nothing to do with personal animosity to Justin Keating. I had been a Christian Democrat before I joined Fine Gael, therefore for me the possibility of serving the European cause was always a high consideration. When the opportunity came up I offered myself and it was largely accepted by my Fine Gael colleagues. Garret lobbied very hard for Justin with people like Pat Cooney, Peter Barry and Tom Fitzpatrick, people he thought might have been shiftable, capable of being moved on this. He didn't go near the likes of Richie or Donegan because he knew these fellows stood solid on the matter.'

In the event because of Garret's advocacy of Keating's claims the issue was pressed to a vote at cabinet. Dick Burke's nomination was agreed by nine votes to six with FitzGerald backing the Labour position but failing to persuade any of his Fine Gael colleagues to follow his lead. Paradoxically the end result of the affair was to make the Labour Ministers more supportive of Cosgrave and less enamoured of FitzGerald.

In the midst of all the drama Cosgrave travelled to the United States in 1976 for that country's bi-centennial celebrations. He was proud of the fact that he was asked to address a joint sitting of Congress as his father had done 50 years before. Michael Mills and the other journalists covering the visit remember Cosgrave's almost childish delight in all aspects of the visit but particularly his speech to Congress.

16

LOST OPPORTUNITY

In the early days of 1974 when the Government was coming up to its first anniversary Cosgrave could see nothing but difficulties on every front. The economy was reeling from the oil crisis and motorists were angered by the prospect of petrol rationing. The first year's membership of the European Community had not brought the expected bonanza. Republican prisoners were on hunger-strike in Britain and the IRA was planting hoax bombs in Dublin. The traditional Irish ambivalence to the Republican violence was reflected in media coverage. In the North the hopes of a bright new dawn were fading fast as Brian Faulkner's power-sharing Executive came under increasing pressure.

Northern Ireland was the first major issue confronted by Cosgrave's Government and it was to dominate his term of office. In fact Cosgrave and some of his potential Ministers flew to London for a meeting with Ted Heath, even before they formally took office. At that stage the IRA campaign was at its height, internment still in force and the British desperately searching for a political solution to the problem. Just six days before Cosgrave became Taoiseach the British Government published a white paper on the North which was to mark the signpost on the road to Sunningdale.

Within both Fine Gael and Labour attitudes on the North had undergone a transformation since the beginning of The Troubles. Conor Cruise O'Brien provided the intellectual argument for change within the Labour Party from traditional Republican thinking to a recognition of the consent principle but it was resisted by a significant number of his colleagues.

In Fine Gael, which is still subtitled the 'United Ireland Party', old attitudes were also changing. It was not that there was any sympathy for the IRA or its campaign of violence but even in 1970 there was still a broad acceptance of the traditional Nationalist view that the central problem was partition and the British presence in the North. That view was changed mainly by Garret FitzGerald and Paddy Harte.

Initially Cosgrave was slow to go along with the new thinking on the North. He was very consciously part of the Sinn Féin tradition and was proud of his father's role in 1916. While Cosgrave was decidedly anti-IRA he was also anti-British and held that the mis-government of the North for 50 years was the root cause of the problem there.

However, the increasing brutality of IRA violence in the early 1970s shocked the population of the Republic and prompted a reassessment of received Nationalist wisdom which had been unchallenged since partition in 1922. Before they took office in March 1973, both Fine Gael and Labour were edging towards an analysis of the North which saw a divided community, rather than partition, as the nub of the problem, and which recognised that there could be no change in the constitutional status of the North without the agreement of the majority of the people there.

In a speech in Blackrock, Co. Dublin, a few months after taking office Cosgrave said:

> 'We must be prepared to recognise the right of the two communities in Northern Ireland to set aside their different views of the eventual shape of Irish political institutions and to establish institutions that will provide the North with a system of government designed to reconcile the two communities in peace and harmony.'

Cosgrave's speech was regarded by the Unionist leader, Brian Faulkner, as 'the most important by a Prime Minister of the Republic for years'. It was made against a background of intense political activity in relation to the North by both the British and Irish Governments. The British white paper had been published only days after Cosgrave took office and its broad thrust was acceptable to Dublin stressing as it did the need for a power-sharing Government in the North and some form of Council of Ireland to recognise the Irish dimension to the problem.

On the Irish side primary responsibility for Northern Ireland policy has always rested with the Taoiseach rather than the Minister for Foreign Affairs although the two usually work in tandem. Despite their personal dislike of one another Cosgrave and FitzGerald worked well in Government. 'Indeed the tensions that had previously existed between Liam Cosgrave and myself completely evaporated in Government and the differences in our attitudes to Northern Ireland that had caused problems in Opposition also disappeared,' writes Garret.

One hugely important development was the appointment of Dermot Nally as assistant secretary to the Government with responsibility for Northern affairs in the Taoiseach's Department. Nally was to play a more significant role than any other Irish official on Northern policy for the next 20 years, spanning Sunningdale, the Anglo-Irish agreement and the Downing Street Declaration. In 1973 he ensured that relations between the Taoiseach's Department and Foreign Affairs ran smoothly.

An unusual feature of Northern policy in the Cosgrave Government was the influence of the Minister for Posts and Telegraphs, Conor Cruise O'Brien who was also responsible for the Government Information Service. O'Brien, as Labour Party spokesman and Corish's advisor on the North, carried that role into Government. Cosgrave accepted without a quibble O'Brien's involvement in everything to do with Northern policy. FitzGerald, while he made the best of it at the time, came to resent O'Brien's influence.

On the formation of the Government the two men regarded each other as political allies but O'Brien gradually moved closer to Cosgrave and began to have deep suspicions about the capacity and influence of the Department of Foreign Affairs on Northern policy. FitzGerald recalls that, on the advice of his wife Joan, O'Brien appointed as head of the Government Information Service, Muiris Mac Conghail, a top television producer. 'Cosgrave assigned responsibility to me for the GIS,' says O'Brien. 'Muiris was picked for the job and it was agreed that he would report to me. The choice of Muiris had been recommended to me by Joan FitzGerald. I think she must have thought that Muiris would work for Garret. I made the choice and he reported to me. I knew what was going on in the press world through him. He was very close to the ground, very bright. He was completely loyal to the coalition government as a whole, to the Taoiseach and the Tánaiste. He was a great help.' Richie Ryan attributes O'Brien's deep distrust of the Department of Foreign Affairs to the jousts he had with Garret at this time. Detailed work went on during the summer and autumn of 1973 on Northern Ireland

and on 17 September came a crucial meeting at Baldonnel military airport outside Dublin between Ted Heath and the Taoiseach.

Cosgrave says:

'The meeting at Baldonnel between Mr Heath and myself arranged the Sunningdale Conference. That was the start of the arrangements for it. Fianna Fáil was not involved in the preparation for it. Fianna Fáil had left office in March 1973 and Corish and I saw Heath before we assumed office. I met him [Heath] again in London before Baldonnel. There were preliminaries but Baldonnel set the scene for Sunningdale. It lasted all day between Mr Heath and myself.'

Garret FitzGerald has a very different account of the meeting saying that it did not go well and describing the encounter as 'a dialogue of the deaf'. He says there was no agreement on whether a power-sharing government in the North should be established before or after a conference between the two Governments and the Northern parties on the Council of Ireland. In the end the structure of the Executive was agreed but it would not formally take office before the conference.

Within the Irish Government there had already been a heated debate on the Council of Ireland proposal as O'Brien recalls.

'There was a division not between Fine Gael and Labour but between the rest of the cabinet and myself. I demurred over the proposals for a Council of Ireland with three tiers and executive powers because I feared that it would undermine the Unionist partners in the joint executive, which is what happened. But none of my colleagues, neither Liam nor Brendan Corish supported me on that. But the opposition to me was led by Garret FitzGerald, not by Liam, who didn't take a stand at all. He didn't utter — as often he didn't. But Garret and Declan Costello were terribly sure that they understood the North so well that there could be no demur to the whole thing. Garret now concedes that I was right but adds that this has given me the illusion that I am also right on other things.'

O'Brien feels that Cosgrave may have been somewhat sympathetic to his position but the Taoiseach didn't intervene and followed the line advocated by the rest of the Government. It took a couple of months to iron out all the difficulties but after agreement in principle on a power-sharing arrangement had been worked out an extraordinary delegation set out from Ireland to Sunningdale Park in Berkshire on 5 December. Cosgrave led a team of nearly 40 people, virtually the entire cabinet and the top rank of the Irish civil service to the conference. In all 120 politicians and officials from the Republic, the North and Britain attended the conference which was designed to end the Northern problem once and for all and put Anglo-Irish relations on a proper footing for the first time in history.

Before he went Cosgrave tried to discourage the belief gaining widespread currency in the Irish media that a major step on the road to a united Ireland was about to be agreed with the British. He urged the Irish public not to 'pin exaggerated hopes on what these talks can produce in the immediate future'.

Nonetheless the strength of the Irish delegation and the presence of so many cabinet Ministers indicated that Cosgrave saw the talks as the most important since the Treaty negotiations of 1921. The fact that the negotiations began on the 52nd anniversary of the signing of the Treaty added to this impression of history making although Cosgrave himself dismisses it as a coincidence. Unlike the Treaty negotiations, not only the Irish and British Governments but politicians from Northern Ireland were at the talks. The chairman of the executive designate, Brian Faulkner, and Gerry Fitt and John Hume of the SDLP were among the delegates. With agreement on power sharing already in place Sunningdale was essentially about the structure of a Council of Ireland, the North–South dimension which still in 1996 is a thorny political issue.

Cosgrave and Faulkner quickly established a rapport which cemented the process. In his autobiography *Memoirs of a Statesman* Faulkner recalls that he first met Cosgrave in the early 1950s:

'My wife and I spent many holidays in the South, often caravanning with the children in Achill or Connemara or Kerry. It was in the early 1950s on a fair day in the village of Claremorris in County Mayo that I first met Mr Cosgrave, later Prime Minister of the Republic. I had gone to hear what he had to say at a political meeting in the square and afterwards I went up to have a word with him and he invited me into the pub for a drink.'

Both men also shared a passion for horses and hunting which was to prove a common bond when they met at Sunningdale. FitzGerald describes how he was having breakfast with Faulkner on the first morning of the talks when they were joined by Cosgrave.

'They had already met on the hunting field, I gathered, and within minutes they were chatting away about mutual acquaintances. They were quickly on good terms, strolling around the grounds together during breaks in the meetings.'

This ability of Cosgrave, who was basically a shy man, to strike up a rapport with the most unlikely of people was one of his strongest political attributes. Other politicians instinctively trusted him and this was the key to his political success. Peter Barry remembers the easy rapport which was quickly established between the prime ministers of North and South. 'Cosgrave got on very well with Faulkner. There was a marvellous photograph to the two of them in the papers walking into the woods at Sunningdale.' Cosgrave's approach to the talks was in line with his handling of the Irish cabinet. For most of the discussions he deliberately held himself in reserve allowing the key members of his delegation, particularly FitzGerald, to argue the Irish case. It was only when sticking points cropped up that he became directly involved as the final authority. FitzGerald recalls one afternoon during the interminable negotiations:

'As we awaited developments we watched racing on television, Liam Cosgrave and Pat Cooney being racing enthusiasts. The rest of us were amused to see the expression on Cosgrave's face when, in the middle of a race, he was told that Heath was anxious to have a word with him. I think, but cannot be certain, that he watched the end of the race before responding to this request.'

The key issues for negotiation were the Council of Ireland and the building of mutual confidence between Unionists and Nationalists. The Irish Government accepted for the first time that unity could only come about with the consent of the people of the North. The British for their part accepted that if the people of Northern Ireland ever wanted unity they would support this wish. These two principles have since become the basis for all subsequent approaches by the two Governments to the Northern problem. Extradition was another thorny subject which was discussed in the talks but the negotiations centered on the shape and powers of a Council of Ireland.

The agreement on a power-sharing administration for the North, which had been arrived at months earlier, was ratified at Sunningdale. The 11-member executive, with Faulkner at its head, which took office on 1 January 1974, contained six Unionist, four SDLP and one Alliance members.

The settlement was designed to isolate the gunmen on both the Republican and Loyalist sides but both sets of extremists continued their violence unabated and Faulkner gradually lost the support of his own party. The Council of Ireland became the focus for Unionist hostility and ultimately proved Conor Cruise O'Brien right, being one step too far.

Shortly after the Sunningdale agreement was signed Kevin Boland launched a legal challenge against it, claiming that it was repugnant to Articles 2 and 3 of the Republic's constitution because the territorial claim could not be reconciled with the recognition of Northern Ireland's constitutional status. The Government naturally defended the action but when the legal defence was leaked to the newspapers in January 1974, it caused a sensation in Northern Ireland. The defence mounted by Attorney General, Declan Costello, claimed that the Government had not actually recognised Northern Ireland as being outside the Republic's jurisdiction.

The defence case came as a severe embarrassment to Faulkner. Cosgrave rang him and agreed that the matter should have been discussed earlier; he suggested an early meeting and Faulkner flew to Baldonnel on 14 January 1974. The Northern premier told Cosgrave that his position had been eroded since Sunningdale and that the Irish Government had been partly responsible. Faulkner added that the acceptance of the consent principle and the reassuring effect that was meant to have for the Unionist community had been blurred by the submission in the Boland case. The fact that 15 suspected terrorists had been picked up by the Gardaí and then released further undermined confidence about the Irish determination to deal with the IRA.

In response Cosgrave explained to Faulkner the merely technical nature of the Irish Government's legal defence to the Boland case so that they could keep within the letter of the constitution if not the spirit. Faulkner again asked if the Irish Government would propose a change to the Constitution but Cosgrave told him he was convinced the time was not ripe for the move and the coalition government would simply lose the referendum.

'Look. We accept Northern Ireland as it is and we want to cooperate with you and that's all there is to it,' Cosgrave told Faulkner, adding that as soon as the court case was over he would make a clear statement to the Dáil to reassure Unionists.

Faulkner wrote:

'As always I found him honest and direct and I had a very great respect for him. He and I were both struggling with deeply rooted traditions which made it difficult for us to work together as we wished but I never doubted his good will and I believe that in time we could have overcome these obstacles.'

As the role and functions of the Council of Ireland continued to be a millstone around Faulkner's neck agreement was reached between the Unionists and the SDLP that the wide-ranging powers for the body, as originally proposed, were unrealistic. Faulkner and his team of Ministers met Cosgrave and his senior Government colleagues at Hillsborough in February to hammer out the precise 'executive and harmonising' functions which were to be allocated to the Council of Ireland. Despite Faulkner's political difficulties the Irish side, acting on the advice of FitzGerald and Iveagh House, insisted on a Council of Ireland with a permanent headquarters and executive functions across a range of issues. When Cosgrave saw how opposed all the Northern parties were to the plan he quickly dropped it and settled for a much more modest proposal.

'The ever talkative Garret FitzGerald went on at great length about his ideas for the Council of Ireland and eventually had to be silenced by Cosgrave when it was clear that we had made up our minds and would not be shifted,' recalled Faulkner.

In the end it was agreed that the executive functions of the Council would be confined to the racing board, drainage, fisheries, aspects of tourism, animal health and other minor non-politically contentious areas. During the meeting Faulkner was disconcerted when Pat Cooney, the Irish Minister for Justice, lashed British security policies in South Armagh and said they had failed in their duty by allowing it to come under IRA control. 'The Army brief with which we had come proved woefully inadequate to answer his arguments.'

The watering down of the Council of Ireland came too late to help Faulkner. In February 1974, a British general election was called by Ted Heath and the Conservatives narrowly lost power to Labour. In Northern Ireland the anti-Faulkner Unionists swept the boards winning every seat except West Belfast which was held by Gerry Fitt. The writing was on the wall for the power-sharing executive. In May came the Ulster Workers' Council strike and the spineless capitulation of the Wilson Government to it. The short-lived experiment in power sharing was over, killed by Unionist intransigence on the one hand and an over ambitions Nationalist agenda on the part of the Irish Government and the SDLP. The continuing campaign of IRA violence only hardened attitudes all around.

Just as the UWC strike was starting Dublin and Monaghan were bombed by Loyalists. The bombs went off on 17 May killing 28 people instantly and injuring another 137. Some of the injured subsequently

died making the atrocity the worst terrorist outrage in Ireland or
Britain during The Troubles.

'The Cruiser said at the time that the Council of Ireland
overloaded it and there is a bit of truth in that,' says Peter Barry. 'The
change of government in Britain didn't help either and there was a
story that the Labour Party were afraid to issue orders to the British
army in case they were disobeyed. I have said that to some Labour
politicians but they have always denied it. One way or another the
failure of Sunningdale was a huge tragedy.'

Cosgrave was impressed with Heath's commitment and believes
that if he had remained in government Sunningdale would ultimately
have succeeded.

> 'Sunningdale mainly collapsed because of the weakness of the Labour
> Government. Indeed I think it is true of all British Labour
> Governments ... they hadn't the guts to put the thing through and
> they didn't stand up to the workers' strike. Now if they had stood up
> to it I think Sunningdale might have worked.'

He also points to the deal that Callaghan and Michael Foot did with
the Unionists later in the 1970s to get their support in the Commons.
'The Labour Government on all that were very unrealistic and
untrustworthy,' Cosgrave told Ursula Halligan. In retrospect he
agreed that the settlement was too ambitious for the time. 'I suppose
Sunningdale was a very conscious effort to try and settle the thing but
once it didn't work, looked at now, it either came too late or too soon
and it is a matter of opinion which.' Michael Mills recalls Cosgrave
saying that the Wilson Government should have dealt with the strikers
by 'hosing them off the streets'.

In this gloomy atmosphere the coalition concentrated on domestic
security and particularly the threat posed by the IRA to the Republic
itself. In the autumn of 1973 the Ministers were told that they and
their families now faced the threat of kidnap by extreme Republicans.
Cosgrave initiated a cabinet discussion of the issue and it was agreed
that if any member of their family was kidnapped they would opt out
of the discussion on the matter and that regardless of the threats no
concessions would be made to the kidnappers. The security provided
for Ministers was upped from the normal armed Garda driver to an
escort car with two armed detectives.

Weeks after the Government took office the gun-running ship, the
Claudia, was intercepted off the Waterford coast as a result of a British
intelligence tip off. The arms cargo was seized and senior IRA-man,

Joe Cahill, was arrested and convicted. Minister for Defence, Paddy Donegan, indelicately said the crew deserved a kick up the transom. The remark tended to trivialise the incident. Later there were IRA break-outs from Mountjoy and Portlaoise and at times it appeared as if the country was in danger of being submerged in a Republican wave.

One of the most shocking IRA atrocities in the Republic took place in March 1974, when the IRA murdered Senator Billy Fox, a Fine Gael politician and a Presbyterian from Monaghan. Fox was murdered when he called at his fiancée's house. When he arrived at the house it was in the process of being ransacked by a dozen members of the IRA who threw the family bible into the fire during the raid. Fox was chased from the house into a field, gunned down and left to die in agony. The IRA tried to cover up this brutal sectarian killing by denying responsibility for the attack, sending a wreath to his funeral, claiming that Fox was sympathetic to their cause and blaming the UDA for the murder. However, the Gardaí captured some members of the IRA gang and all were ultimately arrested and given long prison sentences.

Another ominous development as far as Cosgrave was concerned was the increasing contact between the British Government and the IRA towards the end of 1974. This resulted in an IRA ceasefire before Christmas which was extended for the best part of nine months although sporadic Republican violence continued. IRA leaders, including Gerry Adams, were flown to London for talks with British Ministers and officials in the North were in constant touch with Sinn Féin activists to monitor the ceasefire.

Cosgrave had no faith at all in the ceasefire believing, rightly as it transpired, that the whole episode was a tactic by Sinn Féin-IRA to persuade the British to end internment while also providing an opportunity for them to re-group and re-arm. Cosgrave banned any official meetings between Irish civil servants and Republicans and there was never any question of Ministers meeting representatives of Sinn Féin. As Cosgrave had anticipated once all the internees were released and the IRA in a better position to inflict violence the campaign began again.

The Taoiseach explained his position to the British in March 1976 when he travelled with Corish to meet Wilson and Merlyn Rees after the collapse of the constitutional convention which followed the failure of the power-sharing executive. During the meeting Rees complained about Northern parties and said he would stop meeting them. Cosgrave remarked that it was important that talks should not begin with paramilitaries. He added that negotiations with paramilitary groups weakened the authority of elected politicians because the effect of meeting Republicans was that the IRA would believe the prospect of British withdrawal was attainable.

The Cosgrave attitude to Sinn Féin and the IRA was consistent with the approach of successive governments since his father defeated the Republicans in the Civil War. The policy was continued by successive governments after him until the 'peace process' of the early 1990s when the government of Albert Reynolds and Dick Spring tried to cut a deal with the IRA, reversing long-established precedent.

During Cosgrave's period as Taoiseach there were a number of spectacular jail breakouts by Republicans as well as hunger strikes and frequent civil disturbances. In 1974 IRA prisoner Michael Gaughan died in Parkhurst prison in Britain after a 65-day hunger strike. The funeral in Ireland provided the IRA with an opportunity for massive public demonstrations of support. Another hunger striker, Frank Stagg, was ordered by the IRA to stop after Gaughan's death but he resumed again a year later. He died on 12 February 1976 and the IRA again tried to use it as a huge propaganda exercise despite the fact that the dead man's widow and his brother Emmet Stagg wanted a private funeral. Garret FitzGerald recalls that the British did a deal to hand the body over to the IRA who proposed to parade the coffin through the streets of Dublin. The Irish Government reacted with fury and the British changed their plans and handed the body to the Irish authorities at Heathrow airport. The plane bringing the body back was diverted from Dublin to Shannon to prevent demonstrations in the capital. Stagg was buried in Ballina and his grave cemented over by the authorities but the IRA later exhumed the coffin and buried it in a Republican plot.

In 1975 the feared spectacular kidnapping took place but it was not a Minister but a Dutch industrialist, Tiede Herrema, who was abducted. His kidnappers demanded the release of three high profile IRA prisoners, Rose Dugdale, Kevin Mallon and James Hyland, and threatened that Herrema would be killed within 48 hours if they were not released. Cruise O'Brien remembers Cosgrave's response.

'His style was very laconic, very efficient and quick. He didn't go in for debates. I remember the most decisive stand he took was over the Herrema kidnapping. Some of my colleagues gave the impression afterwards that there had been a debate in the cabinet about what to do. The debate consisted of this:

'Liam Cosgrave: "We have a demand here from these fellows that if we don't hand over Dugdale to them they are going to do all sorts of things. Kill Herrema and all sorts of other people. I take it that we refuse this demand. Next item."

'That was it. Nobody was for arguing against the point. I think Garret and probably Justin Keating would have argued it but they knew what they were up against. If there had been a vote there would have been a majority in support of Cosgrave. Corish would have supported him and most of the Labour people would. It was pretty solid on law and order, that particular government.'

After the cabinet meeting a statement was issued which put the position of Cosgrave and his government quite clearly.

'What the kidnappers are asking is that we open the gates and let subversive criminals loose in society with immunity — people whose organisation wants to bring down the institutions of this State. The Government has no choice in this matter. The position we adopt is a simple one politically, although from an emotional and psychological point of view, when a man's life is at stake, it is difficult.'

Cosgrave's tough tactics worked. The kidnappers did not carry out their threat to kill Herrema. Gardaí tracked the kidnap gang to a house in Monasterevin and a three-week siege ensued which culminated in the Dutch businessman's release unharmed.

17

THUNDERING DISGRACE

CEARBHALL Ó DÁLAIGH became president of Ireland because a cabinet Minister was hard of hearing. It was an accident that was to have profound effects for Liam Cosgrave and his government. What happened was that Erskine Childers died suddenly in November 1974, a little over a year after he had been elected president, and neither the Government or the Fianna Fáil Opposition wanted an election.

'Cosgrave and Lynch did a bit of tic tacking and came up with a list of three possible replacements,' says Peter Barry. 'Rita Childers, the widow of the late President was number one on the list and the others were the president of the GAA, Donal Keenan, and Cearbhall Ó Dálaigh, a former chief justice of the Supreme Court who was then in the European Court.

'Cosgrave told us at a cabinet meeting on a Friday morning that he had discussed the matter with Lynch and that Rita Childers was acceptable. But he emphasised that it was absolutely confidential because the proposal must, for Lynch's own sake, appear to have come from him.'

That same night the Skibbereen urban district council met and passed a resolution asking the Government to invite Mrs Childers to be the next president of Ireland. The following morning Tom O'Donnell, the Minister for the Gaeltacht, who was very hard of hearing, was at home in Limerick when he was approached by the *Irish Independent* reporter for the region, Noel Smith. Having read a story in the *Examiner* that morning about the Skibbereen resolution Smith asked O'Donnell if Mrs Childers was going to be president.

'Tom couldn't hear properly, because he wouldn't wear a hearing aid. He thought the story was out and gave Noel the whole thing,' says

Peter Barry. Smith wrote a lead story for the *Sunday Independent* of 24 November which appeared under the headline 'Mrs Childers for President'. The story quoting government sources as saying Mrs Childers could have the presidency if she wanted it caused consternation in Fianna Fáil. 'Lynch went up like a rocket. He thought Cosgrave had broken confidentiality. That meant Mrs Childers was out and we ended up with Cearbhall. I told Jack Lynch the whole story at the inauguration of Cearbhall,' says Peter Barry.

Cearbhall Ó Dálaigh had reached the pinnacle of his legal career as a member of the European Court of Justice when he was asked to succeed Childers as president. Since his student days he had been involved in politics as an active member of Fianna Fáil and was appointed Attorney General at the age of 35 by Eamon de Valera in 1946. Having unsuccessfully contested the elections of 1948 and 1951 as a Fianna Fáil candidate he was reappointed Attorney General in 1951 and two years later was appointed to the Supreme Court where he ultimately took over as Chief Justice before moving to Europe. Cosgrave and Ó Dálaigh had never hit it off, even as young men, and as President and Taoiseach their relationship was purely formal, without any personal warmth. Ó Dálaigh by temperament was the opposite of Cosgrave. Exuberant, opinionated, a bit of a show-off and quick to stand on his dignity he had virtually nothing in common with the taciturn Taoiseach.

The President was known to believe that Cosgrave was not assiduous enough in observing the Constitutional proprieties by keeping him informed of political developments but the Taoiseach in his turn felt that too much was being asked of him.

'The role of the presidency was something which he found difficult,' says Muiris Mac Conghail. 'I remember accompanying him when he went to brief both President Childers and subsequently President Ó Dálaigh. It was the visit of a man to a house that he didn't know, and he didn't know what to say. He tried to brief them but then he was a man of few words. Then they complained about the fact that he wasn't telling them a whole lot. Well, his attitude was "What do you want to know?" He didn't arrive up with a kind of agenda. They may have seen it differently but I don't imagine President de Valera was all too well briefed during his period.'

Mac Conghail says that both Childers and Ó Dálaigh hankered after the British constitutional convention where the prime minister goes to the Palace to kiss hands with the Queen and brief her on major issues.

'The office of president was uneasily situated in relation to government here and still is. The strain was nothing to do with the fact that they were Fianna Fáil presidents. I remember on one occasion we went up to see President Childers and we were all dressed up for the purpose and he [Cosgrave] said, "This is the strangest place I have ever been in." He would not have had any great constitutional sense of the office.'

The tension between the two men continued as the coalition struggled with the security threat posed by terrorists. The country was stunned on 21 July 1976, when the British Ambassador, Christopher Ewart-Biggs was murdered by the IRA in Sandyford, Co. Dublin. The atrocity provoked widespread calls for tough anti-terrorist measures. The Government responded with the Offences Against the State Amendment Act which allowed terrorist suspects to be detained for up to seven days. However, this legislation was not introduced until the Dáil returned after the summer recess and by that time civil liberties groups and the media queried whether extra powers for the Gardaí were necessary.

When the legislation was passed by the Dáil Fianna Fáil attacked it strongly and President Ó Dálaigh instead of signing it decided, as he was entitled to do under the Constitution, to consult the Council of State about referring it to the Supreme Court. As the legislation was passed under the terms of the 1939 Emergency coalition Ministers were convinced that its constitutionality could not be in doubt and there was some resentment at the President's action. One of the people who attended the Council of State meeting summoned by the President vividly remembers what transpired.

'To my mind Cearbhall Ó Dálaigh was more intent on proving to everybody that he could refer emergency legislation to the Supreme Court than he was with the contents of the Bill itself. Tom O'Higgins was there as Chief Justice and said that since the matter might come to the Supreme Court he wouldn't give any advice to the President. But Tom Finlay was there as President of the High Court and he gave devastating advice that there was no point referring it to the Supreme Court. The legislation was so clearly constitutional that it was a waste of time. Cearbhall kept trying to say there was a suggestion that he could not refer emergency legislation but Finlay was quite clear that as it was emergency legislation there was no doubt about its constitutionality. After that meeting I was of the opinion that Cearbhall was being irresponsible.'

Cosgrave himself was at that meeting and was seething at Ó Dálaigh's attitude.

Ó Dálaigh did refer the Bill to the Supreme Court to the annoyance of most Ministers although FitzGerald says he believed at the time that it was wise to have the legislation tested in this manner rather than at some later stage when a person was in detention. The Bill was referred to the Supreme Court and found to be constitutional as Tom Finlay had argued at the Council of State. In the meantime, though, Minister for Defence, Paddy Donegan, made a dramatic intervention which had very serious consequences for the Government.

Donegan attended a ceremony at Columb Barracks in Mullingar on 18 October where he made a short speech during which he attacked the decision of the President to refer the bill to the Supreme Court.

> 'It was amazing that when the President sent the Emergency Powers Bill to the Supreme Court he did not send the powers of the Army, he did not send the seven years maximum penalty for membership, he did not send the ten years maximum penalty for inciting people to join the IRA to the Supreme Court. In my opinion he is a thundering disgrace. The fact is that the Army must stand behind the state.'

A young journalist, Don Lavery, who was then working for the *Westmeath Examiner*, was present at the ceremony and he reported Donegan's comments for the national newspapers. In the days following there were persistent rumours that Donegan had used stronger language than 'thundering disgrace' and it was also widely rumoured that he was drunk at the time.

Donegan himself always maintained that he wasn't drunk on that occasion but was feeling under the weather because he had been involved in a car crash that morning. He was also emotional over the murder by the IRA a few days before of Garda Michael Clerkin. The death of the garda, who was blown up by a bomb, was regarded at the time as the Republican movement's response to the emergency legislation. Whatever the motive for the Minister's remarks the coalition was plunged into an immediate political crisis as a result.

Pat Cooney, the Minister for Justice, was also present at the function in Mullingar and he immediately rang the Taoiseach's office to alert Cosgrave to what had happened. When Cooney's call came through Cosgrave was at home for lunch and he didn't hear about it until he returned. When the message was relayed to him Cosgrave called all the available cabinet Ministers to his office and asked that they be briefed on what had been said. They listened in horror as Cooney's story was repeated by Ted Nealon. When he had finished there was a silence which was finally broken by Cosgrave. 'I think this calls for a drink,' he said cryptically, going over to the drinks' cabinet and pulling out a bottle of whiskey.

When Donegan returned to Dublin later in the day and realised the implications of an attack on the President he went to the Taoiseach and offered to resign but Cosgrave refused to accept it. Instead Donegan sought an appointment with the President to apologise. Ó Dálaigh refused to meet the Minister even though he drove up to the Phoenix Park hoping to be admitted to Áras an Uachtaráin and waited for a time in the Park as efforts were made to get the President to receive him. Failing to get in the Minister returned to Government Buildings and later issued a public statement:

> 'I regret the remarks which arose out of my deep feelings for the security of our citizens. I intend to offer my apologies to the President as soon as possible.'

The following day Cosgrave summoned his Ministers to meet him in his room and read out a letter from the President protesting at the Minister's remarks. The letter said that the relationship between the President and the Minister had been irreparably breached and went on to ask whether the remarks could be construed otherwise than as an insinuation that the President did not stand behind the State: had the Minister any conception of his responsibilities as a Minister, and in particular as Minister for Defence?

Garret FitzGerald recalls that at this stage other Ministers were inclined to draw some comfort from the absence of a direct threat to resign in the letter but having read it he was worried.

> 'I did not, however, feel in a good position to challenge strongly the optimistic view formed before my arrival, not least because to have done so would in effect have been to demand Paddy Donegan's resignation, and as my relationship with him had for many years been one of some distance, I felt ill-placed to be the one person pressing the issue. I contented myself therefore with voicing a measure of pessimism about the more generally accepted interpretation, without attempting to take the matter further.'

Two days later the issue was raised in the Dáil when Fianna Fáil leader, Jack Lynch, moved a motion calling for Donegan to resign. Cosgrave expressed his regret for the incident but also defended Donegan's record as Minister.

'The Minister for Defence did not attack our institutions. He made what he and I regard as a serious comment on what the President did in a disrespectful way. He immediately announced his intention of apologising for this comment and offered to do so personally. As the President was not available the Minister made a full and unreserved written apology. I regret that the Minister for Defence made any remark which slighted the President ... There is a need to realise the efficient way in which the Minister has built the strength of the Army to the highest possible level in personnel and equipment in peacetime. That fact indicates his dedication to strengthening one of the institutions of State to which, as I have often said, we are all trustees.'

Cosgrave's reply was immediately attacked by the Opposition. 'If I had not been in this House since 10.30 this morning and seen and heard the Taoiseach's contribution to this debate in reply to the leader of the Opposition I do not think I would have believed it,' said Des O'Malley. 'To put it mildly it was no reply. It was the most pathetic, half-hearted attempt to half disapprove of what the Minister for Defence said,' he added.

In his autobiography Garret FitzGerald takes a similar view of Cosgrave's reply.

'Even ignoring the weakness of the syntax, which could have been perversely read as suggesting that it was the President who had been disrespectful, it was a somewhat half-hearted apology and Liam Cosgrave's statement that he as well as Paddy Donegan regarded the latter's remarks as "serious comment", however disrespectfully expressed, was unwise to the point of provocation.'

The following day President Ó Dálaigh resigned. Mid afternoon Cosgrave was informed that a dispatch rider was on his way from the Áras with a message which he immediately knew contained his resignation. The Taoiseach called senior Ministers to his office and having discussed the issue he rang Donegan and accepted his resignation. However, it was too late to stop the President's move. 'The damage done to the Government was immense. Liam Cosgrave had been fatally betrayed by his own excessive loyalty to one of his Ministers,' was Garret's verdict.

The resignation of the President caused a sensation and Fianna Fáil put down a motion of no confidence in the Government which was debated by the Dáil on 28 October. The Government took a pasting during the debate but the stability of the coalition was not damaged as Fianna Fáil had hoped. 'Once it was clear that Cosgrave was not going to require the head of Donegan there was no way we were going to look for his head because we didn't think it was an issue on which to bring down a government,' says Brendan Halligan. 'So Corish gave a speech leading off for the Government which I helped him to draft and I remember him saying "this is the most unhappy speech I have ever given". He didn't deliver it with great enthusiasm but it wasn't an issue on which to bring down a government. No such issue ever arose during that coalition.'

Cosgrave himself sailed through the Dáil debate as if it was a matter of routine. His speech was typically pithy and in response to some Fianna Fáil deputies who claimed his position as Taoiseach had been put in jeopardy by the crisis he replied:

'The Opposition are always worrying about me. When I was in Opposition they were afraid I would be toppled from one day to the other. When I am in Government they are still afraid I will be toppled.'

'[Mr Colley:] You are the best friend we have.'

'[Taoiseach:] May I say this? Thank God, whether in Government or in Opposition I was always able to look after myself and, please God, when I am not I shall call it a day.

'The main thing in the debate is this: the Opposition have had their say; they have made what speeches they could; they have tried to make much more of it than it was worth. When all is said and done the Deputies supporting the Government and me will vote confidence in the Government, and in the last analysis, that it what counts.'

The coalition won the division by 73 votes to 67. From a narrow perspective Cosgrave's Dáil analysis was right; in political terms the row revealed that the coalition parties were ready to stick together through thick and thin and the Fianna Fáil motion was a failure. However, in terms of public opinion the coalition suffered grievously. O'Dalaigh's resignation was a body blow from which the Government never recovered in terms of public esteem and it had a decisive effect on the 1977 Election.

Conor Cruise O'Brien remembers that the incident caused strains in government but not between Fine Gael and Labour.

'In a coalition government a lot of the arguments go on off stage inside the two parties and I think there were signs of strain within Fine Gael. I think Liam didn't want to sacrifice him but I think Garret and others did, on grounds of constitutional propriety. I argued on the other hand that as Donegan had gone to the Park — gone to Canossa if you like — it should be allowed to rest there. What Cosgrave did was to put him out of Defence and leave him in the cold for a while and then the post of Minister for Fisheries was created and I argued Paddy Donegan would be very suitable and Cosgrave accepted that. I mean it was a terrible thing to say but everyone knew he was drunk at the time. Of course it was wrong that as Minister for Defence he should be drunk at a gathering of that kind and OK there was a case for giving him the boot. But I thought it would have been a bit heavy in the circumstances. There was no Fine Gael–Labour division. Justin Keating was somewhat different from the rest of us in that he was closer to Garret than he was to any of his Labour colleagues. But none of the Labour people pressed for Donegan's head. Corish didn't tell me not to defend Donegan to the extent I did.'

'There is a public and private side to everything and people very well understood what the private side was,' says Halligan. 'Politics is a profession like anything else and professionals have a fellow feeling for each other and in the case of Donegan everybody well understood what the problem was. The question was were they going to crucify him for it. The answer was they weren't. I think that there was a feeling that Ó Dálaigh was behaving unreasonably as well as a simultaneous feeling that he was behaving reasonably.'

Peter Barry feels that Cosgrave should have accepted Donegan's resignation at the beginning of the controversy.

'Loyalty was a very big thing with him, to a fault, and he didn't like Cearbhall. I understand his loyalty but politically Cosgrave should have accepted Donegan's resignation. I think Paddy would have been a lot happier; I am surmising now but I feel Paddy would not have minded doing his penance. It damaged the Government and it damaged Liam. He had to chose between a friend and the right thing and he choose a friend. Paddy was a very undisciplined loose cannon on a very wobbly ship.'

One liberal Fine Gael politician who was not regarded as a Cosgrave supporter had sympathy with him on this issue. 'I felt Donegan made a fair charge, although his language was very inappropriate. It was so typical of Liam just defending his Minister.'

Seán Duignan tells a story about the inauguration of Patrick Hillery who was the agreed choice of Government and Opposition to replace

Ó Dálaigh. Up on the platform with the other members of the cabinet for the ceremony was Donegan. It was shortly after the canonisation of Maria Goretti in Rome at which the man who murdered her was brought from his prison cell to witness the ceremony. Duignan asked Donegan how he felt.

'Like the poor hoor who murdered Maria Goretti,' replied the Minister in his inimitable Louth accent.

The negative public reaction to the coalition over the resignation of Ó Dálaigh was compounded by a series of reports in *The Irish Times* around the same period which indicated that terrorist suspects were being ill-treated by the Gardaí. The stories written by Joe Joyce and Don Buckley caused serious public concern about the tactics being used by the so-called 'heavy gang' to extract confessions from Republicans suspected of serious crime. Minister for Justice, Pat Cooney, strenuously rejected the stories as did Cosgrave. FitzGerald remembers meeting two senior Gardaí who told him of their worry about the way some confessions had been extracted. He tried to raise the issue at cabinet but got short shrift from Cosgrave and Cooney. He even contemplated resignation from the Government over the issue but decided against it.

Cosgrave's absolute conviction that the security of the State was the overriding concern of any government led him into direct conflict not just with the liberal media and some in Fine Gael but with an institution for which he had deep respect — the Catholic Church. Relations between the Taoiseach and the Papal Nuncio, Mgr. Alibrandi, were frosty because of the Nuncio's known strong support for Irish Republicans. This boiled over into a diplomatic incident in April 1977 when Cosgrave reacted furiously to what he saw as an attempt by the Catholic Church to interfere in Irish politics.

The incident arose following a hunger strike by Republican prisoners in Portlaoise which had met with an uncompromising response from the Government. Bishop Daly of Derry made a statement on prison conditions during the hunger strike which annoyed Cosgrave and senior Ministers who believed it would only encourage prisoners to pursue the protest to the death. The cabinet considered the issue and decided, in the absence of FitzGerald, who was abroad on official business, to send a diplomatic protest to the Holy See through normal diplomatic channels. When FitzGerald arrived back in Ireland he persuaded Cosgrave that a protest to Rome might be an over reaction and the plan was dropped.

However, unknown to either Cosgrave or FitzGerald at this stage the Vatican had already made an official protest to the Government about its handling of the hunger strike. FitzGerald recalls in his autobiography that Cardinal Benelli, the top-ranking Vatican official, presented a note of protest to the Irish Ambassador on the issue. The Ambassador turned the note around on the desk so that it faced Benelli again, a traditional diplomatic manoeuvre to indicate that the contents would not be acceptable to the Irish Government and should not be pressed. Benelli ignored the hint and turned the note back. The Ambassador then warned the Archbishop about the Taoiseach's possible reaction but to no avail.

FitzGerald was out of the country again the following week when the contents of the Vatican note were delivered to the Government. Cosgrave reacted with fury and he drafted a very strongly worded reply telling the Vatican that the hunger strike had been organised by people convicted of murder and other serious crimes in the course of a terrorist campaign which had led to the deaths of 2,000 Irish people. The note said that Irish Government policy was based on the rule of law and it emphasised that strong exception was taken to interference by the Vatican in a matter affecting the security of the state. Foreign Affairs officials, worried about the strong tone of the reply contacted FitzGerald in Reykjavik to ask whether it should be delivered.

'I could see why my officials had decided to phone me for instructions but I could not conceivably tell them not to deliver the note, especially after I had been responsible for the failure to implement the Government's earlier decision,' says FitzGerald. Instead he added a memorandum of his own explaining the strength of the reaction by the Taoiseach and the Government. Cruise O'Brien remembers that during the IRA hunger strike Cosgrave told the cabinet that he had a request from the Nuncio to visit the prisoners in Portlaoise. 'I refused of course,' he told his Ministers. 'When the Church collided with law and order the State won,' says Cruise O'Brien.

'Although he was a very religious man he drew the line at Church interference on issues that affected the security of state,' says Mac Conghail. 'I can remember an occasion when the late Cardinal Conway had come to see him to discuss the conditions of the prisoners on hunger strike. I can remember being in a room when Cardinal Conway said to him something to the effect "Do you realise these people are only on water?" and the then Taoiseach turned to me and said "Water is too good for them". So he had a very strong view about the national security situation.'

With security concerns uppermost in his mind Cosgrave delivered an emotional speech to his party's Árd Fheis in the Mansion House in Dublin in May 1977. He curtly dismissed complaints in the media that the rights of some IRA suspects had been violated by asking what civil rights has been possessed by Billy Fox or by the two gardaí murdered in the course of their duty. He called an *Irish Times* investigation 'a malicious campaign of vilification' against the Gardaí. Then to thunderous applause he declared:

> 'Not for the first time has this party stood between the people of this country and anarchy. And remember, those people who comment so freely and write so freely — some of them aren't even Irish — no doubt many of you are familiar with an expression in some parts of the country where an outsider is described as a blow-in. Some of these are blow-ins. Now as far as we're concerned they can blow out or blow up.'

This speech became as famous as his 'mongrel foxes' declaration five years earlier. As in 1972 the targets of his criticism were unclear but those in the know claimed that among the 'blow-ins' he was referring to were journalist Bruce Arnold, who was English by birth. Arnold had criticised the Government vigorously over the wealth tax and was highly critical of the coalition. The net effect of the speech was to cause further negative publicity for the coalition on the eve of the general election.

18

ELECTION DISASTER

On 25 May 1977, Liam Cosgrave made the biggest blunder of his political career. He asked President Hillery to dissolve the 20th Dáil and called a general election for 16 June. The cabinet was equally divided over whether to hold an election in June or wait until the autumn when the economic upswing would have had more time to percolate through to the voters. The disastrous decision to go to the country in June was taken by Cosgrave himself. Not alone was the timing wrong, the Government had made no preparations of any kind for a June campaign. Incredibly the coalition parties only commissioned an opinion poll to measure the public mood after the election was called. The same applied to the policies on which the election was fought: they were cobbled together after the date was announced.

This dreadful preparation for the campaign stemmed from deep disagreement among Ministers about the best date for an election and from a complacency which had developed in the coalition due to the so-called Tullymander. Jim Tully, the Minister for Local Government had overseen a constituency revision early in the life of the Government which was widely regarded as making the re-election of the coalition a certainty. The proliferation of three-seat constituencies in Dublin was designed to maximise the number of Fine Gael and Labour seats at the expense of Fianna Fáil. The theory was that on the figures Fianna Fáil would only get one out of three seats instead of a possible two out of four if the constituencies were drawn differently. The Opposition was so perturbed by the revision that Jack Lynch pledged an independent constituency commission if Fianna Fáil won the election.

'I never believed that Jimmy Tully had tailored the constituencies to ensure Fianna Fáil would stay in Opposition,' says Richie Ryan. 'The new situation gave an enhanced margin to whoever had the tide running in their favour. We postponed the census from 1975 to 1976 and I was made go into the Dáil and say we were doing it to save £1 million because of the tight budgetary situation. I was in favour of holding the census in 1975 and so was Garret FitzGerald but the cabinet didn't want to upset the Tully gerrymander. So they had to think of a good excuse. Somebody later asked me why I hadn't resigned but I didn't see it as a resigning matter. The reason we didn't hold it in 1975 was that the results would have been out and there would have had to be some redrawing before the next election and it was decided to leave it until 1976 when there wouldn't be enough time.'

On top of the Tullymander the coalition parties were very encouraged by solid performances in the seven by-elections held during the Government's lifetime. In particular the victory of Enda Kenny in Mayo West in November 1975, and Brendan Halligan in Dublin South West in June 1976, combined with Fianna Fáil's loss of Donegal North East to Patrick Keaveney of Independent Fianna Fáil, appeared to indicate that the tide was turning in the coalition's favour.

The imminence of a general election was widely speculated on by the media from early in 1977. The January budget was well-received and the media accepted the view that the turn-around in the economy had taken place. 'After the budget of February 1977, a poll showed a big swing in the Government's favour and there was some talk about an election. Charlie Haughey told me "God, I couldn't have done better myself",' says Richie Ryan.

One of Cosgrave's central objectives was to prove that coalition governments could work and that they need not fall apart in disarray as the two inter-party governments had. This objective had been achieved by the spring of 1977 when the Government achieved four years in office and an election some time that year was inevitable. Fianna Fáil prepared for it well in advance devising policies and strategies for an all-out effort to win back power. Fine Gael and Labour, preoccupied by the cares of office, hardly focused on the election at all, apart from debating the best date to go to the country.

Richie Ryan and Garret FitzGerald were among the strongest supporters of an autumn election. Justin Keating and Michael O'Leary shared the same view but other Ministers were equally convinced that June was the best time to go. Cosgrave discussed the issue with the entire cabinet in early May and found his colleagues equally divided. He had separate consultations with Brendan Corish and that swayed him in favour of the June date. Richie Ryan recalls how he was informed of the decision late in May when he was summoned to the Taoiseach's office.

> '"Richie, we are going to the country," said Cosgrave. "Corish came to me earlier in the week and he is wobbling like a jellyfish. He says the Labour Party might not stick together over the summer. Thornley is in a bad way and there are other tensions in the party. And if we don't go now the Government could collapse over Labour's internal squabbles."
>
> '"Oh Liam it is too soon," I responded. "People are still not convinced that the economy is turning around. The autumn would be the time to go."
>
> '"I have already told Brendan [Corish] so we have to go and I want you to be Director of Elections."
>
> '"Oh for God's sake Liam listen, I have been stuck in my office for the last four and a half years. I have lost touch with the organisation."
>
> '"Oh, you are the man for it," said Cosgrave and that was that.
>
> 'It would be unimaginable now. We went into an election without having a poll to establish what the position was,' says one senior Fine Gael figure from that time.

Jack Jones of MRBI was commissioned to conduct the poll and he produced the results nine days after the election was called to a meeting of the campaign committee in Government Buildings. Around the table at 10 a.m. on Saturday, 4 June, were Richie Ryan, Garret FitzGerald, Michael O'Leary, Justin Keating, Conor Cruise O-Brien, Brendan Halligan, Senator Jim Dooge and Senator Alexis Fitzgerald. The information supplied by Jones left the coalition leaders reeling. Fianna Fáil was on 59% of the vote, Fine Gael 25%, Labour 10%, unspecified coalition 4% and Others 2%. Raymond Smith in his book *Garret: The Enigma* quotes FitzGerald as remarking: 'Can we un-dissolve the Dáil.' Michael O'Leary remembered 'coffee cups tinkling against saucers was the only sound to be heard in the room as the figures of impending defeat were read out.'

Jim Dooge was given the unenviable task of taking the information to Liam Cosgrave but there were no histrionics when the bad news was imparted, he just listened patiently until Dooge had finished.

'Can you trust these things,' remarked Cosgrave who had never made a secret of his own doubts about polls.

'Well you can trust them to within 4 or 5%,' responded Dooge. 'This means we have no real chance,' said Cosgrave.

'I think it does,' replied Dooge and no more was said about it.

'Cosgrave fought the whole campaign facing that disaster but he never betrayed a hint of it. He typically fought the campaign scrupulously refusing to use government resources, the same as Garret did afterwards. He wouldn't even use a government xerox machine. It was really amazing in hindsight but Liam fought a very good campaign knowing that he had no chance,' said one Fine Gael figure.

Meanwhile Fianna Fáil launched its famous give-away manifesto which was to cost the country dear in the long term but which proved very attractive to voters in 1977. Rates on houses were to be abolished as was car tax. Grants for first-time house buyers and a huge expansion of the public service to create new jobs was also promised but it was the straight forward give-aways that proved so attractive. Although some senior Fianna Fáil figures, particularly Charles Haughey, were privately appalled at the profligate nature of the manifesto it put the party in the driving seat for the whole campaign.

While senior coalition figures knew the disaster they were facing they didn't inform their junior colleagues or give any public hint of it. The media made the Government the clear favourites to win the election. On 2 June, before the Government got its bad poll news, *The Irish Times* printed its own poll results under the heading 'Survey Indicates Fianna Fáil lead over Coalition'. Incredibly no figures for party support were produced in the poll with figures simply being given for how the electorate perceived Government and Opposition in relation to the issues.

'I don't think most people were anticipating a coalition defeat,' says John Bruton. 'Of course politicians took their cue from the media and, strangely, had a tendency to believe that what appeared in the papers must be right, which isn't always the case now. Certainly Fianna Fáil seized the initiative and captured the public imagination, if that is not too elevated a word to use for the greed that motivated people.'

Cosgrave in his election speeches stressed the unity of the coalition.

'The Government is a cohesive, united one and I believe it is not immodest of me to say that the team I selected are talented and have done their jobs well and thoroughly. They have come through the most testing of times with determination and drive,' he said praising individual Fine Gael and Labour Ministers by name.

On 5 June Cosgrave toured North Tipperary. By this time he knew the bad poll results but he didn't let it show. Dick Walsh who accompanied him wrote for the following day's *Irish Times.* 'The script tells the official story. Unscripted, Mr Cosgrave was direct and nearly jovial. He emphasised rates and raised a cheer when he derided Fianna Fáil's promise to abolish road tax.' Getting a dig in at local Fianna Fáil TD, Michael O'Kennedy, who had bought a house in Dublin, Cosgrave praised the two coalition TDs for the constituency saying, 'you haven't to travel 100 miles to find them.' He asked Fine Gael voters to continue their preferences for Labour TD, John Ryan. 'Lift your pencil and don't waste a vote,' he said.

The following day Cosgrave was struck down with a bout of laryngitis and he was out of action for a few days. His son Liam, Jr, delivered a speech on his behalf focusing on the battle for power in Fianna Fáil between the Lynch and the Haughey factions and asking which of these two contending power blocks would get their hands on the levers of power if the Opposition won.

On Saturday 11 June, Jack Jones presented the results of a second poll to the coalition campaign committee. It showed that Fianna Fáil had dropped 8% to 51% and gave Fine Gael and Labour some hope that the tide was now running in their favour. However, the campaign was now entering its final days and there was not enough time to make further inroads into the Fianna Fáil vote.

In the last days of the campaign Cosgrave focused on law and order, which didn't go down very well with an electorate now preoccupied with bread and butter politics as a result of the Fianna Fáil promises. Attacking media commentators who had criticised the Gardaí and highlighted the conditions of Republican prisoners in Portlaoise the Taoiseach was in fighting form. He said that the prisoners had been jailed for 'most heinous crimes of murder, shooting and robbery. They aren't there for not having lights on their bikes. Where else should they be but in prison.'

The Taoiseach's focus on security was echoed by Cruise O'Brien who also attacked Charles Haughey in a BBC radio interview. Richie Ryan and Garret FitzGerald felt this attack played straight into Fianna Fáil's hands and tried to rein in the Cruiser. 'The only argument we had in the coalition at that time, and it didn't involve Liam, was between myself and Garret,' remembers Cruise O'Brien. 'I was for having a go at Haughey and I started doing this and then I was told, absurdly in retrospect, that the thing to do was concentrate on the economic issues. We would have lost anyway but would have lost by a smaller margin if we had concentrated on 'Haughey is not a safe man' type of charge. There was a good case to be made for that and it would at least, have diverted some attention from the promises.'

The media was totally unaware of the problems besetting the coalition from the beginning of the campaign. Even the massive and warm public response to Fianna Fáil leader, Jack Lynch, in his nationwide tour didn't shake the assumption that Cosgrave was going to lead the coalition back to power, a feat which had never been achieved by a coalition leader in the history of the state. On the Sunday before the election the country's top political correspondents interviewed on RTE radio confidently predicted that Fine Gael and Labour would win an overall majority. Seán Duignan summed up the prevailing media mood when he said that if Fianna Fáil managed to win it would be 'the greatest comeback since Lazarus.'

When the boxes were opened on 17 June it quickly became apparent that Lazarus had nothing on Fianna Fáil who were sweeping the country. The party's vote was up to 51%, a feat achieved only once by Eamon de Valera. In terms of seats the Fianna Fáil performance was awesome. The party's strength in the Dáil increased from 69 in 1973 to 84. Fine Gael slumped from 54 to 43 while Labour declined from 19 to 17. The Tullymander which had been designed to win the election for the coalition actually made things worse than they need have been for the Government. Three senior Ministers, Cruise O'Brien, Keating and Cooney lost their seats in the rout which gave Fianna Fáil a massive 20-seat majority in the Dáil. Jack Lynch was as stunned as his opponents by the scale of the victory.

'I didn't think it was going to be as bad. I was one of the more optimistic,' recalls Cruise O'Brien. Looking back Brendan Halligan believes that the 1977 campaign was a tribute to Cosgrave. 'A final judgement on Cosgrave as Taoiseach and as a party leader in coalition is that we went out united and fought a united campaign. Now that is the best judgement that can be made from the point of view of the Labour Party and indeed his own party. If that had not been the case it would have been an index of relationships. The fact that they went out together to face into the hurricane says a lot for both men.' Peter Barry remembers the disillusionment that followed. 'When the Government changed we were depressed and demoralised because we thought we had done a good job. We knew we had been psyched out of it.'

The day after the election there was some press speculation about Cosgrave's future but there was no serious consideration given to the possibility that he would step down as party leader at the age of 57. As all the parties assessed the situation over the weekend *The Irish Times* carried a story suggesting that Cosgrave and Corish might not continue as party leaders. Garret FitzGerald was quoted as saying that he would respond to the demands of the party should Liam Cosgrave decide to resign.

This was regarded as ominous by some close supporters of Cosgrave but the majority of Fine Gael TDs did not even consider the possibility that Cosgrave would step down. FitzGerald in his memoirs says that there was speculation about Brendan Corish but not about Cosgrave. 'Those of us who felt we knew Liam Cosgrave thought it unlikely that he would opt out of political life at such an early age; he was only 57.'

However, one week after the election at the first party meeting to review the result Cosgrave announced his resignation. There had been no prior consultation with anyone and the announcement caused consternation. In his speech to the party he paid tribute to his Fine Gael colleagues in government but he mentioned only one by name and that was FitzGerald. Given their relationship this nonplussed FitzGerald as much as it did Cosgrave's own strong supporters. Paddy Donegan got to his feet to urge Cosgrave not to resign but the Taoiseach was in no mood to reconsider.

Cosgrave's sudden departure at the age of 57 is still something that puzzles some of his former colleagues but others were not all that surprised when they thought about it.

'I think he knew that Garret would have been out to challenge him,' says Richie Ryan. 'Garret wouldn't have defied him in the open but he would have had his minions going around and undermining him and Liam decided that to crawl back up again would be extremely difficult in those circumstances. I was away when he announced he was going. I was in Washington at an IMF meeting. I got a message from RTE to do an interview about the leadership and that was the first I knew of it. So he did go very suddenly, and he hadn't told anybody but that would be Liam's form. I know there was a belief that Cosgrave and I were extremely close and that we shared secrets and confidences and all that kind of thing. If Liam sought my advice I gave it. I probably expressed opinions to him from time to time, even when he hadn't sought them.'

Even those who had been given a hint of Cosgrave's move in advance were surprised. The day before the party meeting Jim Dooge went to Liam immediately after the Dáil election to say he was not going to run for the Seanad again and Cosgrave remarked, 'Well I always knew you were a realist like myself.' Despite the hint Dooge was as surprised as anyone else at the decision. So was John Bruton who says:

'I was surprised he resigned so quickly. In fact I was surprised that he resigned at all. Few enough people would have blamed him for the defeat. Most people would have felt the Government as a whole had been culpably complacent in the way it went into the election and that it hadn't prepared properly. The party machine had been allowed to run down and that was a collective failure for which Liam Cosgrave had his share of responsibility but he shouldn't have had to take all the responsibility by resigning. I was shocked when he went because I expected him to go on. He probably remembered the bleak period he had gone through from 1965 until 1973 and didn't want to repeat that performance. I also know he didn't think we would be back in power for a very long time because he said it to me. He was clearly thinking back to the 16 years Fine Gael had been out of office.' I was not happy at the speed with which he went. I would have thought that if he had hung on for another six months and then resigned there would have been a calmer atmosphere in Fine Gael as to who should succeed him. Garret came in and there was really no other choice that could be made at the time. There would have been people rallying to me but they would have been only rallying to me in the hope that I could stop Garret and that wasn't a good reason. In a calmer time I don't think they would have made a different choice but there would have been less opposition to Garret inside the parliamentary party. People like Donegan and those were sniping at Garret all the time.'

Richie Ryan was in the United States for the announcement and he rang Peter Barry to arrange a meeting in Cork. Barry remembers the meeting.

'I got a room at Cork airport and we had a chat. He was trying to mount a "Stop Garret" campaign and he wanted me as the person who would do that. Ted Nealon told me later that if I had stood I would have gotten more votes than Garret in the party and I knew there was a chance of that but I also knew it would have been an anti-Garret vote and not a pro-Barry vote. That wouldn't have been any good for the party and anyway the humour of the grassroots was that they were so shocked by the defeat in the election they could only see knights on white horses and Garret appeared to be that. I would have to say that Garret, with all the problems he would present to you on a personal basis and on a party basis, chasing after every little wisp, jumping up and down in the Dáil and not thinking things out, he was a visionary. There was an awful lot wrong with this country and he shook this party and this country into the 1990s.'

FitzGerald recalls ringing Peter Barry to compare notes on their respective levels of support in the 62-member parliamentary party. 'I reckoned that I had the support of something like 43, leaving Peter with just under 20. He on the other hand believed that he had 25 supporters and was slightly upset that our figures did not tally.'

As Fine Gael TDs considered whom they would appoint as their new leader Cosgrave took one further step, which upset the liberals in his own party as well as Fianna Fáil. In the interregnum before the Government changed he looked after a number of his prominent supporters. John Grattan Esmonde, the defeated Fine Gael TD for Wexford was made a Circuit Court judge, Brendan Toal, defeated TD for Monaghan, was made a Land Commissioner. Frank Roe, a friend and political ally of many years was offered promotion from the circuit Court to the High Court but refused. Instead the job went to James D'Arcy. A number of other state vacancies were filled and promotions given before the Government's tenure ended on 5 July.

This spate of appointments naturally attracted criticism but Cosgrave saw it in terms of looking after people who had sacrificed their own careers to serve with him. Ted Nealon believes it is to his credit that he acted as he did.

'There were an awful lot of casualties in that election and he worked extremely hard trying to ensure that various people around him who might be out of work because of the change of government were fixed up. He sought to help them out in whatever way he could. He was extraordinarily concerned like that and made no apology for it. He came in for an awful lot of criticism in the papers but did what he believed was right.'

Cosgrave's successor was chosen on 1 July. Peter Barry did not enter the contest, instead he proposed FitzGerald who was the unanimous choice of the party. The Cosgrave era ended formally on 5 July 1977 when the Dáil met and elected Jack Lynch Taoiseach. Fine Gael took a new direction under FitzGerald who in the early 1980s brought the party to greater heights in terms of popular support than Cosgrave ever achieved. Yet by the end of his tenure in 1987 Fine Gael plunged to a much lower ebb than it had ever been under Cosgrave. It took the party nearly a decade to get into government again and it has still not recovered the level of support that Cosgrave managed on his worst election outing in 1977.

John Bruton reflects:

'There was certainly a sense once Garret took over that the party was taking a new course, almost cutting off its links with its past. We have since learned that he was somebody who had voted Fianna Fáil in 1961 and while that wasn't said publicly until recently a lot of people might have suspected it. There was a lot of vacant space in the Irish political spectrum which Garret was well fit to occupy but it wasn't space that would belong to Fine Gael in any long-term sense.'

19

CHAIRMAN AND CHIEF

In HIS time as Taoiseach Liam Cosgrave earned the enduring respect of almost all his Ministers, including his Labour colleagues. It was ironic that leading figures in the party who had campaigned against him in 1969 as an arch conservative opponent ultimately came to respect and like him in a way some of his more liberal Fine Gael colleagues never did.

'It was a coalition which on the whole worked remarkably smoothly because there grew up a relation of confidence between Cosgrave and Corish, personally,' recalls Conor Cruise O'Brien. 'They trusted one another and therefore they didn't get into flaps about things.'

Brendan Halligan, who was very close to the centre of power all through the lifetime of coalition as Corish's right-hand man, believes that Cosgrave's authority was seriously underestimated by commentators at the time and since.

> 'The first thing to be said is that, taking Brian Farrell's categorisation of chairman or chief, it would be a profound mistake to put Cosgrave into the category of chairman, as is often done. I think that in public he was the chairman in private he was the chief. He behaved as if he was Taoiseach; he had a natural authority about him; nobody at all ever contested his authority during the four years and nobody called his judgement into account. He was simply treated with enormous respect by the Labour Ministers.'

Both Halligan and Dick Burke make the point that Cosgrave had a relationship with senior Labour figures which transcended politics. 'For example Conor Cruise O'Brien had been a civil servant, which must not be forgotten and had served under Liam Cosgrave as Minister for Foreign Affairs. This very heavily influenced Conor's relationship with Cosgrave as Taoiseach. He had this enormous respect that a civil servant would have for a Minister or a Minister would have for a Taoiseach. Cosgrave never had the slightest problem with Conor and the expectation was that he would,' says Halligan.

'The same was true of Tully. Here the link was a psychological link; it was the Army. Now Tully had only been an NCO but Tully had the NCOs respect for an officer. In the case of Justin I couldn't put a finger on it but I know there were no problems at all and in the case of Mick O'Leary it was one politician's respect for another because we all recognised that Cosgrave was an extremely good politician.'

'Cosgrave had a great relationship with fellows like Tully and the Cruiser,' says Dick Burke. 'There was an old long-standing relationship between Liam and Conor going back to their days in Foreign Affairs. But again Liam Cosgrave was an absolutely fair man. And a stickler for the proprieties of office. He would treat Ministers properly at all times.'

Richie Ryan remembers his handling of the Government.

'He was a marvelous chairman at government meetings. It wouldn't be easy to control when you had prima donnas like Conor Cruise and Garret FitzGerald and Justin Keating jumping in and prepared to carry on extraordinarily lengthy debates with all kinds of esoteric ideas. Liam would suffer for a while and then would give a little sniff and say "Look I think we have heard enough of that now" and he would move on with the agenda and carry on the argument elsewhere. He would be on the phone to the two participants later in the afternoon and he'd say, "Maybe you should cool it a bit. Would you come down to me and we'll see what we can do," and he had this great capacity, some people would call it wheel and deal", but he had a great capacity for finding consensus.'

Cruise O'Brien remembers an episode at the beginning of the Government which was both highly amusing and instructive.

'De Valera, who was president of course, and then very old, very near the end of his days, gave a dinner for the new Government which we weren't expecting. He could have been excused on the grounds of age and it was known that he didn't approve very much of non-Fianna Fáil governments. But he not only gave the dinner with graciousness, as everyone would expect when he was the host, but he also spoke and I remember this because Liam had a rather unexpected hair-trigger laugh. He would see something as funny and he would suddenly explode with a kind of horsey whinny. We were all arranged every which way and I was sitting beside Cosgrave and Dev began his speech with the following immortal words. He said in his old creaky voice:

'"I have always been opposed to the system of election known as proportional representation, because I foresaw that, if persisted in, this would one day lead to coalition government," and then Liam exploded,' recalls Cruise O'Brien with a chuckle.

'He had his glass to his lips and he splashed his Irish and soda all over the table. But then Dev went on and it was rather interesting. He went on to say: "I have put to myself the question. How can a coalition government be reconciled with stability in the governance of the State? And I have a reached a conclusion which I wish to convey to you all. It is that the central principle in any given coalition should be that of loyalty to the Taoiseach." So Liam looked quite pleased with that. And I must say it influenced me and some of my colleagues in what we actually did and it helped the stability of the coalition government.'

The Government press secretary, Muiris Mac Conghail, remembers the same evening vividly.

'It was a very long lecture and quite provocative. At the end of it Cosgrave got up and simply said "I wish President de Valera and Bean de Valera every happiness in their retirement". After dinner drinks we gathered around Dev for a chat. I was sitting quite close to him on the floor because I was speaking Irish to him and I remember looking around and there was John Maurice Kelly, Michael O'Leary, Peter Barry and Conor Cruise O'Brien and the conversation was going on in Irish and he turned to me and said, "*Conas na raibh rialtas mar sin agamsa.*"[2]'

That key relationship in the Government was between Taoiseach and Tánaiste and it was warm from the very beginning. Whatever their differences in the past the two men developed an enormous respect and even affection for each other in government. 'They were very familiar and very easy with each other and liked each other,' remembers Halligan. 'Of course they had been in cabinet together but also, and this may seem very trite, people who like each other must have at least one common interest, and in their case it was horses. Small talk is very important because you can't talk business all the time. So what did they talk about — horses.'

'They liked one another. Neither of them were very talkative or flag- waving sort of people. They wouldn't inflict much ideology on each other,' says Cruise O'Brien. Both were essentially self-effacing,

---

2. Why did I not have a government like this?

devout Catholics who had simple tastes and no desire to hog the limelight.

'I enjoyed working in that cabinet a lot,' says Peter Barry. 'He allowed Ministers to take responsibility but he expected them, if they had a problem, to go and tell him about it and not to have to read it in the paper. I think most people were pretty loyal to him. He got closer and closer to Corish and they ran a two-man government if you like. He did what Albert Reynolds never did. He recognised that he wasn't the total boss in the Government and that other people had to be brought along with him and he consulted all the time.'

Halligan agrees:

'Cosgrave never, ever, regarded the coalition as a two-party arrangement in which one was trying to get advantage over another. He regarded it almost as a one-party arrangement, with two parts for which there must be mutual benefit and he very well understood all of the time that unless we felt that we were getting as much out of it as Fine Gael the thing wouldn't endure.'

Cosgrave's approach was in stark contrast to more recent coalitions and even to that of FitzGerald in the 1980s. Ironically, given Garret's role as almost the sixth Labour Minister in the Cosgrave Cabinet, he never established an easy rapport with the Labour Ministers in his own governments. The contrast with the administrations of Haughey and Reynolds, in which a basis of trust between the coalition parties was never established in the first place, is even more pointed.

'The relationship was so good that I can remember a number of by-elections, in which we fought common campaigns,' says Halligan. 'I can remember once or twice discussing internal Labour Party arrangements with him and it was always done with enormous respect and he would enquire as to what the situation was and he might say what he would ideally like to see happen. I remember on one occasion saying quite clearly to him, "That is not possible" and he simply said, "Fine, I accept that." There was no attempt to interfere at all but he was always trying to reinforce us. And allowing us both collectively and individually to get as much credit as we could out of it. It was an extraordinary and subtle way of running an administration.'

'Relations were very good and there were no party divisions,' recalls Dick Burke. 'There were some strains but they were not related to party politics. I don't think it is any secret that Garret was more inclined towards the social democratic type of things than some of the others in Fine Gael. But he was so involved, and beneficially and worthily involved in the European thing, that he wasn't that involved in domestic affairs.'

Brendan Halligan confirms that FitzGerald was regarded as virtually the sixth Labour Minister in the cabinet. He sided regularly with the majority of Labour Ministers against his Fine Gael colleagues but the arguments at cabinet rarely split along clear party lines.

FitzGerald says that Labour's weight in the Government was even greater than the two-to-one ratio of cabinet seats would indicate.

'In the first place, Brendan Corish's decision to delegate full authority over his Social Welfare Department to Frank Cluskey, his parliamentary secretary, virtually gave them a sixth government seat, as Frank had to be present whenever Social Welfare matters were discussed — which, given our extensive programme of social reform was very frequently — and Liam Cosgrave's respect for Frank Cluskey's political judgement led him sometimes to suggest that he remain on afterwards to join in discussion of other matters.

'Second, at the very start of the new Government Conor Cruise O'Brien persuaded Liam Cosgrave to give him responsibility for the Government Information Service, which had hitherto always answered directly to the Taoiseach of the day through its — uniquely — politically appointed head. Third, the combination of the exceptional intellectual calibre of some of the Labour Party Ministers and the weight of the portfolios they collectively commanded gave them a higher profile than their numbers alone would account for.'

FitzGerald adds that the Labour influence did not mean that the Government leaned ideologically to the left because he claims Tully was to the right of most Fine Gael Ministers while Cruise O'Brien's concern for law and order also tended to pull the Government to the right. 'Liam Cosgrave's own conservatism, the respect in which the Labour Party Ministers held him and the pragmatic manner in which we addressed our agenda as a government all combined to ensure a balanced approach to most problems and to minimise ideological tensions.'

FitzGerald like other Ministers makes the point that they dealt with cabinet business in such a way as to ensure the solidarity of the Government. 'The Labour Party sought to avoid becoming isolated on potentially contentious issues and if there was any danger of this happening at least one Fine Gael Minister joined them in the relevant vote — frequently myself (usually by conviction) or in my absence some other Fine Gael Minister (sometimes as a matter of political prudence).'

The cabinet met twice a week on Tuesdays and Thursdays at 11 a.m. Meetings went on until 1 p.m. and sometimes resumed again for the afternoon after a break for lunch. Ministers sat around the table in the order they had seated themselves for the first cabinet meeting and they did not sit in party groupings. Apart from the cabinet Ministers the chief whip, John Kelly, and the secretary to the Government, Donal O'Sullivan, attended all meetings. Attorney General, Declan Costello, was at most meetings and Frank Cluskey attended regularly at Cosgrave's request.

Cosgrave and Corish were the only members of the coalition who had previous cabinet experience and it took the other Ministers some time to adapt to the protocol of government decision making. Cabinet agendas were long and demanding due in part to the fact that the nature of government decision making was becoming much more complex in a period of change with a big expansion in the role of the State as well as Ireland's accession to the EEC. Northern Ireland also occupied a huge swathe of government time while the various crisis which plagued the country during the mid-1970s added to the weight of cabinet business.

'At cabinet he let other people speak. He never showed any signs of agreement or disagreement. Except to the extent of the free vote on contraception and the very hard and fast line laid down immediately over the Herrema kidnapping,' says Cruise O'Brien.

'Cosgrave was an excellent chairman of a meeting in the sense that people said their piece but he would never go for stirring up the discussion again,' says Dick Burke. It wasn't so much that he didn't seek consensus but he distilled the consensus himself after a certain amount of talking and said well I think that is agreed now.'

FitzGerald also says that Cosgrave proved to be an effective chairman of the Government and he was helped in this by the fact that although he was only 53 he was older than most other Ministers and had far more government experience than anybody else.

Mac Conghail says Cosgrave was a man who took advice well and also had a great political sense of what he should say.

'I know that some of his colleagues in government have rubbished him from time to time, because leaders tend to hear these stories about themselves, and therefore the then Minister for Foreign Affairs or the then Minister for Industry and Commerce may have been quite critical of him behind his back, but when it came to cabinet meetings they weren't like that.'

Some former Ministers, however, believe that at times Cosgrave was not decisive enough. He irritated them from time to time by his concern to get everybody's point of view and search for consensus when it was quite clear what the majority view was but this was an occasional failing. Cabinet meetings during FitzGerald's tenure in office went on for much, much longer, but other modern Taoisigh have followed the Cosgrave style of a tighter rein on cabinet meetings. Haughey and Reynolds usually dispatched business at one meeting a week and that one meeting was often concluded by lunchtime, having started at 11 a.m. The three-party coalition led by John Bruton also tends to wrap up its business at one meeting a week but a big change in the decision-making process has taken place since the 1970s. Now programme managers sort out most problems and arguments before the cabinet even considers major issues. That has reduced the time given by the cabinet to making decisions.

'Liam Cosgrave faced into big issues in a clear way and cabinet meetings were usually quite short,' says Mac Conghail. 'They would start at 11 o'clock and would be over well before lunch mostly although they could occasionally drag on. He was a man who believed the less said the less needed to be mended and he didn't want to have a kind of theatre at a cabinet meeting. He read his brief well and marked up everything he had to do. He did it exactly as he would mark the racing page in the *Irish Independent*. Everything was prepared for him and he would take a brief from the secretary to the Government, Dan O'Sullivan, Dermot Nally the assistant secretary, myself or Frank Murray, his private secretary, on the issue to be addressed. He took a note on each one of those things and would generally use it well but he didn't always slavishly follow the civil service line. He would often say "I'm sorry I didn't follow your line on that but I decided to go another way". The Minister for Foreign Affairs sometimes went on at length at cabinet meetings but Cosgrave's attitude was that people couldn't hang around all day.'

John Bruton says he learned a lot from Cosgrave.

'I would try to be like him in the way I would handle meetings and the way I would handle people. He gave a very good example of how to manage a government as a collection of human beings, recognising their strengths and weaknesses. I think he set an excellent example and in so far as I can I follow that. I have obviously an asset in terms of back-up that he wouldn't have had. It is also important to recognise that relations between Labour and Fine Gael were pretty bad before they went into government in 1973. Distrust had developed during the 1960s and Labour were very ideological.'

Cosgrave had the difficulty not only of trying to weld Ministers of two parties into a coherent government but the potentially much stickier problem of building up a good working relationship with people like FitzGerald and Cooney who had been deadly rivals of his only a few months before the Government took office. His impatience with Garret sometimes broke through as Richie Ryan recalls.

'I remember well one day at a cabinet meeting Justin Keating saying that he wouldn't be present the following week because he had to be in Brussels and he asked that an important item be deferred until his return.'

As Ryan recalls it Garret said:

'"Ridiculous, you can get a plane from Brussels to Birmingham and from Birmingham on to somewhere else and you can easily be here in time."

'"Well my office tells me that I can't. It is not possible to be here on time," said Justin.

'"Oh, of course it is," said Garret reeling off plane times.

'"Look," said Cosgrave. "This is not a travel agency. If Justin says he can't be here that is that."'

Cruise O'Brien recalls that Cosgrave's relations with his Ministers were very good, on the whole.

'He would originally have had some doubts about Pat Cooney, who was regarded as a liberal in Fine Gael and Cosgrave had a slight tendency to see Fine Gael liberals as Provos which was by no means fair to Pat among others. Then when he found Cooney starting to get a bad name from the press over the Heavy Gang and so on Liam felt he could relax and they became quite closely associated. Indeed I think Peter Barry and Pat Cooney were the Fine Gael Ministers that were closest to him. He liked Paddy Donegan personally but he regarded him as a bit unstable. I don't think either party knew much about what was going on in the other, except what Garret and Justin would learn from one another. They were close.'

The Taoiseach's principal concern from the beginning was to foster trust among his disparate team. This took a lot of delicacy on his part, given the diverse political backgrounds of his Ministers, not to mention their intellectual abilities and political rivalries. He succeeded in obtaining from them all total loyalty to himself and a high degree of loyalty to each other. While his reluctance to force issues irritated different Ministers at times his circuitousness prevented confrontations which could have isolated particular Ministers. If a Minister felt strongly on an issue Cosgrave was very reluctant to cut short discussion and force a quick decision. Cosgrave said looking back at his period in office:

> 'I always endeavoured to allow a full discussion without too much repetition because otherwise meetings tend to become excessively long and people get a bit exasperated and frustrated.'

Cosgrave's style is best appreciated when put into the context of coalitions since his time. Dick Spring walked out on Garret FitzGerald in 1987, Des O'Malley forced Charles Haughey to sack his Tánaiste, Brian Lenihan, from the cabinet in 1990 and then forced Haughey himself to step down as Taoiseach in February 1992. Haughey's successor Albert Reynolds and Des O'Malley between them brought down the Fianna Fáil–PD Government in November 1992 and in November 1994 Dick Spring walked out on Albert Reynolds, after months of clashes, and joined a government under the leadership of John Bruton.

By contrast Cosgrave's Ministers remained utterly loyal to him and he to them, to the extent that today he is still very reluctant to discuss his political life in detail for fear of being in any way disloyal to the men who served him in government. The Labour perspective according to Cruise O'Brien was that 'of course we saw it as loyalty to the Taoiseach and the Tánaiste'.

His opponent for so many years, Garret FitzGerald, summed up Cosgrave's style of leadership thus:

> 'Although he could relax and become a warm personality on informal occasions, when he found the company congenial, he had an instinct for the exercise of authority combined with a reticence and a certain remoteness that did not encourage over-familiarity, with the result that where he clearly had a strongly held view most Ministers were reluctant to challenge him. In Opposition, without the extra authority of office, these attributes had not been sufficient to protect him for challenges over issues on which his conservatism tended to isolate him; in government they proved effective in safeguarding his authority.'

Cosgrave himself believed that the role of a Taoiseach was to facilitate the taking of decisions by the Government but he believed consensus was desirable and he often allowed extra time to establish if it was possible. 'Generally, delayed decisions were due to complexity or to a conflict of views, well, the complexity might justify a delay but if it is a conflict of view, if it is not going to be solved by agreement or compromise then you have to take a decision,' he told Ursula Halligan.

There was no strict pecking order of Ministers as far as Cosgrave was concerned. Each one was allowed to express their views on all the issues coming before cabinet although clearly the Minister for Finance, Richie Ryan, had a pivotal role on all issues relating to Finance. 'All Ministers rank equally. All are entitled to speak at government meetings. They all have just one vote if it comes to a vote. Take for instance a department like the Gaeltacht, which is a very small department, the Minister would have the same voice and vote like anybody else,' he said. To encourage all Ministers to give their views on important issues he arranged special cabinet meetings to deal with specific topics, usually relating to the economy or the North.

He was also scrupulous about not interfering in the day-to-day running of his Ministers' departments. Each Minister was left to get on with his work and it was only in exceptional circumstances, when he felt important matters were not being attended to that he interfered. This sometimes had the effect of allowing the less dynamic Ministers in the Government to slow things down but in general it worked and certainly promoted a feeling of team-spirit.

Although he has never said it, the Minister in the Government with whom Cosgrave had the poorest personal relations was FitzGerald. Apart from the political antipathy generated by Garret's attempts to push him out of the leadership, the two men were chalk and cheese and never had any basis of mutual understanding. Cosgrave simply didn't trust FitzGerald's judgement which was why he wouldn't make him Minister for Finance. Even though FitzGerald maintains that they worked well in government, after their earlier difficulties in Opposition, other Ministers remember that the old antipathies never completely died away.

'Garret was leaking away all the time,' says Cruise O'Brien. 'He had his confidants in the press and he talked aloud and whatever he talked aloud was always with an anti-Cosgrave line, always cutting him down. And I think Garret wasn't too sorry that we lost that election in 1977 because it was the end of Cosgrave. The two who leaked were Garret and Justin. They did so pretty constantly and their colleagues knew that they were doing it and didn't like it. The trouble is that when a colleague is leaking you know it but you can never prove it.'

'He was very impatient with Garret,' says Peter Barry. 'He would have recognised his considerable ability but would have considered him a bit frothy, lacking stability and he would have a wry smile for the Tony O'Reilly comment "that's all very well in practice but will it work in theory". He would have thought of Garret a bit like that.'

Cosgrave's complete absence of egomania or pomposity, his impartiality and his total loyalty to all his cabinet prompted a reciprocal loyalty to him and it was the bedrock of his authority. 'I'll tell you what I think grew up around his office when he was Taoiseach — authority — an aura of authority,' says Michael O'Leary who adds that whatever commentators said about his weakness on television the people who served in government with him had no doubt 'that the authority of his office was absolutely unquestioned'.

On the rare occasions when tempers did get frayed at cabinet Cosgrave usually intervened to lower the temperature and, if necessary, arranged one-to-one meetings between the people concerned so that they could sort out their differences and return to the cabinet table. The fact that the Taoiseach never favoured Fine Gael Ministers over their Labour colleagues impressed the smaller party very much. The late John Kelly told Ursula Halligan in 1982 that Cosgrave never hesitated to take a vote if things became intractable.

> 'Liam gave everybody their head but when discussions had got to a point he'd say "Well look, we have to make a decision about this," and if there was a difference of view at the table he would go around and take a head count. He was quite businesslike about the whole thing.'

Once decisions were taken that was the end of it as far as the Taoiseach was concerned. 'He didn't have an obsessive interest in the nuts and bolts and shape of policy. The policy had been agreed and that was it. He didn't lie awake at night sweating about it. I think that is a very important quality in a Taoiseach,' said Kelly.

His basic view of the Taoiseach's role as somebody whose job it is to harness the combined wisdom of a group of people rather than develop a charismatic style of leadership is a distinctively Fine Gael view of the office, drawing its inspiration from W.T. Cosgrave and John A. Costello, as Ursula Halligan perceptively pointed out. 'As Taoisigh, both favoured a low profile emphasising instead the cooperative nature and team function of the cabinet. By contrast, Fianna Fáil Taoisigh usually appeared as strong cult figures around whom their cabinets revolved. The status of the leader was a long-standing point of difference, distinguishing the two parties.'

Since Cosgrave's period in office Garret FitzGerald has proved
something of an exception to this rule but John Bruton, when he took
over as leader of a three-party coalition in 1994, made no secret of the
fact that he modelled his style on that of Liam Cosgrave. Despite
previous poor relations with Labour leader, Dick Spring, Bruton as
Taoiseach, went out of his way to build trust in government and draw a
distinction between the way Fianna Fáil and Fine Gael operated within
coalitions.

Cosgrave had a clear and simple view of government:

'Under the system of government here, which is usually known as
cabinet government, to function properly it must work as a team.
Each Minister should run his own department but accept his share of
the responsibility as a member of the cabinet. If a government is
successful all can share in the achievement but when things go wrong
no one should try to escape the burden.'

Cosgrave was undoubtedly closer to some Ministers than others. On
the Fine Gael side of the cabinet Clinton, Burke and Donegan were
sometimes regarded by colleagues as being especially close to the
Taoiseach but he never allowed a kitchen cabinet to develop. Among
Labour, Ministers O'Brien and Tully were closest to him but again
nobody got too close. One result of his determination to remain
impartial was that nobody ever got really friendly with him on a
personal level; there was always a sense of reserve and aloofness which
discouraged over-familiarity. This quality added to his authority.

In the Dáil Cosgrave didn't make flamboyant speeches or indulge
in overblown rhetoric but he was an effective performer and Fianna
Fáil found it very difficult to score points against him. 'If the Dáil was
televised, as it is today, I think Cosgrave's public image would have
changed profoundly,' says Brendan Halligan. 'The public regarded
him as a dry old character and all the rest of it because the media
portrayed him as that. But in the chamber I could not think of a better
debater. Take any speech at random on the adjournment, Cosgrave
would speak in a very self-confident and very authoritative manner
and with a cutting witticism. A withering witticism directed at Fianna
Fáil. When you sat behind him on the benches listening you felt very
secure, you felt somewhat proud, you were reassured. This man gave
Fianna Fáil a terrible time. They never, ever, dominated him once in
the Dáil at Question Time. I think that side of him, the parliamentary
performer, is a side of him that is not sufficiently appreciated.'

Halligan also makes the point that it was not only at cabinet where relations between Fine Gael and Labour were good.

'We had joint parliamentary party meetings from time to time. They were held in the Fine Gael rooms, which was an interesting concession by the Labour Party. And Cosgrave at these meetings would be at his best. Here was the quintessential politician. He knew everybody in the room, he knew intimately their constituency details and concerns, he knew everything about them as persons, including the Labour Party deputies. He had an extraordinary relationship with Stevie Coughlan and everybody would have said this was one of the most delicate relationships, given what Stevie had been doing before the coalition. Coughlan adored him and was always up defending him if it was required.

'Chairing the meeting Cosgrave would listen intently to every crib, and of course every constituency deputy was concerned about themselves. These would all be very carefully noted and would be routed to Ministers "You look after that, Brendan". And he always used first names here and then he would give a rousing round-up. Cosgrave's view of coalition was very simple. The two parties had agreed to a deal and that meant they would sink or swim together. There was no tactical manoeuvering for position but absolute loyalty of each side to the other, whatever the circumstances.'

Years later, on the anniversary of Ireland joining the EU, Halligan was sitting beside Cosgrave at a dinner and the former Taoiseach laughed and said,

'"They never understood how I did it."

'What he meant was that it was all so simple. He just treated us as he would have expected to be treated himself. They always wondered how it could be done and looked for the magic secret, there wasn't any, it was all so obvious. The cabinet was extraordinarily cohesive.'

20

PARALLEL LIVES

THE CONTRIBUTION of the Cosgrave family to Irish public life has been enormous. It is remarkable that father and son both attained the highest office in the land. Neither had the obvious attributes of the successful Irish politician; they were not easy men of the people like so many TDs down the years nor did they possess the quality of demagoguery which has marked out some of Ireland's political leaders.

The very ordinariness of W.T. and Liam was their striking feature, yet they both showed great courage. They shared many qualities, both were modest, droll, pious, politically cunning but utterly lacking flamboyance. Yet they each possessed a self-reliance and a strength of character that made them resilient and successful statesmen.

In their personal lives they were also similar. Both were dedicated family men, ardent Catholics who loved their Church. On the other hand they liked an occasional drop of whiskey and both enjoyed horse racing as their favourite form of relaxation.

Both men also had an enigmatic quality which often baffled their contemporaries. Their friends and allies, as well as their enemies, found it difficult to get to grips with this personality trait. Kevin O'Higgins at times found W.T.'s political style and his apparent indecisiveness infuriating. Garret FitzGerald often had a similar reaction to his son. Liam's decision to vote against his own government's contraceptive legislation in 1974, without telling any of his colleagues beforehand, was an extreme example of his sphinx-like approach.

Liam Cosgrave came to power in a very different Ireland from that of his father yet he too suffered, if that is the word, from an excess of modesty. That often led his opponents into fatally underestimating him, because he had a steely resolve and an acute political brain. What often appeared as indecisiveness in both father and son when faced with enormous obstacles was, rather, the oldest and most successful political tactic in the book — playing for time.

'One of the most touching things about Liam Cosgrave is his devotion to his father,' says Peter Barry. 'It is not that he idolised him, he didn't, but he respected him. He thought he was a great man who had taken this country through a very difficult time, without any experience of how a country should be run. And I think they were good friends. He mightn't necessarily do the same but he would think 'what would my father do?'

The contribution of W.T. and Liam Cosgrave to Irish democracy is incalculable. The overriding imperative for both men was not personal or party advantage but the deep-seated conviction that the will of the people was paramount. The democratic institutions and the rule of law we have today were established by W.T. to ensure that the people were the ultimate arbiters of Ireland's destiny rather than self-appointed military groups. Liam's overriding concern was to ensure that the institutions of the State would be preserved against the same forces. The Cosgrave legacy has largely been taken for granted by the Irish public and neither man has received his due but neither was arrogant enough to worry what posterity might think of them.

'Liam Cosgrave had a very strong sense of what this State had achieved since 1921. In certain senses in his own physical presence he embodied the flinty integrity that created this state,' said Taoiseach, John Bruton in September 1996.

> 'I have a strong sense, which I have acquired from him, of the fact that this State has its own achievements to its name. Ours is the fourth oldest continuous democracy in Europe and it was founded by a Cosgrave. We shouldn't forget that. As people try and draw us in beyond our better judgement into tantalising issues *vis-à-vis* Northern Ireland we have got to be very careful that in getting involved we don't lose what we have already created here in this State which is a tolerant democracy based on laws that are fairly applied.

> 'We must not allow any blurring of the principles upon which our own State is founded in our endeavour to solve problems in Northern Ireland and I think Cosgrave saw that danger quite clearly. He drew a very clear line upon that subject, a line which continues to this day in Irish politics. Some people believe that we should not be proud of what this State has achieved because it is considered to be incomplete,

because it does not include the six counties. But that is a reality and we should not allow it to prevent us from seeing what in fact we have achieved. And we shouldn't allow what we have achieved to be undermined by adventures of any kind.'

Bruton added that he had been substantially influenced by Liam Cosgrave in the attitude he took to violence.

'There can be no ambiguity in this area. Either you support democratic institutions and the democratically appointed forces of order or you do not. You can't be half a democrat. You have to be fully supportive of non-violent politics. Liam Cosgrave expressed that very eloquently and very simply and he certainly influenced my approach to that matter.'

The overriding commitment of both Cosgraves to protecting the institutions of the State established in so much bitterness and blood in 1922 was their strength but it was also the source of their political weakness. W.T. Cosgrave was so determined to prove the Treaty had worked that he never emphasised the enormous gains in sovereignty made during his ten years in office through the Imperial conference of 1923 and the Statute of Westminster. Neither did he take account of the popular appeal Fianna Fáil's policies which played on the endemic anti-English sentiment of the Irish electorate.

His Cumann na nGaedheal party also grew distant from the concerns of the electorate during the 1920s. To a large extent this was unavoidable because of the sacrifices which had to be imposed on the entire community to get the new State built on firm foundations. The destruction wrought by Republicans during the Civil War cost the country billions in today's money. Cosgrave's government had to introduce a succession of hair shirt budgets to prevent the new State from collapsing but this period of austerity was used as a political weapon to unseat him by the very people who had caused the destruction in the first place.

Liam Cosgrave also had a fierce commitment to the institutions of the State, particularly the Army and the Gardaí. This loyalty meant that he was loath to cast a critical eye on their activities. His refusal to take seriously the heavy gang allegations and his casual attitude to Paddy Donegan's insult to President Ó Dálaigh did his government enormous damage.

The very flintyness which made him a safe pair of hands also made it appear at times that he did not understand the concerns of ordinary people. Fine Gael as a party too often wallowed in its reputation for doing the right thing rather than the popular thing and the result was the massive defeat in 1977.

Yet at the end of the day his attitude was the right one. The really important consideration for serious politicians should not be to hold on to power for its own sake but to do the State real service. This both W.T and Liam Cosgrave unquestionably did.

'The central thing about Cosgrave was his reverence for the institutions of the State,' says Brendan Halligan. 'His party had created the State and its institutions were sacrosanct. Politics he regarded as a sacred and solemn public duty. This was a great attribute of Cumann an nGaedheal which many of us did not appreciate when we were younger.'

Liam Cosgrave's reverence for the institutions of the State was also influenced by his period in the Army. In August 1996, he marched proudly wearing his Army medals with other veterans of the Emergency. 'I said when we left office that the further away we get from that government the better it will look and I have little doubt that is going to be the verdict of history. The manner of his going, immediately after the election of 1977, says a great deal about Cosgrave and also about Corish,' is Brendan Halligan's tribute.

Barry Desmond, who was assistant Government whip between 1973 and 1977 and shared a constituency with the Taoiseach says that Cosgrave strongly reflected at all times the political philosophy of his father.

> 'Liam Cosgrave's father's influence and his three years in the Army during the Emergency, shaped his passionate preoccupation with the security of the institutions of the state. His second characteristic was his intense Catholicism. It permeated his public approach to every moral and social issue before Dáil Éireann. His third attribute was that one knew precisely where Liam Cosgrave stood on almost all issues, local and national. This may seem to some a somewhat mundane observation but in Leinster House, where so many deputies perpetually head to the populist political issues of the day, particularly in their own constituencies, Liam Cosgrave stood out.

> 'Many sons of many founding fathers of the State have disappointed in their political careers. Liam Cosgrave can legitimately claim, though claim he never did and never will, that he successfully contributed to the democratic development of our country.'

Since he left public life Cosgrave has studiously avoided any intervention in either national politics or the internal workings of Fine Gael. He has also refused to give interviews relating to his time as

Taoiseach. He regularly attends race meetings and state occasions but carefully avoids any hint of public controversy. He has observed Irish politics from the sidelines for almost 20 years, keeping in discreet touch with some of his contemporaries, visiting friends in hospital, attending funerals and speaking at the graves of departed colleagues.

It is on these occasions that he has occasionally been prompted to make oblique comments on current events. Delivering the oration at the graveside of Gerry L'Estrange in 1996 during the controversy over Eithne Fitzgerald's Ethics in Government Bill he remarked 'Gerry L'Estrange never needed an act of parliament to show people he was an honest man.' At the age of 76 Cosgrave still looks very fit and goes riding most days. He hasn't lost his sense of humour or his sense of proportion on departing high office and has enjoyed an active and fruitful life away from the spotlight.

FURTHER READING

Browne, Vincent (Ed.) *The Magill Book of Irish Politics,* 1981.

Caulfield, Max, *The Easter Rebellion* (Four Square, London, 1965).

Coogan, Tim Pat, *Michael Collins* (Hutchinson, London, 1990).

Ibid., *De Valera* (Hutchinson, London, 1993).

Curran, Joseph M., *The Birth of the Irish Free State* (University of Alabama Press, 1980).

Dáil Debates, 1919 to 1977.

de Vere White, Terence, *A Fretful Midge* (Routledge and Keegan Paul, London, 1957).

Ibid., *Kevin O'Higgins* (Anvil, Dublin, 1994).

Fanning, Ronan, *Independent Ireland* (Helicon, London, 1983).

Farrell, Brian, *Chairman or Chief: The Role of the Taoiseach in Irish Government* (Gill & Macmillan, Dublin, 1971).

Ibid., *The Creation of the Dáil* (Blackwater, Dublin 1994).

FitzGerald, Garret, *All in a Life* (Gill & Macmillan, Dublin, 1991).

Gaughan, J. Anthony, *Tom Johnson* (Kingdom Books, 1980).

Gogarty, Oliver St John, S*ackville Street and Other Stories* (Rich and Cowan, London, 1936).

Halligan, Ursula, 'The Cosgrave Coalition 1973–1977', MA thesis, University College Dublin, 1985.

Lee, Joseph, *Ireland 1912–1985: Politics and Society* (Cambridge University Press, Cambridge, 1989).

Lindsay, Patrick, *Memories* (Blackwater Press, Dublin, 1992).

Macardle, Dorothy, *The Irish Republic* (Corgi, 1968).

Manning, Maurice, *The Blueshirts* (Gill & Macmillan, Dublin, 1970).

Manning, Maurice, *Irish Political Parties* (Gill & Macmillan, Dublin, 1972).

Mitchell, Arthur, *Revolutionary Government in Ireland*, 1919–22 (Gill & Macmillan, Dublin, 1972).

Ó Broin, Leon, *W.E. Wylie and the Irish Revolution* (Gill & Macmillan, Dublin, 1989).

O'Connor, Ulick, *Oliver St John Gogarty* (Jonathan Cape, London, 1964).

O'Leary, Cornelius, *Irish Elections* 1918–1977 (Gill & Macmillan, Dublin, 1979).

O'Sullivan, Michael, *Seán Lemass* (Blackwater Press, Dublin, 1994).

Sinnott, Richard, *Irish Voters Decide* (Manchester University Press, 1995).

Smith, Raymond, *Garret the Enigma* (Aherlow Publishers, Dublin, 1985).

Ryan, Desmond, *Michael Collins* (Anvil Books, Dublin, 1932).

Walker, Brian, (Ed.) *Parliamentary Election Results in Ireland*, 1918–1992 (Royal Irish Academy, Dublin 1992).

Name Index

Dolan, Charles 7
Donegan, Paddy 79, 115, 120, 141,
    171, 181, 187–192, 201–
    202, 212, 216, 220
Donnellan, Mick 67
Dooge, Jim 70, 88, 95–96, 104, 110,
    112, 126, 128–129, 134,
    139, 197–198, 202
Downey, Jim 96
Drago, Miss 18
Dugdale, Rose 182
Duignan, Seán 152, 191, 200
Dunbar-Harrison, Letitia 46
Dunne, Sean 95

E

Edward VII 6
Ennis, Mary 61
Esmonde, Anthony 120
Ewart-Biggs, Christopher 186
Eyre 15

F

Fanning, Ronan 45, 48, 71
Farrell, Brian 43, 67, 205
Faulkner, Brian 172–173, 176–179
Feetham, Justice 49
ffrench Mullen, Douglas 11
Finlay, Dick 72
Finlay, Tom 72, 187
Fisher, J. R. 49
Fitt, Gerry 176, 179
FitzGerald, Alexis 85, 110, 134,
    154, 197
FitzGerald, Desmond 61
Fitzgerald, Eithne 222
FitzGerald, Garret 39, 60–61, 70,
    81–82, 85, 88–97, 99–101,
    110–112, 115–120, 123,
    127, 130, 132, 134, 137–
    141, 143, 151, 159–161,
    163, 165, 167, 170–171,
    173–177, 179, 187–189,
    192–193, 196–197, 199,
    201, 203, 206, 208–214,
    216, 218
Fitzgerald, Gene 114
Fitzgerald, Grace 85
FitzGerald, Joan 138, 174
Fitzpatrick, Tom 171
Flanagan, Alderman 18
Flanagan, Bird 18, 63
Flanagan, Louise 18
Flanagan, Oliver 79, 96, 121, 156
Fogarty, Bishop 43, 45, 53
Fogarty, Patrick 61
Foot, Michael 180
Fox, Billy 181, 194

G

Gallagher, Frank 25
Gallagher, James 12
Gallagher, Michael 164
Gaughan, Michael 182
Geoghegan, Johnny 105
George V 22
George, Lloyd 22–23, 29
Gibbons, Jim 110
Gilmartin, Archbishop 46
Glennon, Chris 152
Gogarty, Oliver St John 6, 18, 28,
    31, 45, 47, 77
Goretti, Maria 192
Governey, Des 168
Grattan Esmonde, John 203
Greenwood, Hamar 29
Griffith, Arthur 2, 6, 8, 14, 16–17,
    20, 22–25, 27, 29–34, 102,
    109, 156

H

Hales, Sean 38
Hall, Frank 163
Halligan, Brendan 93, 95–96, 98,
    103, 106, 109–111, 113–
    114, 126–133, 136, 139,

Pearse, Patrick 6
Plunkett, Count 14, 17
Plunkett, Joseph Mary 14
Plunkett, Sir Horace 40
Pope Pius XII 74

R

Rabbitte, Pat 66–67, 130
Ramsay, Lt 10
Redmond, John 6–8
Redmond, Willie 14, 51
Rees, Merlyn 181
Reynolds, Albert 142, 182, 208, 211, 213
Robinson, Lennox 47
Robinson, Mary 170
Robinson, Nick 170
Roe, Frank 203
Roe, Patrick Joseph 61
Ryan, Desmond 17, 23
Ryan, Frank 56
Ryan, John 199
Ryan, Richie 79, 84, 100–102, 111–112, 118, 122, 125–126, 128–130, 135, 137–139, 141, 148–149, 154–164, 168, 196–197, 199, 201–202, 206, 212, 214

S

Sanfey, Jim 113, 126, 130, 149

Sheehy, Eugene, Fr 8
Sherlock, Lorcan 12
Sinclair, Maynard 68
Smith, Noel 184
Smith, Raymond 197
Smylie, Bertie 50
Spring, Dan 166–167
Spring, Dick 182, 213, 216
Stack, Austin 15, 24–26, 41
Stagg, Emmet 182
Stagg, Frank 182
Sweetman, Gerald 76, 78–79, 81–85, 87, 91–94, 96–97, 100–102, 110

T

Thornley, David 98
Toal, Brendan 203
Tully, Jim 95, 126, 141, 158, 170, 195–196, 206, 209, 216
Tunney, James 61

W

Walsh, Dick 152, 199
Warmington, Captain 10
Wilson, Harold 68
Wylie, W. E. 12

Y

Yeats, W.B. 47